W9-CCW-293

THE MILKY WAY AND BEYOND

STARS, NEBULAE, AND OTHER GALAXIES

AN EXPLORER'S GUIDE TO THE UNIVERSE

THE MILKY WAY AND BEYOND

STARS, NEBULAE, AND OTHER GALAXIES

EDITED BY ERIK GREGERSEN, ASSOCIATE EDITOR, ASTRONOMY AND SPACE EXPLORATION

Britannica
Educational Publishing

IN ASSOCIATION WITH

ROSEN
EDUCATIONAL SERVICES

Published in 2010 by Britannica Educational Publishing
(a trademark of Encyclopædia Britannica, Inc.)
in association with Rosen Educational Services, LLC
29 East 21st Street, New York, NY 10010.

Distributed exclusively by Rosen Educational Services.
For a listing of additional Britannica Educational Publishing titles, call toll free (800) 237-9932.

First Edition

Britannica Educational Publishing
Michael I. Levy: Executive Editor
Marilyn L. Barton: Senior Coordinator, Production Control
Steven Bosco: Director, Editorial Technologies
Lisa S. Braucher: Senior Producer and Data Editor
Yvette Charboneau: Senior Copy Editor
Kathy Nakamura: Manager, Media Acquisition
Erik Gregersen: Associate Editor, Astronomy and Space Exploration

Rosen Educational Services
Jeanne Nagle: Senior Editor
Nelson Sá: Art Director
Matthew Cauli: Designer
Introduction by Greg Roza

Library of Congress Cataloging-in-Publication Data

The Milky Way and beyond / edited by Erik Gregersen.—1st ed.
    p. cm.—(An explorer's guide to the universe)
"In association with Britannica Educational Publishing, Rosen Educational Services."
Includes index.
ISBN 978-1-61530-024-2 (lib. bdg.)
1. Milky Way—Popular works. 2. Galaxies—Popular works. I. Gregersen, Erik.
QB857.7.M55 2010
523.1'13—dc22

2009037980

Manufactured in the United States of America

On the cover: Thousands of sparkling young stars are nestled within the giant nebula
NGC 3603, one of the most massive young star clusters in the Milky Way Galaxy. *NASA,
ESA, and the Hubble Heritage (STScI/AURA)-ESA/Hubble Collaboration*

CONTENTS

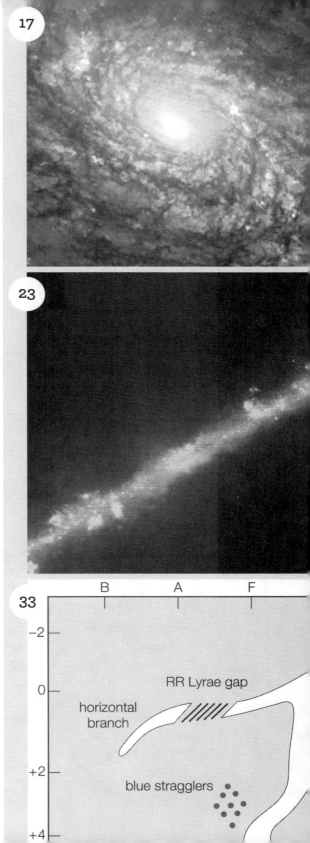

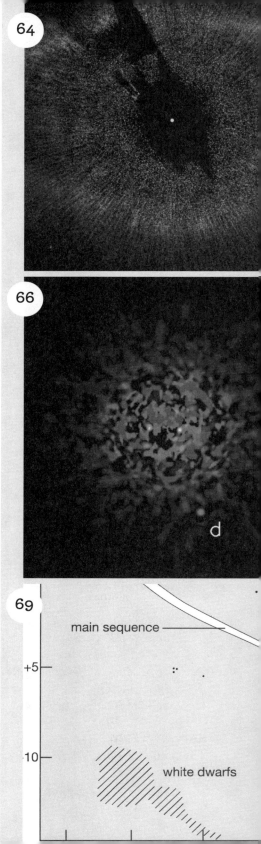

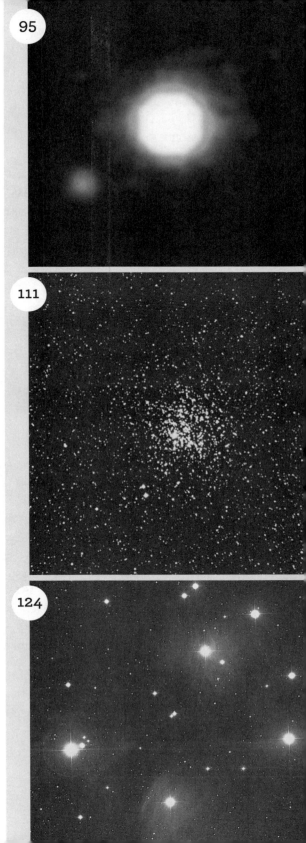

95

111

124

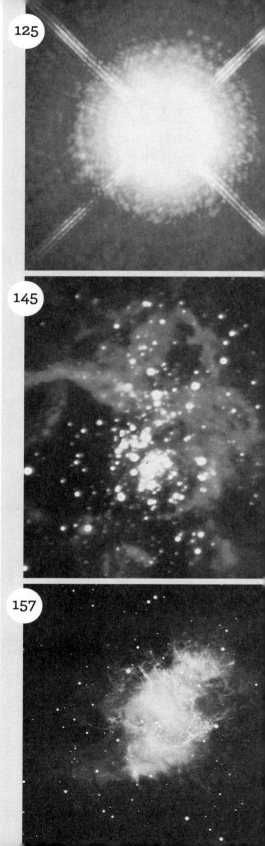

161

164

181

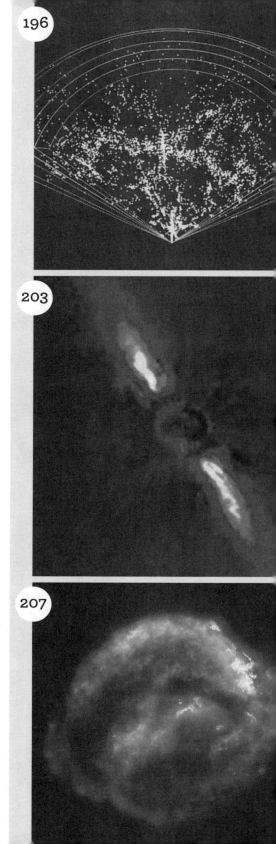

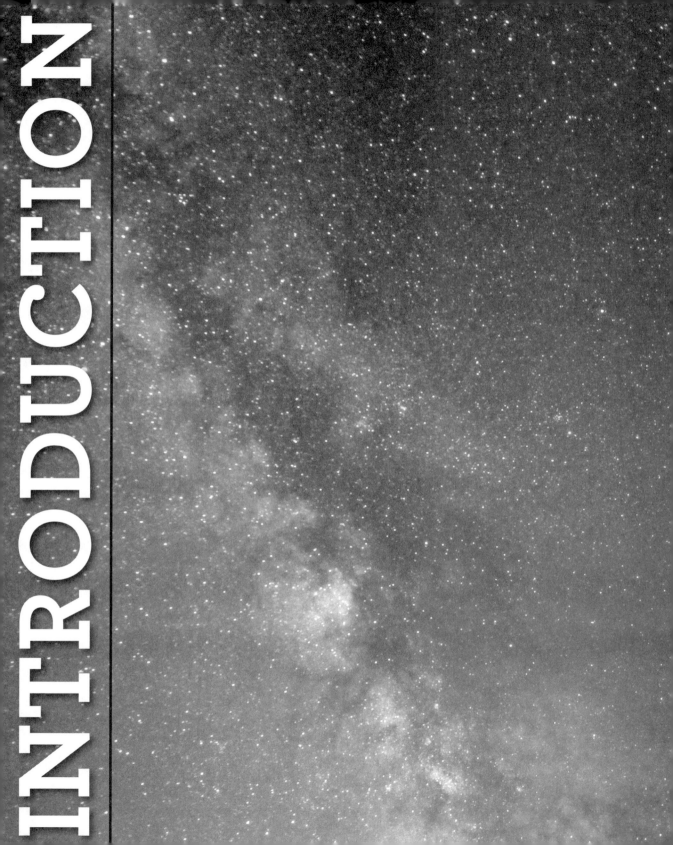

INTRODUCTION

For thousands of years, astronomers have worked to unlock the mysteries of the heavens. As they observed the stars and planets that parade majestically across the sky, one great source of wonder was a huge faint trail of light that was called the Milky Way Galaxy because it looked like milk, spilled across the darkness of night. When scientists started using telescopes in the 1600s, they began to understand more about the Milky Way. But it wasn't until the 20th century that new technology allowed scientists to take the full measure of this galaxy and others scattered across the universe. What they have uncovered is richly detailed in the pages of this book.

The primary elements of any galaxy are stars. A star is a massive body of gas that shines by radiation resulting from internal energy sources. There are so many stars in the universe it would be impossible to count them all. Only a very small fraction are actually visible to the unaided eye. In the Milky Way Galaxy alone there are hundreds of billions of stars. The easiest of these for scientists to study is the Sun, the star closest to Earth. It is about 150 million kilometres (93 million miles) away from us. It has a radius of about 700,000 km (430,000 miles.). Its mass is about the same as that of 330,000 Earth masses. It creates approximately 4×10^{23} kilowatts (4×10^{33} ergs) of luminosity per second, making it average in size, mass, and brightness. Scientists use these measurements as benchmarks when discussing other stars, which can be bigger or smaller, more or less bright, depending on their type and age.

While 150 million kilometres may sound like a very long distance, it is tiny in cosmic terms. The next closest star to Earth is Proxima Centauri, which is the smallest of three stars making up the triple star Alpha Centauri. Proxima Centauri is approximately 4.22 light years from Earth—or about 3.99×10^{16} metres (2.48×10^{13} miles). Even the fastest modern spacecraft would take countless lifetimes to reach this distant star.

Scientists have used several different methods to determine the distances from Earth to the stars. The earliest method, which is still used to determine the distances of closer stars, is a trigonometric parallax, which involves observing a star from two points on opposite sides of Earth's orbit. This technique depends on using the relatively unchanged backdrop of distant space for precise measurements. More-distant stars require other techniques, most of which rely on comparing luminosities.

Depending on its mass, a star may "live" 10 million years or 10 billion years.

Milky white stars and interstellar dust cascade across the sky to form the Milky Way Galaxy, a spiral galaxy that is home to the solar system. www.istockphoto.com/Shaun Lowe

During this time, it goes through many dramatic changes. Stars begin as clouds of interstellar gases, mostly hydrogen. Molecules in the clouds slowly begin to collapse and clump together, eventually forming areas of greater density. The clumps begin to rotate slowly as they grow more massive. In time, one or more of the clumps begins to collapse in on itself due to gravity. Often, several stars form from the same cloud, resulting in star groups.

Mass, gravity, and other forces cause the cloud to form a disk shape around the young star core. The temperature within the core continually rises, and when the temperature is high enough, hydrogen fusion begins, which allows stars to radiate tremendous amounts of heat and light. Soon after, the star has become fully formed. With a star the size of the Sun, this might take tens of millions of years. More massive stars, which burn hotter and more quickly, may take just a few hundred thousand years to reach this point.

For most of its life, a star continues to create helium through hydrogen fusion. This part of a star's life is called the main sequence. Fusion creates the light and heat that stars radiate and turns hydrogen into helium in the process. The power created by fusion is constantly pushing outward and fighting against the massive gravitational pull of the core. In time, as the hydrogen fuel in the core decreases, the core is converted to helium. Hydrogen is then burned on the surface of the helium core at a higher rate, which causes

the outer layers of the star to expand. This is called the red giant stage. It can take anywhere from about a million years to hundreds of billions of years for a star to reach this stage.

Eventually, due to the lack of hydrogen, the fusion reaction begins to die down. Not all stars die in the same manner. They differ depending on how they formed, how dense they are, how big they are, and their age. In less-massive stars, the outer layers may drift away into space, leaving the slowly cooling core called a white dwarf. More-massive stars can explode as a supernova. The most-massive stars go supernova, then collapse in on themselves due to immense gravitational force. The result is a black hole—a force so powerful nothing, not even light, can escape its grasp.

Stars are not the only bright points of light in the night sky. A few of those twinkling specks are nebulae. A nebula is an interstellar cloud of gas and dust. The matter that makes up nebulae is called the interstellar medium, which can be found just about everywhere in the universe, although it is more dense in nebulae. The composition of nebulae is approximately 90 percent hydrogen and nearly 10 percent helium, with a very small amount of other elements mixed in, namely oxygen, carbon, neon, and nitrogen. Many of the characteristics of nebulae are determined by the physical state of the hydrogen in them.

Based on their components and behaviour, there are two main

The interstellar medium (gas and dust) that make up nebulae can take many shapes, including this aptly named Bow Tie Nebula. NASA, ESA, R. Sahai and J. Trauger (Jet Propulsion Laboratory) and the WFPC2 Science Team

categories of nebulae, dark and bright. Dark nebulae, which are also called molecular clouds, are dense and cold. While molecular clouds can contain approximately 60 different kinds of molecules, the majority of their composition is molecular hydrogen (H_2). They are opaque because of the relatively high concentration of solid grains in them. Densities generally are millions of hydrogen molecules per cubic centimetre. These are the clouds from which most new stars form through gravitational collapse.

Although a very small percentage of the interstellar medium, like that found in dark nebulae, is in solid grains, that percentage is very important to the creation of stars and solar systems. Unlike the gases in dark nebulae, solid grains absorb starlight. In turn, they are able to heat and cool the gases.

Bright nebulae are usually not as dense as the dark variety. However, as the name suggests, they are visible. There are several different kinds of bright nebulae. Reflection nebulae are molecular clouds just like dark nebulae. However, they are visible because light from nearby stars reflect off of their solid grains.

H II regions are cosmic clouds that glow because they have been ionized by the radiation produced by a neighbouring hot star. Ionization occurs when the hydrogen atoms in the cloud separate into positive hydrogen ions (H^+) and free electrons, causing the cloud to glow. Another kind of nebula, called the diffuse nebula, is visible due to the ionization of hydrogen, nitrogen, and sulfur. Diffuse nebulae require the most energy of all the kinds of nebulae and are found in the vicinity of the hottest and most-massive stars.

When a star goes supernova, the resulting explosion can last for several weeks. After the supernova dies down, a bright, colourful nebula, sometimes called a supernova remnant, is left behind. Stars that don't go supernova can create planetary nebulae. This occurs when the envelope of gases around the dying star begins to expand and spread out. Planetary nebulae often have a round, compact shape. Scientists believe the Milky Way Galaxy contains about 20,000 planetary nebulae.

Despite their many differences, nebulae have basic traits in common. For example, all nebulae exhibit chaotic motions scientists call turbulence. This is similar to the ripples and whirlpools we see when we add a coloured liquid to a clear liquid. The disorganized flow of gases creates energy and heat. Scientists know that turbulence has a great effect on the behaviour of nebulae, but they do not fully understand why or how. They hope to learn more about turbulence and nebulae by continuing to study known nebulae and by discovering new ones.

Galaxies are massive, self-contained collections of stars. Scientists believe that most galaxies formed shortly after the birth of the universe, about 13 billion years ago. They can look very different, based on how they formed and evolved. Some are very small, while others, like the Milky Way, have huge spiral arms reaching deep into space.

Scientists have had difficulty studying the Milky Way because of a thick layer of interstellar medium that obscures their view of it, even with powerful telescopes. Many think the galaxy's diameter is about 100,000 light-years, and that our sun resides in a spiral arm about 30,000 light-years from the galaxy's center.

The Milky Way is one galaxy in a cluster of galaxies called the Local Group. Galaxy clusters are groups of galaxies

The arms of spiral galaxies, such as the Milky Way and this dusty spiral (pictured), are thought to be produced by density waves that compress and expand galactic material. NASA Headquarters - GRIN

that can be hundreds of millions of light-years across. The word "cluster," however, might be a bit misleading. The Magellanic Clouds are two satellite galaxies orbiting the Milky Way. They are probably between 160,000 and 190,000 light-years away. Scientists have learned much about nebulae and stars by observing these neighbouring galaxies.

The Andromeda Galaxy is the closest spiral galaxy beyond the Milky Way galaxy cluster. The Andromeda Galaxy cluster is one of the most-distant objects that can be seen from Earth with the unaided eye. At one time, scientists thought the Andromeda Galaxy was a nebula in the Milky Way. However, we now know that it is about 2,480,000 light-years from Earth and is twice the size of the Milky Way galaxy. Scientists believe this galaxy has a history of "consuming" smaller galaxies. In fact, the two galaxies are moving toward each other and will some day—billions of years from now—merge to form a single galaxy.

Beyond the Andromeda Galaxy, countless other galaxies with countless stars and nebulae are scattered to the farthest corners of the cosmos. We may never travel past the distant limits of our own solar system, and those galaxies may always be just colourful specks visible only through our most-powerful telescopes. However, scientists will continue to study them and search for new stars, nebulae, and galaxies in the hope of learning more about our place in the vast cosmos. With billions upon billions of galaxies—each of which are home to billions upon billions of stars—there will no doubt be plenty for scientists to study for many years to come.

CHAPTER 1

THE MILKY WAY GALAXY

On a very dark clear night, if you look upward at the heavens, you will see an irregular luminous band of stars and gas clouds that stretches across the sky. This band is called the Milky Way. The Milky Way is actually a large spiral system, a galaxy, consisting of several billion stars, one of which is the Sun. Although Earth lies well within the Milky Way Galaxy (sometimes simply called the Galaxy), astronomers do not have as complete an understanding of its nature as they do of some external star systems. A thick layer of interstellar dust obscures much of the Galaxy from scrutiny by optical telescopes. Astronomers can determine its large-scale structure only with the aid of radio and infrared telescopes, which can detect the forms of radiation that penetrate the obscuring matter.

THE STRUCTURE AND DYNAMICS OF THE MILKY WAY GALAXY

The first reliable measurement of the size of the Galaxy was made in 1917 by American astronomer Harlow Shapley. He arrived at his size determination by establishing the spatial distribution of globular clusters. Shapley found that, instead of a relatively small system with the Sun near its centre, as had previously been thought, the Galaxy is immense, with the Sun nearer the edge than the centre. Assuming that the globular clusters outlined the Galaxy, he determined that it has a diameter of about 100,000 light-years and that the Sun lies about 30,000 light-years from the centre. (A light-year is the distance traveled by light in one year and is roughly 9,460,000,000,000 km, or 5,880,000,000,000 miles.) His values have held up remarkably well over the years. Depending in part on the particular component being discussed, the stellar disk of the Milky Way system is just about as large as Shapley's model predicted, with neutral hydrogen somewhat more widely dispersed and dark (i.e., unobservable) matter perhaps filling an even larger volume than expected. The most distant stars and gas clouds of the system that have had their distance reliably determined lie roughly 72,000 light-years from the galactic centre, while the distance of the Sun from the centre has been found to be approximately 25,000 light-years.

Structure of the Spiral System

The Milky Way Galaxy's structure is fairly typical of a large spiral system. This structure can be viewed as consisting of six separate parts: (1) a nucleus, (2) a central bulge, (3) thin and thick disks (4) spiral arms, (5) a spherical component, and (6) a massive halo. Some of these components blend into each other.

The Nucleus

At the very centre of the Galaxy lies a remarkable object—in all likelihood a massive black hole surrounded by an accretion disk of high-temperature gas. Neither the central object nor any of the material immediately around it can be observed at optical wavelengths because of the thick screen of intervening dust in the Milky Way. The object, however, is readily detectable at radio wavelengths and has been dubbed Sagittarius A* by radio astronomers. Somewhat similar to the centres of active galaxies, though on a lesser scale, the galactic nucleus is the site of a wide range of activity apparently powered by the black hole.

Infrared radiation and X-rays are emitted from the area, and rapidly moving gas clouds can be observed there. Data strongly indicate that material is being pulled into the black hole from outside the nuclear region, including some gas from the z direction (i.e., perpendicular to the galactic plane). As the gas nears the black hole, its strong gravitational force squeezes the gas into a rapidly rotating disk, which extends outward about 5–30 light-years from the central object. Rotation measurements of the disk and the orbital motions of stars (seen at infrared wavelengths) indicate that the black hole has a mass 4,310,000 times that of the Sun.

The Central Bulge

Surrounding the nucleus is an extended bulge of stars that is nearly spherical in shape and that consists primarily of old

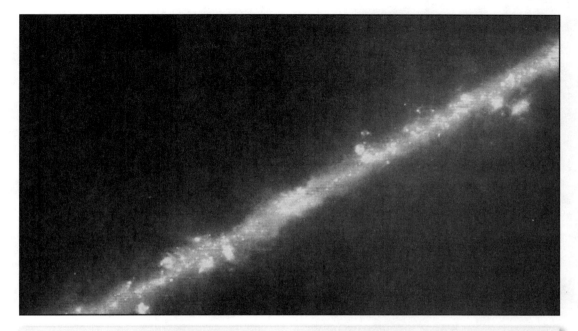

Image of the centre of the Milky Way Galaxy, produced from the observations made by the Infrared Astronomy Satellite (IRAS). The bulge in the band is the centre of the Galaxy. NASA

stars, known as Population II stars, though they are comparatively rich in heavy elements. Mixed with the stars are several globular clusters of similar stars. Both the stars and clusters have nearly radial orbits around the nucleus. The bulge stars can be seen optically where they stick up above the obscuring dust of the galactic plane.

THE DISK

From a distance the most conspicuous part of the Galaxy would be the disk, which extends from the nucleus out to approximately 75,000 light-years. The Galaxy resembles other spiral systems, featuring as it does a bright, flat arrangement of stars and gas clouds that is spread out over its entirety and marked by a spiral structure.

The disk can be thought of as being the underlying body of stars upon which the arms are superimposed. This body has a thickness that is roughly one-fifth its diameter, but different components have different characteristic thicknesses. The thinnest component, often called the "thin disk," includes the dust and gas and the youngest stars, while a thicker component, the "thick disk," includes somewhat older stars.

THE SPIRAL ARMS

Astronomers did not know that the Galaxy had a spiral structure until 1953, when the distances to stellar associations were first obtained reliably. Because of the obscuring interstellar dust and the interior location of the solar system, the spiral structure is very difficult to detect optically. This structure is easier to discern from radio maps of either neutral hydrogen or molecular clouds, since both can be detected through the dust. Distances to the observed neutral hydrogen atoms must be estimated on the basis of measured velocities used in conjunction with a rotation curve for the Galaxy, which can be built up from measurements made at different galactic longitudes.

From studies of other galaxies, it can be shown that spiral arms generally follow a logarithmic spiral form such that

$$\log r = a - b\phi,$$

where ϕ is a position angle measured from the centre to the outermost part of the arm, r is the distance from the centre of the galaxy, and a and b are constants. The range in pitch angles for galaxies is from about 50° to approximately 85°. The pitch angle is constant for any given galaxy if it follows a true logarithmic spiral. The pitch angle for the spiral arms of the Galaxy is difficult to determine from the limited optical data, but most measurements indicate a value of about 75°. There are five optically identified spiral arms in the part of the Milky Way Galaxy wherein the solar system is located.

Theoretical understanding of the Galaxy's spiral arms has progressed greatly since the 1950s, but there is still no complete understanding of the relative importance of the various effects thought to determine their structure. The overall pattern is almost certainly the result of a general dynamical effect known as a density-wave pattern. The American astronomers Chia-Chiao Lin and Frank H. Shu showed that a spiral shape is a natural result of any large-scale disturbance of the density distribution of stars in a galactic disk. When the interaction of the stars with one another is calculated, it is found that the resulting density distribution takes on a spiral pattern that does not rotate with the stars but rather moves around the nucleus more slowly as a fixed pattern. Individual stars in their orbits pass in and out of the spiral arms, slowing down in the arms temporarily and thereby causing the density enhancement. For the Galaxy, comparison of neutral hydrogen data with the calculations of Lin and Shu have shown that the pattern speed is 4 km/sec per 1,000 light-years.

Other effects that can influence a galaxy's spiral shape have been explored. It has been demonstrated, for example, that a general spiral pattern will result simply from the fact that the galaxy has differential rotation; i.e., the rotation speed is different at different distances from the galactic centre. Any disturbance, such as a sequence of stellar formation events that are sometimes found drawn out in a near-linear pattern, will eventually take on a spiral shape simply because of the differential rotation. For example, the outer spiral structure in some galaxies may be the result of tidal encounters with other galaxies or galactic cannibalism. Distortions that also can be included are the results of massive explosions such as supernova events. These, however, tend to have only fairly local effects.

THE SPHERICAL COMPONENT

The space above and below the disk of the Galaxy is occupied by a thinly populated extension of the central bulge. Nearly spherical in shape, this region is populated by the outer globular clusters, but it also contains many individual field stars of extreme Population II, such as RR Lyrae variables and dwarf stars deficient in the heavy elements. Structurally, the spherical component resembles an elliptical galaxy, following the same simple mathematical law of how density varies with distance from the centre.

THE MASSIVE HALO

The least-understood component of the Galaxy is the giant massive halo that is exterior to the entire visible part. The existence of the massive halo is demonstrated by its effect on the outer rotation curve of the Galaxy. All that can be said with any certainty is that the halo extends considerably beyond a distance of 100,000 light-years from the centre and that its mass is several times greater than the mass of the rest of the Galaxy taken together. It is not known what its shape is, what its constituents are, or how far into intergalactic space it extends.

MAGNETIC FIELD

It was once thought that the spiral structure of galaxies might be controlled by a strong magnetic field. However, when the general magnetic field was detected by radio techniques, it was found to be too weak to have large-scale effects on galactic structure. The strength of the galactic field is only about 0.000001 times the strength of Earth's field at its surface, a value that is much too low to have dynamical effects on the interstellar gas that could account for the order represented by the spiral-arm structure. This is, however, sufficient strength to cause a general alignment of the dust grains in interstellar space, a feature that is detected by measurements of the polarization of starlight.

In the prevailing model of interstellar dust grains, the particles are shown to be rapidly spinning and to contain small amounts of metal (probably iron), though the primary constituents are ice and carbon. The magnetic field of the Galaxy can gradually act on the dust particles and cause their rotational axes to line up in such a way that their short axes are parallel to the direction of the field. The field itself is aligned along the Milky Way band, so that the short axes of the particles also become aligned along the galactic plane. Polarization measurements of stars at low galactic latitudes confirm this pattern.

ROTATION

The motions of stars in the local stellar neighbourhood can be understood in terms of a general population of stars that have circular orbits of rotation around the distant galactic nucleus, with an admixture of stars that have more highly elliptical orbits and that appear to be high-velocity stars to a terrestrial observer as Earth moves with the Sun in its circular orbit. The general rotation of the disk stars was first detected through studies made in the 1920s, notably those of the Swedish astronomer Bertil Lindblad, who correctly interpreted the apparent asymmetries in stellar motions as the result of this multiple nature of stellar orbital characteristics.

The disk component of the Galaxy rotates around the nucleus in a manner similar to the pattern for the planets of the solar system, which have nearly circular orbits around the Sun. Because the rotation rate is different at different distances from the centre of the Galaxy, the measured velocities of disk stars in different directions along the Milky Way exhibit different patterns. The Dutch astronomer Jan H. Oort first interpreted this effect in terms of galactic rotation motions, employing the radial velocities and proper motions of stars. He demonstrated that differential rotation leads to a systematic variation of the radial velocities of stars with galactic longitude following the mathematical expression:

$$\text{radial velocity} = Ar \sin 2l,$$

where A is called Oort's constant and is approximately 15 km/sec/kiloparsec (1 kiloparsec is 3,260 light-years), r is the distance to the star, and l is the galactic longitude.

A similar expression can be derived for measured proper motions of stars. The agreement of observed data with Oort's formulas was a landmark demonstration of the correctness of Lindblad's ideas about stellar motions. It led to the modern understanding of the Galaxy as consisting of a giant rotating disk with other more spherical, and more slowly rotating, components superimposed.

MASS

The total mass of the Galaxy, which had seemed reasonably well-established during the 1960s, has become a matter of considerable uncertainty. Measuring the mass out to the distance of the farthest large hydrogen clouds is a relatively straightforward procedure. The measurements required are the velocities and positions of neutral hydrogen gas, combined with the approximation that the gas is rotating in nearly circular orbits around the centre of the Galaxy. A rotation curve, which relates the circular velocity of the gas to its distance from the galactic centre, is constructed. The shape of this curve and its values are determined by the amount of gravitational pull that the Galaxy exerts on the gas. Velocities are low in the central parts of the system because not much mass is interior to the orbit of the gas; most of the Galaxy is exterior to it and does not exert an inward gravitational pull. Velocities are high at intermediate distances because most of the mass in that case is inside the orbit of the gas clouds and the gravitational pull inward is at a maximum. At the farthest distances, the velocities decrease because nearly all the mass is interior to the clouds.

This portion of the Galaxy is said to have Keplerian orbits, since the material should move in the same manner that the German astronomer Johannes Kepler discovered the planets to move within the solar system, where virtually all the mass is concentrated inside the orbits of the orbiting bodies. The total mass of the Galaxy is then found by constructing mathematical models of the system with different amounts of material distributed in various ways and by comparing the resulting velocity curves with the observed one. As applied in the 1960s, this procedure indicated that the total mass of the Galaxy was approximately 200 billion times the mass of the Sun.

During the 1980s, however, refinements in the determination of the velocity curve began to cast doubts on the earlier results. The downward trend to lower velocities in the outer parts of the Galaxy was found to have been in error. Instead, the curve remained almost constant, indicating that there continue to be substantial amounts of matter exterior to the measured hydrogen gas. This in turn indicates that there must be some undetected material out there that is completely unexpected. It must extend considerably beyond the previously accepted positions of the edge of the Galaxy, and it must be dark at virtually all wavelengths, as it remains undetected even when searched for with radio, X-ray, ultraviolet, infrared, and optical telescopes. Until the dark matter is identified and its distribution determined, it will be impossible to measure the total mass of the Galaxy, and so all that can be said is that the mass is several times larger than thought earlier.

The nature of the dark matter in the Galaxy remains one of the major questions of galactic astronomy. Many other galaxies also appear to have such undetected matter. The possible kinds of material that are consistent with the nondetections are few in number. Planets and rocks would be impossible to detect, but it is extremely difficult to understand how they could materialize in sufficient numbers, especially in the outer parts of galaxies where there are no stars or even interstellar gas and dust from which they could be formed. Low-luminosity stars, called brown dwarfs, are so faint that only a few have been detected directly. In the 1990s, astronomers carried out exhaustive lensing experiments involving the study of millions of stars in the galactic central areas and in the Magellanic

Clouds to search for dark objects whose masses would cause lensed brightenings of background stars. Some lensing events were detected, but the number of dark objects inferred is not enough to explain completely the dark matter in galaxies and galaxy clusters. It appears likely that there is more than one form of dark matter, with the most important being hypothetical types of objects, such as WIMPs (weakly interacting massive particles).

STAR POPULATIONS AND MOVEMENT

The Milky Way Galaxy is made up of about one hundred billion stars. Stars come in many different masses, from a few percent that of the Sun to a hundred times greater. Stars also appear in different colours, from a dim, cool red to an incandescent blue. Despite their different properties, stars can be divided into populations. The differences between the populations can also be seen in how stars are distributed and how they move.

STARS AND STELLAR POPULATIONS

The concept of different populations of stars has undergone considerable change over the last several decades. Before the 1940s, astronomers had been aware of differences between stars and had largely accounted for most of them in terms of different masses, luminosities, and orbital characteristics around the Galaxy. Understanding of evolutionary differences, however, had not yet been achieved, and, although differences in the chemical abundances in the stars were known, their significance was not comprehended. At this juncture, chemical differences seemed exceptional and erratic and remained uncorrelated with other stellar properties. There was still no systematic division of stars even into different kinematic families, in spite of the advances in theoretical work on the dynamics of the Galaxy.

PRINCIPAL POPULATION TYPES

In 1944 the German-born astronomer Walter Baade announced the successful resolution into stars of the centre of the Andromeda Galaxy, M31, and its two elliptical companions, M32 and NGC 205. He found that the central parts of Andromeda and the accompanying galaxies were resolved at very much fainter magnitudes than were the outer spiral arm areas of M31. Furthermore, by using plates of different spectral sensitivity and coloured filters, he discovered that the two ellipticals and the centre of the spiral had red giants as their brightest stars rather than blue main-sequence stars, as in the case of the spiral arms.

This finding led Baade to suggest that these galaxies, and also the Milky Way Galaxy, are made of two populations of stars that are distinct in their physical properties as well as their locations. He applied the term Population I to the stars that constitute the spiral arms of Andromeda and to most of the stars that are visible in the Milky Way system in the neighbourhood of the Sun. He found that these Population I objects were limited to the flat disk of the spirals and suggested that they were absent from the centres of such galaxies and from the ellipticals entirely. Baade designated as Population II the bright red giant stars that he discovered in the ellipticals and in the nucleus of Andromeda. Other objects that seemed to contain the brightest stars of this class were the globular clusters of the Galaxy. Baade further suggested that the high-velocity stars near the Sun were Population II objects that happened to be passing through the disk.

As a result of Baade's pioneering work on other galaxies in the Local Group (the cluster of star systems to which the Milky Way Galaxy belongs), astronomers immediately applied the notion of two stellar populations to the Galaxy. It is possible to segregate various components of the Galaxy into the two population types by applying both the idea of kinematics of different populations suggested by their position in the Andromeda system and the dynamical theories that relate galactic orbital properties with z distances (the distances above the plane of the Galaxy) for different stars. For many of these objects, the kinematic data on velocities are the prime source of population classification. The Population I component of the Galaxy, highly limited to the flat plane of the system, contains such objects as open star clusters, O and B stars, Cepheid variables, emission nebulae, and neutral hydrogen. Its Population II component, spread over a more nearly spherical volume of space, includes globular clusters, RR Lyrae variables, high-velocity stars, and certain other rarer objects.

As time progressed, it was possible for astronomers to subdivide the different populations in the Galaxy further. These subdivisions ranged from the nearly spherical "halo Population II" system to the very thin "extreme Population I" system. Each subdivision was found to contain (though not exclusively) characteristic types of stars, and it was even possible to divide some of the variable-star types into subgroups according to their population subdivision. The RR Lyrae variables of type ab, for example, could be separated into different groups by their spectral classifications and their mean periods. Those with mean periods longer than 0.4 days were classified as halo Population II, while those with periods less than 0.4 days were placed in the "disk population." Similarly, long-period variables were divided into different subgroups, such that those with periods of less than 250 days and of relatively early spectral type (earlier than M5e) were considered "intermediate Population II," whereas the longer period variables fell into the "older Population I" category. As dynamical properties were more thoroughly investigated, many astronomers divided the Galaxy's stellar populations into a "thin disk," a "thick disk," and a "halo."

An understanding of the physical differences in the stellar populations became increasingly clearer during the 1950s with improved calculations of stellar evolution. Evolving-star models showed that giants and supergiants were evolved objects recently derived from the main sequence (a distinctive, primary band of stars) after the exhaustion of hydrogen in the stellar core. As this became better understood, it was found that the luminosity of such giants was not only a function of the masses of the initial main-sequence stars from which they evolved, but was also dependent on the chemical composition of the stellar atmosphere. Therefore, not only was the existence of giants in the different stellar populations understood, but differences between the giants with relation to the main sequence of star groups came to be understood in terms of the chemistry of the stars.

At the same time, progress was made in determining the abundances of stars of the different population types by means of high-dispersion spectra obtained with large reflecting telescopes having a coudé focus arrangement. A curve of growth analysis demonstrated beyond a doubt that the two population types exhibited very different chemistries. In 1959 H. Lawrence Helfer, George Wallerstein, and Jesse L. Greenstein of the United States showed that the giant stars in globular clusters have chemical abundances quite different from those of Population I stars such as typified by the Sun. Population II stars have considerably lower abundances of the heavy elements—by amounts ranging from a factor of 5 or 10 up to a factor of several hundred. The total abundance of heavy elements, Z, for typical Population I stars is 0.04 (given in terms of the mass percent for all elements with atomic weights heavier than helium, a common practice in calculating stellar models). The values of Z for halo population globular clusters, on the other hand, were typically as small as 0.003.

A further difference between the two populations became clear as the study of stellar evolution advanced. It was found that Population II was exclusively made up of stars that are very old. Estimates of the age of Population II stars have varied over the years, depending on the degree of sophistication of the calculated models and the manner in which observations for globular clusters are fitted to these models. They have ranged from 10^9 years up to 2×10^{10} years. Recent comparisons of these data suggest that the halo globular clusters have ages of approximately $1.1–1.3 \times 10^{10}$ years. The work of American astronomer Allan Sandage and his collaborators proved without a doubt that the range in age for globular clusters was relatively small and that the detailed characteristics of the giant branches of their colour-magnitude diagrams were correlated with age and small differences in chemical abundances.

On the other hand, stars of Population I were found to have a wide range of ages. Stellar associations and galactic clusters with bright blue main-sequence stars have ages of a few million years (stars are still in the process of forming in some of them) to a few hundred million years. Studies of the stars nearest the Sun indicate a mixture of ages with a considerable number of stars of great age—on the order of 10^9 years. Careful searches, however, have shown that there are no stars in the solar neighbourhood and no galactic clusters whatsoever that are older than the globular clusters. This is an indication that globular clusters, and thus Population II objects, formed first in the Galaxy and that Population I stars have been forming since.

In short, as the understanding of stellar populations grew, the division into Population I and Population II became understood in terms of three parameters: age, chemical composition, and kinematics. (A fourth parameter, spatial distribution, appeared to be clearly another manifestation of kinematics.) The correlations among these three parameters were not perfect but seemed to be reasonably good for the Galaxy, even though it was not yet known whether these correlations were applicable to other galaxies. As various types of galaxies were explored more completely, it became clear that the mix of populations in galaxies was correlated with their Hubble type, which separates galaxies into ellipticals, barred spirals, and spirals without bars. Spiral galaxies such as the Milky Way Galaxy have Population I concentrated in the spiral disk and Population II spread out in a thick disk and/or a spherical halo. Elliptical galaxies are nearly pure Population II, while irregular galaxies are dominated by a thick disk of Population I, with only a small number of Population II stars. Furthermore, the populations vary with galaxy mass; while the Milky Way Galaxy, a massive example of a spiral galaxy, contains no stars of young age and a low heavy-metal abundance, low-mass galaxies, such as the dwarf irregulars, contain young, low heavy-element stars, as the buildup of heavy elements in stars has not proceeded far in such small galaxies.

THE STELLAR LUMINOSITY FUNCTION

The stellar luminosity function is a description of the relative number of stars of different absolute luminosities. It is often used to describe the stellar content of various parts of the Galaxy or other groups of stars, but it most commonly refers to the absolute number of stars of different absolute magnitudes in the solar neighbourhood. In this form it is usually called the van Rhijn function, named after the Dutch astronomer Pieter J. van Rhijn. The van Rhijn function is a basic datum for the local portion of the Galaxy, but it is not necessarily representative for an area larger than the immediate solar neighbourhood. Investigators have found that elsewhere in the Galaxy, and in the external galaxies (as well as in star clusters), the form of the luminosity function differs in various respects from the van Rhijn function.

The detailed determination of the luminosity function of the solar neighbourhood is an extremely complicated process. Difficulties arise because of (1) the incompleteness of existing surveys of stars of all luminosities in any sample of space and (2) the uncertainties in the basic data (distances and magnitudes). In determining the van Rhijn function, it is normally preferable to specify exactly what volume of space is being sampled and to state explicitly the way in which problems of incompleteness and data uncertainties are handled.

In general there are four different methods for determining the local luminosity function. Most commonly, trigonometric parallaxes are employed as the basic sample. Alternative but somewhat less certain methods include the use of spectroscopic parallaxes, which can involve much larger volumes of space. A third method entails the use of mean parallaxes of a star of a given proper motion and apparent magnitude; this yields a statistical sample of stars of approximately known and uniform distance. The fourth method involves examining the distribution of proper motions and tangential velocities (the speeds at which stellar objects move at right angles to the line of sight) of stars near the Sun.

Because the solar neighbourhood is a mixture of stars of various ages and different types, it is difficult to interpret the van Rhijn function in physical terms without recourse to other sources of information, such as the study of star clusters of various types, ages, and dynamical families. Globular clusters are

the best samples to use for determining the luminosity function of old stars having a low abundance of heavy elements (Population II stars).

Globular-cluster luminosity functions show a conspicuous peak at absolute magnitude $M_V = 0.5$, and this is clearly due to the enrichment of stars at that magnitude from the horizontal branch of the cluster. The height of this peak in the data is related to the richness of the horizontal branch, which is in turn related to the age and chemical composition of the stars in the cluster. A comparison of the observed M3 luminosity function with the van Rhijn function shows a depletion of stars, relative to fainter stars, for absolute magnitudes brighter than roughly $M_V = 3.5$. This discrepancy is important in the discussion of the physical significance of the van Rhijn function and luminosity functions for clusters of different ages and so will be dealt with more fully below.

Many studies of the component stars of open clusters have shown that the luminosity functions of these objects vary widely. The two most conspicuous differences are the overabundance of stars of brighter absolute luminosities and the underabundance or absence of stars of faint absolute luminosities. The overabundance at the bright end is clearly related to the age of the cluster (as determined from the main-sequence turnoff point) in the sense that younger star clusters have more of the highly luminous stars. This is completely understandable

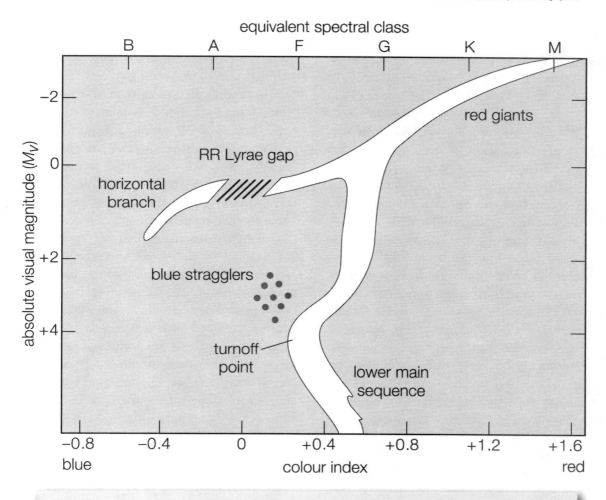

Colour-magnitude (Hertzsprung-Russell) diagram for an old globular cluster made up of Population II stars. From *Astrophysical Journal,* reproduced by permission of the American Astronomical Society

in terms of the evolution of the clusters and can be accounted for in detail by calculations of the rate of evolution of stars of different absolute magnitudes and mass. For example, the luminosity function for the young clusters *h* and χ Persei, when compared with the van Rhijn function, clearly shows a large overabundance of bright stars due to the extremely young age of the cluster, which is on the order of 10^6 years. Calculations of stellar evolution indicate that in an additional 10^9 or 10^{10}

years all of these stars will have evolved away and disappeared from the bright end of the luminosity function.

In 1955 the first detailed attempt to interpret the shape of the general van Rhijn luminosity function was made by the Austrian-born American astronomer Edwin E. Salpeter, who pointed out that the change in slope of this function near M_V = +3.5 is most likely the result of the depletion of the stars brighter than this limit. Salpeter noted that this particular absolute luminosity is very close to the turnoff point of the main sequence for stars of an age equal to the oldest in the solar neighbourhood—approximately 10^{10} years. Thus, all stars of the luminosity function with fainter absolute magnitudes have not suffered depletion of their numbers because of stellar evolution, as there has not been enough time for them to have evolved from the main sequence. On the other hand, the ranks of stars of brighter absolute luminosity have been variously depleted by evolution, and so the form of the luminosity function in this range is a composite curve contributed by stars of ages ranging from 0 to 10^{10} years.

Salpeter hypothesized that there might exist a time-independent function, the so-called formation function, which would describe the general initial distribution of luminosities, taking into account all stars at the time of formation. Then, by assuming that the rate of star formation in the solar neighbourhood has been uniform since the beginning of this process and by using available calculations of the rate of evolution of stars of different masses and luminosities, he showed that it is possible to apply a correction to the van Rhijn function in order to obtain the form of the initial luminosity function. Comparisons of open clusters of various ages have shown that these clusters agree much more closely with the initial formation function than with the van Rhijn function; this is especially true for the very young clusters. Consequently, investigators believe that the formation function, as derived by Salpeter, is a reasonable representation of the distribution of star luminosities at the time of formation, even though they are not certain that the assumption of a uniform rate of formation of stars can be precisely true or that the rate is uniform throughout a galaxy.

It has been stated that open-cluster luminosity functions show two discrepancies when compared with the van Rhijn function. The first is due to the evolution of stars from the bright end of the luminosity function such that young clusters have too many stars of high luminosity, as compared with the solar neighbourhood. The second discrepancy is that very old clusters such as the globular clusters have too few high-luminosity stars, as compared with the van Rhijn function, and this is clearly the result of stellar evolution away from the main sequence. Stars do not, however, disappear completely from the luminosity function; most become white dwarfs and reappear at the faint end. In his early comparisons of formation functions with luminosity functions of galactic clusters, Sandage calculated the number of white dwarfs expected in various clusters; present searches for these objects in a few of the clusters (e.g., the Hyades) have supported his conclusions.

Open clusters also disagree with the van Rhijn function at the faint end—i.e., for absolute magnitudes fainter than approximately M_V = +6. In all likelihood this is mainly due to a depletion of another sort, the result of dynamical effects on the clusters that arise because of internal and external forces. Stars of low mass in such clusters escape from the system under certain common conditions. The formation functions for these clusters may be different from the Salpeter function and may exclude faint stars. A further effect is the result of the finite amount of time it takes for stars to condense; very young clusters have few faint stars partly because there has not been sufficient time for them to have reached their main-sequence luminosity.

DENSITY DISTRIBUTION

The density distribution of stars near the Sun can be used to calculate the mass density of material (in the form of stars) at the Sun's distance within the Galaxy. It is therefore of interest not only from the point of view of stellar statistics but also in relation to galactic dynamics. In principle, the density distribution can be calculated by integrating the stellar luminosity function. In practice, because of uncertainties in the luminosity function at

the faint end and because of variations at the bright end, the local density distribution is not simply derived nor is there agreement between different studies in the final result.

In the vicinity of the Sun, stellar density can be determined from the various surveys of nearby stars and from estimates of their completeness. For example, Wilhelm Gliese's catalog of nearby stars, a commonly used resource, contains 1,049 stars in a volume within a radius of 65 light-years. This is a density of about 0.001 stars per cubic light-year. However, even this catalog is incomplete, and its incompleteness is probably attributable to the fact that it is difficult to detect the faintest stars and faint companions, especially extremely faint stars such as brown dwarfs.

In short, the true density of stars in the solar neighbourhood is difficult to establish. The value most commonly quoted is 0.003 stars per cubic light-year, a value obtained by integrating the van Rhijn luminosity function with a cutoff taken M = 14.3. This is, however, distinctly smaller than the true density as calculated for the most complete sampling volume discussed above and is therefore an underestimate. Gliese has estimated that when incompleteness of the catalogs is taken into account, the true stellar density is on the order of 0.004 stars per cubic light-year, which includes the probable number of unseen companions of multiple systems.

The density distribution of stars can be combined with the luminosity-mass relationship to obtain the mass density in the solar neighbourhood, which includes only stars and not interstellar material. This mass density is 4×10^{-24} g/cm^3.

Density Distribution of Various Types of Stars

To examine what kinds of stars contribute to the overall density distribution in the solar neighbourhood, various statistical sampling arguments can be applied to catalogs and lists of stars. For rare objects, such as globular clusters, the volume of the sample must of course be rather large compared with that required to calculate the density for more common stars.

The most common stars and those that contribute the most to the local stellar mass density are the dwarf M (dM) stars, which provide a total of 0.0008 solar masses per cubic light-year. It is interesting to note that RR Lyrae variables and planetary nebulae—though many are known and thoroughly studied—contribute almost imperceptibly to the local star density. At the same time, white dwarf stars, which are difficult to observe and of which very few are known, are among the more significant contributors.

Variations in the Stellar Density

The star density in the solar neighbourhood is not perfectly uniform. The most conspicuous variations occur in the z direction, above and below the plane of the Galaxy, where the number density falls off rapidly. This will be considered separately below. The more difficult problem of variations within the plane is dealt with here.

Density variations are conspicuous for early type stars (i.e., stars of higher temperatures) even after allowance has been made for interstellar absorption. For the stars earlier than type B3, for example, large stellar groupings in which the density is abnormally high are conspicuous in several galactic longitudes. The Sun, in fact, appears to be in a somewhat lower density region than the immediate surroundings, where early B stars are relatively scarce. There is a conspicuous grouping of stars, sometimes called the Cassiopeia-Taurus Group, that has a centroid at approximately 600 light-years distance. A deficiency of early type stars is readily noticeable, for instance, in the direction of the constellation Perseus at distances beyond 600 light-years. Of course, the nearby stellar associations are striking density anomalies for early type stars in the solar neighbourhood. The early type stars within 2,000 light-years are significantly concentrated at negative galactic latitudes. This is a manifestation of a phenomenon referred to as the Gould Belt, a tilt of the nearby bright stars in this direction with respect to the galactic plane first noted by the English astronomer John Herschel in 1847. Such anomalous behaviour is true only for the immediate neighbourhood of the Sun; faint B stars are strictly concentrated along the galactic equator.

Generally speaking, the large variations in stellar density near the Sun are less conspicuous for the late type dwarf stars (those of lower temperatures) than for the earlier types. This fact is explained as the result of the mixing of stellar orbits over long time intervals available for the older stars, which are primarily those stars of later spectral types. The young stars (O, B, and A types) are still close to the areas of star formation and show a common motion and common concentration due to initial formation distributions. In this connection it is interesting to note that the concentration of A-type stars at galactic longitudes 160° to 210° is coincident with a similar concentration of hydrogen detected by means of 21-cm (8-inch) line radiation. Correlations between densities of early type stars on the one hand and interstellar hydrogen on the other are conspicuous but not fixed; there are areas where neutral-hydrogen concentrations exist but for which no anomalous star density is found.

The variations discussed above are primarily small-scale fluctuations in star density rather than the large-scale phenomena so strikingly apparent in the structure of other galaxies. Sampling is too difficult and too limited to detect the spiral structure from the variations in the star densities for normal stars, although a hint of the spiral structure can be seen in the distribution in the earliest type stars and stellar associations. In order to determine the true extent in the star-density variations corresponding to these large-scale structural features, it is necessary to turn either to theoretical representations of the spiral structures or to other galaxies. From the former it is possible to find estimates of the ratio of star densities in the centre of spiral arms and in the interarm regions. The most commonly accepted theoretical representation of spiral structure, that of the density-wave theory, suggests that this ratio is on the order of 0.6, but, for a complicated and distorted spiral structure such as apparently occurs in the Galaxy, there is no confidence that this figure corresponds very accurately with reality. On the other hand, fluctuations in other galaxies can be estimated from photometry of the spiral arms and the interarm regions, provided that some indication of the nature of this stellar luminosity function at each position is available from colours or spectrophotometry. Estimates of the star density measured across the arms of spiral galaxies and into the interarm regions show that the large-scale spiral structure of a galaxy of this type is, at least in many cases, represented by only a relatively small fluctuation in star density.

It is clear from studies of the external galaxies that the range in star densities existing in nature is immense. For example, the density of stars at the centre of the nearby Andromeda spiral galaxy has been determined to equal 100,000 solar masses per cubic light-year, while the density at the centre of the Ursa Minor dwarf elliptical galaxy is only 0.00003 solar masses per cubic light-year.

VARIATION OF STAR DENSITY WITH z DISTANCES

For all stars, variation of star density above and below the galactic plane rapidly decreases with height. Stars of different types, however, exhibit widely differing behaviour in this respect, and this tendency is one of the important clues as to the kinds of stars that occur in different stellar populations.

The luminosity function of stars is different at different galactic latitudes, and this is still another phenomenon connected with the z distribution of stars of different types. At a height of z = 3,000 light-years, stars of absolute magnitude 13 and fainter are nearly as abundant as at the galactic plane, while stars with absolute magnitude 0 are depleted by a factor of 100.

The values of the scale height for various kinds of objects form the basis for the segregation of these objects into different population types. Such objects as open clusters and Cepheid variables that have very small values of the scale height are the objects most restricted to the plane of the Galaxy, while globular clusters and other extreme Population II objects have scale heights of thousands of parsecs, indicating little or no concentration at the plane. Such data and the variation of star density with z distance bear on the mixture of stellar orbit types. They show the range from those stars having nearly circular orbits that are strictly limited to a very flat volume centred at the galactic plane to stars with highly elliptical orbits that are not restricted to the plane.

Stellar Motions

A complete knowledge of a star's motion in space is possible only when both its proper motion and radial velocity can be measured. Proper motion is the motion of a star across an observer's line of sight and constitutes the rate at which the direction of the star changes in the celestial sphere. It is usually measured in seconds of arc per year. Radial velocity is the motion of a star along the line of sight and as such is the speed with which the star approaches or recedes from the observer. It is expressed in kilometres per second and is given as either a positive or negative figure, depending on whether the star is moving away from or toward the observer.

Astronomers are able to measure both the proper motions and radial velocities of stars lying near the Sun. They can, however, determine only the radial velocities of stellar objects in more distant parts of the Galaxy and so must use these data, along with the information gleaned from the local sample of nearby stars, to ascertain the large-scale motions of stars in the Milky Way system.

Proper Motions

The proper motions of the stars in the immediate neighbourhood of the Sun are usually very large, as compared with those of most other stars. Those of stars within 17 light-years of the Sun, for instance, range from 0.49 to 10.31 arc seconds per year. The latter value is that of Barnard's star, which is the star with the largest known proper motion. The tangential velocity of Barnard's star is 90 km/sec (56 miles/sec), and, from its radial velocity (–108 km/sec [–67 miles/sec]) and distance (6 light-years), astronomers have found that its space velocity (total velocity with respect to the Sun) is 140 km/sec (87 miles/sec). The distance to this star is rapidly decreasing; it will reach a minimum value of 3.5 light-years in about the year 11,800.

RADIAL VELOCITIES

Radial velocities, measured along the line of sight spectroscopically using the Doppler effect, are not known for all of the recognized stars near the Sun. Of the 55 systems within 17 light-years, only 40 have well-determined radial velocities. The radial velocities of the rest are not known, either because of faintness or because of problems resulting from the nature of their spectrum. For example, radial velocities of white dwarfs are often very difficult to obtain because of the extremely broad and faint spectral lines in some of these objects. Moreover, the radial velocities that are determined for such stars are subject to further complication because a gravitational redshift generally affects the positions of their spectral lines. The average gravitational redshift for white dwarfs has been shown to be the equivalent of a velocity of –51 km/sec (–32 miles/sec). To study the true motions of these objects, it is necessary to make such a correction to the observed shifts of their spectral lines.

For nearby stars, radial velocities are with very few exceptions rather small. For stars closer than 17 light-years, radial velocities range from –119 km/sec (–74 miles/sec) to +245 km/sec (+152 miles/sec). Most values are on the order of ±20 km/sec (±12 miles/sec), with a mean value of –6 km/sec (–4 miles/sec).

SPACE MOTIONS

Space motions are made up of a three-dimensional determination of stellar motion. They may be divided into a set of components related to directions in the Galaxy: U, directed away from the galactic centre; V, in the direction of galactic rotation; and W, toward the north galactic pole. For the nearby stars the average values for these galactic components are as follows:

$$U = -8 \text{ km/sec}, V = -28 \text{ km/sec, and}$$
$$W = -12 \text{ km/sec } (U = -5 \text{ miles/sec,}$$
$$V = -17 \text{ miles/sec, and } W = -7 \text{ miles/sec})$$

These values are fairly similar to those for the galactic circular velocity components, which give

$$U = -9 \text{ km/sec}, V = -12 \text{ km/sec, and}$$
$$W = -7 \text{ km/sec } (U = -5 \text{ miles/sec,}$$
$$V = -7 \text{ miles/sec, and } W = -4 \text{ miles/sec})$$

Note that the largest difference between these two sets of values is for the average V, which shows an excess of 16 km/sec (10 miles/second) for the nearby stars as compared with the circular velocity. Since V is the velocity in the direction of galactic rotation, this can be understood as resulting from the presence of stars in the local neighbourhood that have significantly elliptical orbits for which the apparent velocity in this direction is much less than the circular velocity. This fact was noted long before the kinematics of the Galaxy was understood and is referred to as the asymmetry of stellar motion.

The average components of the velocities of the local stellar neighbourhood also can be used to demonstrate the so-called stream motion. Calculations based on the Dutch-born American astronomer Peter van de Kamp's table of stars within 17 light-years, excluding the star of greatest anomalous velocity, reveal that dispersions in the V direction and the W direction are approximately half the size of the dispersion in the U direction. This is an indication of a commonality of motion for the nearby stars; i.e., these stars are not moving entirely at random but show a preferential direction of motion—the stream motion—confined somewhat to the galactic plane and to the direction of galactic rotation.

High-Velocity Stars

One of the nearest 55 stars, called Kapteyn's star, is an example of the high-velocity stars that lie near the Sun. Its observed radial velocity is -245 km/sec (152 miles/sec), and the components of its space velocity are

$$U = 19 \text{ km/sec}, V = -288 \text{ km/sec, and}$$
$$W = -52 \text{ km/sec } (U = 19 \text{ km/sec,}$$
$$V = -288 \text{ km/sec, and } W = -52 \text{ km/sec})$$

The very large value for V indicates that, with respect to circular velocity, this star has practically no motion in the direction of galactic rotation at all. As the Sun's motion in its orbit around the Galaxy is estimated to be approximately 250 km/sec (155 miles/sec) in this direction, the value V of -288 km/sec (-179 miles/sec) is primarily just a reflection of the solar orbital motion.

Solar Motion

Solar motion is defined as the calculated motion of the Sun with respect to a specified reference frame. In practice, calculations of solar motion provide information not only on the Sun's motion with respect to its neighbours in the Galaxy but also on the kinematic properties of various kinds of stars within the system. These properties in turn can be used to deduce information on the dynamical history of the Galaxy and of its stellar components. Because accurate space motions can be obtained only for individual stars in the immediate vicinity of the Sun (within about 100 light-years), solutions for solar motion involving many stars of a given class are the prime source of information on the patterns of motion for that class. Furthermore, astronomers obtain information on the large-scale motions of galaxies in the neighbourhood of the Galaxy from solar motion solutions because it is necessary to know the space motion of the Sun with respect to the centre of the Galaxy (its orbital motion) before such velocities can be calculated.

The Sun's motion can be calculated by reference to any of three stellar motion elements: (1) the radial velocities of stars, (2) the proper motions of stars, or (3) the space motions of stars.

Solar Motion Calculations from Radial Velocities

For objects beyond the immediate neighbourhood of the Sun, only radial velocities can be measured. Initially it is necessary to choose a standard of rest (the reference frame) from which the solar motion is to be calculated. This is usually done by selecting a particular kind of star or a portion of space. To solve for solar motion, two assumptions are made. The first is that the stars that form the standard of rest are symmetrically distributed over the sky, and the second is that the peculiar motions—the motions of individual stars with respect to that standard of rest—are randomly distributed. Considering the geometry then provides a mathematical solution for the motion of the Sun through the average rest frame of the stars being considered.

In astronomical literature where solar motion solutions are published, there is often employed a "K-term," a term that is added to the equations to account for systematic errors, the stream motions of stars, or the expansion or contraction of the member stars of the reference frame. Recent determinations of solar motion from high-dispersion radial velocities have suggested that most previous K-terms (which averaged a few kilometres per second) were the result of systematic errors in stellar spectra caused by blends of spectral lines. Of course, the K-term that arises when a solution for solar motions is calculated for galaxies results from the expansion of the system of galaxies and is very large if galaxies at great distances from the Milky Way Galaxy are included.

Solar Motion Calculations From Proper Motions

Solutions for solar motion based on the proper motions of the stars in proper motion catalogs can be carried out even when the distances are not known and the radial velocities are not given. It is necessary to consider groups of stars of limited dispersion in distance so as to have a well-defined and reasonably spatially-uniform reference frame. This can be accomplished by limiting the selection of stars according to their apparent magnitudes. The procedure is the same as the above except that the proper motion components are used instead of the radial velocities. The average distance of the stars of the reference frame enters into the solution of these equations and is related to the term often referred to as the secular parallax. The secular parallax is defined as $0.24h/r$, where h is the solar motion in astronomical units per year and r is the mean distance for the solar motion solution.

Solar Motion Calculations From Space Motions

For nearby well-observed stars, it is possible to determine complete space motions and to use these for calculating the solar motion. One must have six quantities: α (the right ascension of the star); δ (the declination of the star); μ_a (the proper motion in right ascension); μ_s (the proper motion in declination); ρ (the radial velocity as reduced to the Sun); and r (the distance of the star). To find the solar motion, one calculates the velocity components of each star of the sample and the averages of all of these.

Solar motion solutions give values for the Sun's motion in terms of velocity components, which are normally reduced to a single velocity and a direction. The direction in which the Sun is apparently moving with respect to the reference frame is called the apex of solar motion. In addition, the calculation of the solar motion provides dispersion in velocity. Such dispersions are as intrinsically interesting as the solar motions themselves because a dispersion is an indication of the integrity of the selection of stars used as a reference frame and of its uniformity of kinematic properties. It is found, for example, that dispersions are very small for certain kinds of stars (e.g., A-type stars, all of which apparently have nearly similar, almost circular orbits in the Galaxy) and are very large for some other kinds of objects (e.g., the RR Lyrae variables, which show a dispersion of almost 100 km/sec [62 miles/sec] due to the wide variation in the shapes and orientations of orbits for these stars).

SOLAR MOTION SOLUTIONS

The motion of the Sun with respect to the nearest common stars is of primary interest. If stars within about 80 light-years of the Sun are used exclusively, the result is often called the standard solar motion. This average, taken for all kinds of stars, leads to a velocity

$$V_\odot = 19.5 \text{ km/sec (12 miles/sec)}$$

The apex of this solar motion is in the direction of

$$\alpha = 270°, \delta = +30°.$$

The exact values depend on the selection of data and method of solution. These values suggest that the Sun's motion with respect to its neighbours is moderate but certainly not zero. The velocity difference is larger than the velocity dispersions for common stars of the earlier spectral types, but it is very similar in value to the dispersion for stars of a spectral type similar to the Sun. The solar velocity for, say, G5 stars is 10 km/sec (6 miles/sec), and the dispersion is 21 km/sec (13 miles/sec). Thus, the Sun's motion can be considered fairly typical for its class in its neighbourhood. The peculiar motion of the Sun is a result of its relatively large age and a somewhat noncircular orbit. It is generally true that stars of later spectral types show both greater dispersions and greater values for solar motion, and this characteristic is interpreted to be the result of a mixture of orbital properties for the later spectral types, with increasingly large numbers of stars having more highly elliptical orbits.

The term *basic solar motion* has been used by some astronomers to define the motion of the Sun relative to stars moving in its neighbourhood in perfectly circular orbits around the galactic centre. The basic solar motion differs from the standard solar motion because of the noncircular motion of the Sun and because of the contamination of the local population of stars by the presence of older stars in noncircular orbits within the limits of the reference frame. The most commonly quoted value for the basic solar motion is a velocity of 16.5 km/sec (10 miles/sec) toward an apex with a position

$$\alpha = 265°, \delta = 25°.$$

When the solutions for solar motion are determined according to the spectral class of the stars, there is a correlation between the result and the spectral class. The apex of the solar motion, the solar motion velocity, and its dispersion are all correlated with spectral type. Generally speaking (with the exception of the very early type stars), the solar motion velocity increases with decreasing temperature of the stars, ranging from 16 km/sec (10 miles/sec) for late B-type and early A-type stars to 24 km/sec (15 miles/sec) for late K-type and early M-type stars. The dispersion similarly increases from a value near 10 km/sec (6 miles/sec) to a value of 22 km/sec (14 miles/sec). The reason for this is related to the dynamical history of the Galaxy and the mean age and mixture of ages for stars of the different spectral types. It is quite clear, for example, that stars of early spectral type are all young, whereas stars of late spectral type are a mixture of young and old. Connected with this is the fact that the solar motion apex shows a trend for the latitude to decrease and the longitude to increase with later spectral types.

The solar motion can be based on reference frames defined by various kinds of stars and clusters of astrophysical interest. Data of this sort are interesting because of the way in which they make it possible to distinguish between objects with different kinematic properties in the Galaxy. For example, it is clear that interstellar calcium lines have relatively small solar motion and extremely small dispersion because they are primarily connected with the dust that is limited to the galactic plane and with objects that are decidedly of the Population I class. On the other hand, RR Lyrae variables and globular clusters have very large values of solar motion and very large dispersions, indicating that they are extreme Population II objects that do not all equally share in the rotational motion of the Galaxy. The solar motion of these various objects is an important consideration in determining to what population the objects belong and what their kinematic history has been.

When some of these classes of objects are examined in greater detail, it is possible to separate them into subgroups and find correlations with other astrophysical properties. Take, for example, globular clusters, for which the solar motion is correlated with the spectral type of the clusters. The clusters of spectral types G0–G5 (the more metal-rich clusters) have a mean solar motion of 80 ± 82 km/sec (50 ± 51 miles/sec) (corrected for the standard solar motion). The earlier type globular clusters of types F2–F9, on the other hand, have a mean velocity of 162 ± 36 km/sec (101 ± 22 miles/sec), suggesting that they partake much less extensively in the general rotation of the Galaxy. Similarly, the most distant globular clusters have a larger solar motion than the ones closer to the galactic centre. Studies of RR Lyrae variables also show correlations of this sort. The period of an RR Lyrae variable, for example, is correlated with its motion with respect to the Sun. For type ab RR Lyrae variables, periods frequently vary from 0.3 to 0.7 days, and the range of solar motion for this range of period extends from 30 to 205 km/sec (18 ± 127 miles/sec), respectively. This condition is believed to be primarily the result of the effects of the spread in age and composition for the RR Lyrae variables in the field, which is similar to, but larger than, the spread in the properties of the globular clusters.

Since the direction of the centre of the Galaxy is well established by radio measurements and since the galactic plane is clearly established by both radio and optical studies, it is possible to determine the motion of the Sun with respect to a fixed frame of reference centred at the Galaxy and not rotating (i.e., tied to the external galaxies). The value for this motion is generally accepted to be 225 km/sec (140 miles/sec) in the direction

$$l^{II} = 90°.$$

It is not a firmly established number, but it is used by convention in most studies.

In order to arrive at a clear idea of the Sun's motion in the Galaxy as well as of the motion of the Galaxy with respect to neighbouring systems, solar motion has been studied with respect to the Local Group galaxies and those in nearby space. Hubble determined the Sun's motion with respect to the galaxies beyond the Local Group and found the value of 300 km/sec (186 miles/sec) in the direction toward galactic longitude 120°, latitude +35°. This velocity includes the Sun's motion in relation to its proper circular velocity, its circular velocity around the galactic centre, the motion of the Galaxy with respect to the Local Group, and the latter's motion with respect to its neighbours.

One further question can be considered: What is the solar motion with respect to the universe? In the 1990s the Cosmic Background Explorer first determined a reliable value for the velocity and direction of solar motion with respect to the nearby universe. The solar system is headed toward the constellation Leo with a velocity of 370 km/sec (230 miles/sec). This value was confirmed in the 2000s by an even more sensitive space telescope, the Wilkinson Microwave Anisotropy Probe.

CHAPTER 2

STARS

The Milky Way Galaxy is made up of one hundred billion of those tantalizing points of light called stars, the massive, self-luminous celestial bodies of gas that shine by radiation derived from their internal energy sources. Our Sun is a star. Of the tens of billions of trillions of stars composing the observable universe, only a very small percentage are visible to the naked eye. Many stars occur in pairs, multiple systems, and star clusters. Members of such stellar groups are physically related through common origin and bound by mutual gravitational attraction. Somewhat related to star clusters are stellar associations, which consist of loose groups of physically similar stars insufficient mass as a group to remain together as an organization.

THE NATURE OF STARS

To say that stars are balls of gas that shine through the workings of their internal energy does not do justice to their full nature and complexity. Not all stars are like our Sun. Some stars are massive giants doomed to burn away in merely millions of years. Others are dim brown dwarfs that are in some ways like stars and in others like the even smaller giant planets.

SIZE AND ACTIVITY

The Sun seems like an impressive star. It casts aside the gloom of night and bathes the entire planet in its life-giving rays. However, when the Sun is considered among stars, it is merely average in its size and the activity of its winds.

VARIATIONS IN STELLAR SIZE

With regard to mass, size, and intrinsic brightness, the Sun is a typical star. Its approximate mass is 2×10^{30} kg (about 330,000 Earth masses), its approximate radius 700,000 km (430,000 miles), and its approximate luminosity 4×10^{33} ergs per second (or equivalently 4×10^{23} kilowatts of power). Other stars often have their respective quantities measured in terms of those of the Sun.

The table lists data pertaining to the 20 brightest stars, or, more precisely, stellar systems, since some of them are double (binary stars) or even triple stars. Successive columns give the name of the star, its brightness expressed in units called visual magnitudes and the spectral type or types to which the star or its components belong, the distance in light-years (a light-year being the distance that light waves travel in one Earth year: 9.46 trillion km, or 5.88 trillion miles), and the visual luminosity in terms of that of the Sun. All the primary stars (designated as the A component) are intrinsically as bright as or brighter than the Sun. Some of the companion stars are fainter.

Many stars vary in the amount of light they radiate. Stars such as Altair, Alpha Centauri A and B, and Procyon A are called dwarf stars. Their dimensions are roughly comparable to those of the Sun. Sirius A and Vega, though much brighter, also are dwarf stars; their higher temperatures yield a larger rate of emission per unit area. Aldebaran A, Arcturus, and Capella A are examples of giant stars, whose dimensions are much larger than those of the Sun. Observations with an interferometer (an instrument that measures the angle subtended by the diameter of a star at the observer's position), combined with parallax measurements, which yield a star's distance, give sizes of 12 and 22 solar radii for Arcturus and Aldebaran A. Betelgeuse and Antares A are examples of supergiant stars. The latter has a radius some 300 times that of the Sun, whereas the variable star Betelgeuse oscillates between roughly 300 and 600 solar radii.

Several of the stellar class of white dwarf stars, which have low luminosities and high densities, also are listed. Sirius B is a prime example, having a radius one-thousandth that of the Sun, which is comparable to the size of Earth. Among other notable stars, Rigel A is a young supergiant in the constellation Orion, and Canopus is a bright beacon in the Southern Hemisphere often used for spacecraft navigation.

STELLAR ACTIVITY AND MASS LOSS

The Sun's activity is apparently not unique. It has been found that stars of many types are active and have stellar winds analogous to the solar wind. The importance and ubiquity of strong stellar winds became apparent only through

NAME	VISUAL MAGNITUDE[1] AND SPECTRAL TYPE				DISTANCE IN LIGHT-YEARS[2]	VISUAL LUMINOSITY RELATIVE TO THE SUN	
	A[3]		B[3]			A[3]	B[3]
Sirius	−1.47	A1 V	8.44	DA	8.6	20.8	0.00225
Canopus	−0.72	F0 Ib			310	13,000	
Arcturus	−0.04	K1.5 III			36.7	101.6	
Alpha Centauri	0.01	G2 V	1.34	K0 V	4.4	1.39	0.409
Vega	0.03	A0 V			25.3	45.2	
Capella	0.08[4]	G8 III	0.96	G0 III	42.2	120	53
Rigel	0.12	B8 I	7.5	B9	860	48,000	54
Procyon	0.38	F5 IV-V	10.7	DZ	11.4	6.66	0.0005
Achernar	0.05	B3 V			140	900	
Betelgeuse	0.58 (var.)	M2 I			500	10,500	
Beta Centauri	0.6	B1 III	4	B2 (uncertain)	390	6,400	280
Altair	0.77	A7 V			16.8	10.1	
Alpha Crucis	0.81[4]	B0.5 IV	2.09	B1 V	320	3,600	1,100
Aldebaran	0.85	K5 III			65	141	
Spica	1.04	B1 III–IV			250	1,700	
Antares	1.09 (var.)	M1.5 I	7	B2.5 V	550	8,100	35.2
Pollux	1.15	K0 III			33.7	28.6	
Fomalhaut	1.16	A4 V			25.1	15.7	
Deneb	1.25	A2 I			1,400	47,000	
Beta Crucis	1.30	B0.5 IV			280	1,700	

[1] Negative magnitudes are brightest, and one magnitude difference corresponds to a difference in brightness of 2.5 times; e.g., a star of magnitude −1 is 10 times brighter than one of magnitude 1.5.

[2] One light-year equals about 9.46 trillion km.

[3] A and B are brighter and fainter components, respectively, of the star. A multiple system is ranked by the brightness of its A component.

[4] Combined magnitudes of A and B.

advances in spaceborne ultraviolet and X-ray astronomy, as well as in radio and infrared surface-based astronomy.

X-ray observations that were made during the early 1980s yielded some rather unexpected findings. They revealed that nearly all types of stars are surrounded by coronas having temperatures of one million kelvins (K) or more. Furthermore, all stars seemingly display active regions, including spots, flares, and prominences much like those of the Sun. Some stars exhibit starspots so large that an entire face of the star is relatively dark, while others display flare activity thousands of times more intense than that on the Sun.

The highly luminous hot, blue stars have by far the strongest stellar winds. Observations of their ultraviolet spectra with telescopes on sounding rockets and spacecraft have shown that their wind speeds often reach 3,000 km (roughly 2,000 miles) per second, while losing mass at rates up to a billion times that of the solar wind. The corresponding mass-loss rates approach and sometimes exceed one hundred-thousandth of a solar mass per year, which means that one entire solar mass (perhaps a tenth of the total mass of the star) is carried away into space in a relatively short span of 100,000 years. Accordingly, the most luminous stars are thought to lose substantial fractions of their mass during their lifetimes, which are calculated to be only a few million years.

Ultraviolet observations have proved that to produce such great winds the pressure of hot gases in a corona, which drives the solar wind, is not enough. Instead, the winds of the hot stars must be driven directly by the pressure of the energetic ultraviolet radiation emitted by these stars. Aside from the simple realization that copious quantities of ultraviolet radiation flow from such hot stars, the details of the process are not well understood. Whatever is going on, it is surely complex, for the ultraviolet spectra of the stars tend to vary with time, implying that the wind is not steady. In an effort to understand better the variations in the rate of flow, theorists are investigating possible kinds of instabilities that might be peculiar to luminous hot stars.

Observations made with radio and infrared telescopes, as well as with optical instruments, prove that luminous cool stars also have winds whose total mass-flow rates are comparable to those of the luminous hot stars, though their velocities are much lower—about 30 km (20 miles) per second. Because luminous red stars are inherently cool objects (having a surface temperature of about 3,000 K, or half that of the Sun), they emit very little detectable ultraviolet or X-ray radiation. Thus, the mechanism driving the winds must differ from that in luminous hot stars.

Winds from luminous cool stars, unlike those from hot stars, are rich in dust grains and molecules. Since nearly all stars more massive than the Sun eventually evolve into such cool stars, their winds, pouring into space from vast numbers of stars, provide a major source of new gas and dust in interstellar space, thereby furnishing a vital link in the cycle of star formation and galactic evolution. As in the case of the hot stars, the specific mechanism that drives the winds of the cool stars is not understood. At this time, investigators can only surmise that gas turbulence, magnetic fields, or both in the atmospheres of these stars are somehow responsible.

Strong winds also are found to be associated with objects called protostars, which are huge gas balls that have not yet become full-fledged stars in which energy is provided by nuclear reactions. Radio and infrared observations of deuterium (heavy hydrogen) and carbon monoxide (CO) molecules in the Orion Nebula have revealed clouds of gas expanding outward at velocities approaching 100 km (60 miles) per second. Furthermore, high-resolution, very-long-baseline interferometry observations have disclosed expanding knots of natural maser (coherent microwave) emission of water vapour near the star-forming regions in Orion, thus linking the strong winds to the protostars themselves. The specific causes of these winds remain unknown, but if they generally accompany star formation, astronomers will have to consider the implications for the early solar system. After all, the Sun was presumably once a protostar too.

DISTANCES TO THE STARS

For thousands of years humanity has wondered about how far it was to the stars. Among the ancient Greeks, the fact that the stars did not seem to move was evidence that Earth did not move around the Sun. The real answer was that the stars were very far away. How far away was not known until astronomical technology had advanced far enough for parallax techniques to be used in the 19th century.

DETERMINING STELLAR DISTANCES

Distances to stars were first determined by the technique of trigonometric parallax, a method still used for nearby stars. When the position of a nearby star is measured from two points on opposite sides of Earth's orbit (i.e., six months apart), a small angular (artificial) displacement is observed relative to a background of very remote (essentially fixed) stars. Using the radius of Earth's orbit as the baseline, the distance of the star can be found from the parallactic angle, p. If p = 1" (one second of arc), the distance of the star is 206,265 times Earth's distance from the Sun—namely, 3.26 light-years. This unit of distance is termed the parsec, defined as the distance of an object whose parallax equals one arc second. Therefore, one parsec equals 3.26 light-years. Since parallax is inversely proportional to distance, a star at 10 parsecs would have a parallax of 0.1". The nearest star to Earth, Proxima Centauri (a member of the triple system of Alpha Centauri), has a parallax of 0.7723", meaning that its distance is 1/0.7723, or 1.295, parsecs, which equals 4.22 light-years.

The parallax of Barnard's star, the next closest after the Alpha Centauri system, is 0.549", so that its distance is nearly 6 light-years. Errors of such parallaxes are now typically 0.005", meaning that there is a 50 percent probability that a star whose parallax is 0.065" lies between 14.3 and 16.7 parsecs (corresponding to parallaxes of 0.070" and 0.060", respectively) and an equal chance that it lies outside that range. Thus, measurements of trigonometric parallaxes are useful for only the nearby stars within a few hundred light-years. In fact, of the billions of stars in the Milky Way Galaxy, only about 700 are close enough to have their parallaxes measured with useful accuracy. For more distant stars indirect methods are used. Most of them depend on comparing the intrinsic brightness of a star (found, for example, from its spectrum or other observable property) with its apparent brightness.

NEAREST STARS

The table lists information about the 20 nearest known stars. Only three stars, Alpha Centauri, Procyon, and Sirius, are among the 20 brightest and the 20 nearest stars. Ironically, most of the relatively nearby stars are dimmer than the Sun and are invisible without the aid of a telescope. By contrast, some of the well-known bright stars outlining the constellations have parallaxes as small as the limiting value of 0.001" and are therefore well beyond several hundred light-years distance from the Sun. The most luminous stars can be seen at great distances, whereas the intrinsically faint stars can be observed only if they are relatively close to Earth.

The brightest and nearest stars fall roughly into three categories: (1) giant stars and supergiant stars that are tens or even hundreds of solar radii and extremely low average densities—in fact, several orders of magnitude less than that of water (one gram per cubic centimetre [1 cubic centimetre = .06 cubic inch]); (2) dwarf stars ranging from 0.1 to 5 solar radii and with masses from 0.1 to about 10 solar masses; and (3) white dwarf stars, with masses comparable to that of the Sun but dimensions appropriate to planets, meaning that their average densities are hundreds of thousands of times greater than that of water.

These rough groupings of stars correspond to stages in their life histories. The second category is identified with what is called the main sequence and includes stars that emit energy mainly by converting hydrogen into helium in their cores. The first category comprises stars that have exhausted the hydrogen in their cores and are burning hydrogen within a shell surrounding the core. The white dwarfs represent the final stage in the life of a typical star, when most available sources of energy have been exhausted and the star has become relatively dim.

The large number of binary stars and even multiple systems is notable. These star systems exhibit scales comparable in size to that of the solar system. Some, and perhaps many, of the nearby single stars have invisible (or very dim) companions detectable by their gravitational effects on the primary star; this orbital motion of the unseen member causes the visible star to "wobble" in its motion through space. Some of the invisible companions have been found to have masses on the order of 0.001 solar mass or less, which is in the range of planetary rather than stellar dimensions. Current observations

NAME	VISUAL MAGNITUDE* AND SPECTRAL TYPE				DISTANCE IN LIGHT-YEARS**	VISUAL LUMINOSITY RELATIVE TO THE SUN	
	A***		B***			A***	B***
Proxima Centauri	11.09	M5.5 V			4.2	0.00005	
Alpha Centauri (A and B only)	0.01	G2 V	1.34	K0 V	4.4	1.37	0.403
Barnard's star	9.53	M4 V			6	0.0004	
Wolf 359	13.44	M6			7.8	0.00002	
Lalande 21185	7.47	M2 V			8.3	0.00513	
Sirius	−1.43	A1 V	8.44	DA	8.6	20	0.00225
BL Ceti (A), UV Ceti (B)	12.54	M5.5 V	12.99	M6 V	8.7	0.00005	0.00004
Ross 154	10.43	M3.5			9.7	0.00046	
Ross 248	12.29	M5.5 V			10.3	0.00009	
Epsilon Eridani	3.73	K2 V			10.5	0.26	
Lacaille 9352	7.34	M1.5 V			10.7	0.00971	
Ross 128	11.13	M4 V			10.9	0.00031	
EZ Aquarii	13.33	M5 V	13.27	M6 V	11.3	0.00004	0.00004
Procyon	0.38	F5 IV-V	10.70	DZ	11.4	6.65	0.0005
61 Cygni	5.21	K5 V	6.03	K7 V	11.4	0.0778	0.0366
GJ 725	8.9	M3 V	9.69	M5 V	11.5	0.0027	0.0013
GX Andromedae	8.08	M1.5 V	11.06	M3.5 V	11.6	0.00575	0.00037
Epsilon Indi	4.69	K5	24.47	T1	11.8	0.135	0.000000018
DX Cancri	14.78	M6.5 V			11.8	0.00001	
Tau Ceti	3.49	G8 V			11.9	0.412	

* Negative magnitudes are brightest, and one magnitude difference corresponds to a difference in brightness of 2.5 times; e.g., a star of magnitude −1 is 10 times brighter than one of magnitude 1.5.

** One light-year equals about 9.46 trillion km.

*** A and B are brighter and fainter components, respectively, of star.

suggest that they are genuine planets, though some are merely extremely dim stars (sometimes called brown dwarfs). Nonetheless, a reasonable inference that can be drawn from these data is that double stars and planetary systems are formed by similar evolutionary processes.

STELLAR POSITIONS

Even the basic measurement of where a star is in the sky can yield much useful information. Such observations can tell if a star is related to its neighbours and how it moves through the Galaxy.

BASIC MEASUREMENTS

Accurate observations of stellar positions are essential to many problems of astronomy. Positions of the brighter stars can be measured very accurately in the equatorial system (the coordinates of which are called right ascension [α, or RA] and declination [δ, or DEC] and are given for some epoch—for example, 1950.0 or, currently, 2000.0). Fainter stars are measured by using photographic plates or electronic imaging devices (e.g., a charge-coupled device, or CCD) with respect to the brighter stars, and finally the entire group is referred to the positions of known external galaxies. These distant galaxies are far enough away to define an essentially fixed, or immovable, system, whereas positions of both the bright and faint stars are affected over relatively short periods of time by galactic rotation and by their own motions through the Galaxy.

STELLAR MOTIONS

Accurate measurements of position make it possible to determine the movement of a star across the line of sight (i.e., perpendicular to the observer)—its proper motion. The amount of proper motion, denoted by μ (in arc seconds per year), divided by the parallax of the star and multiplied by a factor of 4.74 equals the tangential velocity, V_T, in kilometres per second in the plane of the celestial sphere.

The motion along the line of sight (i.e., toward the observer), called radial velocity, is obtained directly from spectroscopic observations. If λ is the wavelength of a characteristic spectral line of some atom or ion present in the star, and λ_L the wavelength of the same line measured in the laboratory, then the difference $\Delta\lambda$, or $\lambda - \lambda_L$, divided by λ_L equals the radial velocity, V_R, divided by the velocity of light, c—namely,

$$\Delta\lambda/\lambda_L = V_R/c.$$

Shifts of a spectral line toward the red end of the electromagnetic spectrum (i.e., positive V_R) indicate recession, and those toward the blue end (negative V_R) indicate approach. If the parallax is known, measurements of μ and V_R enable a determination of the space motion of the star. Normally, radial velocities are corrected for Earth's rotation and for its motion around the Sun, so that they refer to the line-of-sight motion of the star with respect to the Sun.

Consider a pertinent example. The proper motion of Alpha Centauri is about 3.5 arc seconds, which, at a distance of 4.4 light-years, means that this star moves 0.00007 light-year in one year. It thus has a projected velocity in the plane of the sky of 22 km per second (14 miles per second). As for motion along the line of sight, Alpha Centauri's spectral lines are slightly blue-shifted, implying a velocity of approach of about 20 km per second. The true space motion, equal to $(22^2 + 20^2)^{1/2}$ or about 30 km per second (19 miles per second), suggests that this star will make its closest approach to the Sun (at three light-years' distance) some 280 centuries from now.

LIGHT FROM THE STARS

The light that stars emit does more than beautify the night sky. It tells us much about the stars themselves. All we know about what the stars are made of, how massive they are, and the temperatures of their surfaces all comes from starlight.

Stellar Magnitudes

Stellar brightnesses are usually expressed by means of their magnitudes, a usage inherited from classical times. A star of the first magnitude is about 2.5 times as bright as one of the second magnitude, which in turn is some 2.5 times as bright as one of the third magnitude, and so on. A star of the first magnitude is therefore 2.5^5 or 100 times as bright as one of the sixth magnitude. The magnitude of Sirius, which appears to an observer on Earth as the brightest star in the sky (save the Sun), is –1.4. Canopus, the second brightest, has a magnitude of –0.7, while the faintest star normally seen without the aid of a telescope is of the sixth magnitude. Stars as faint as the 30th magnitude have been measured with modern telescopes, meaning that these instruments can detect stars about four billion times fainter than can the human eye alone.

The scale of magnitudes comprises a geometric progression of brightness. Magnitudes can be converted to light ratios by letting l_n and l_m be the brightnesses of stars of magnitudes n and m; the logarithm of the ratio of the two brightnesses then equals 0.4 times the difference between them—i.e.,

$$\log(l_m/l_n) = 0.4(n - m).$$

Magnitudes are actually defined in terms of observed brightness, a quantity that depends on the light-detecting device employed. Visual magnitudes were originally measured with the eye, which is most sensitive to yellow-green light, while photographic magnitudes were obtained from images on old photographic plates, which were most sensitive to blue light.

Today, magnitudes are measured electronically, using detectors such as CCDs equipped with yellow-green or blue filters to create conditions that roughly correspond to those under which the original visual and photographic magnitudes were measured. Yellow-green magnitudes are still often designated V magnitudes, but blue magnitudes are now designated B. The scheme has been extended to other magnitudes, such as ultraviolet (U), red (R), and near-infrared (I). Other systems vary the details of this scheme. All magnitude systems must have a reference, or zero, point. In practice, this is fixed arbitrarily by agreed-upon magnitudes measured for a variety of standard stars.

The actually measured brightnesses of stars give apparent magnitudes. These cannot be converted to intrinsic brightnesses until the distances of the objects concerned are known. The absolute magnitude of a star is defined as the magnitude it would have if it were viewed at a standard distance of 10 parsecs (32.6 light-years). Since the apparent visual magnitude of the Sun is -26.75, its absolute magnitude corresponds to a diminution in brightness by a factor of $(2,062,650)^2$ and is, using logarithms,

$$-26.75 + 2.5 \times \log(2,062,650)^2,$$
$$\text{or } -26.75 + 31.57 = 4.82.$$

This is the magnitude that the Sun would have if it were at a distance of 10 parsecs—an object still visible to the naked eye, though not a very conspicuous one and certainly not the brightest in the sky. Very luminous stars, such as Deneb, Rigel, and Betelgeuse, have absolute magnitudes of -7 to -9, while an extremely faint star, such as the companion to the star with the catalog name BD + 4°4048, has an absolute visual magnitude of +19, which is about a million times fainter than the Sun. Many astronomers suspect that large numbers of such faint stars exist, but most of these objects have so far eluded detection.

STELLAR COLOURS

Stars differ in colour. Most of the stars in the constellation Orion visible to the naked eye are blue-white, most notably Rigel (Beta Orionis), but Betelgeuse (Alpha Orionis) is a deep red. In the telescope, Albireo (Beta Cygni) is seen as two stars, one blue and the other orange. One quantitative means of measuring stellar colours involves a comparison of the yellow (visual) magnitude of the star with its magnitude measured through a blue filter. Hot, blue stars appear brighter through the blue filter, while the opposite is true for cooler, red stars.

In all magnitude scales, one magnitude step corresponds to a brightness ratio of 2.512. The zero point is chosen so that white stars with surface temperatures of about 10,000 K have the same visual and blue magnitudes. The conventional colour index is defined as the blue magnitude, B, minus the visual magnitude, V; the colour index, $B - V$, of the Sun is thus

$$+5.47 - 4.82 = 0.65.$$

MAGNITUDE SYSTEMS

Problems arise when only one colour index is observed. If, for instance, a star is found to have, say, a $B - V$ colour index of 1.0 (i.e., a reddish colour), it is impossible without further information to decide whether the star is red because it is cool or whether it is really a hot star whose colour has been reddened by the passage of light through interstellar dust. Astronomers have overcome these difficulties by measuring the magnitudes of the same stars through three or more filters, often *U* (ultraviolet), *B*, and *V*.

Observations of stellar infrared light also have assumed considerable importance. In addition, photometric observations of individual stars from spacecraft and rockets have made possible the measurement of stellar colours over a large range of wavelengths. These data are important for hot stars and for assessing the effects of interstellar attenuation.

BOLOMETRIC MAGNITUDES

The measured total of all radiation at all wavelengths from a star is called a bolometric magnitude. The corrections required to reduce visual magnitudes to bolometric magnitudes are large for very cool stars and for very hot ones, but they are relatively small for stars such as the Sun. A determination of the true total luminosity of a star affords a measure of its actual energy output. When the energy radiated by a star is observed from Earth's surface, only that portion to which the energy detector is sensitive and that can be transmitted through the atmosphere is recorded. Most of the energy of stars like the Sun is emitted in spectral regions that can be observed from Earth's surface. On the other hand, a cool dwarf star with a surface temperature of 3,000 K has an energy maximum on a wavelength scale at 10000 angstroms (Å) in the far-infrared, and most of its energy cannot therefore be measured as visible light. (One angstrom equals 10^{-10} metre, or 0.1 nanometre.) Bright, cool stars can be observed at infrared wavelengths, however, with special instruments that measure the amount of heat radiated by the star. Corrections for the heavy absorption of the infrared waves by water and other molecules in Earth's air must be made unless the measurements are made from above the atmosphere.

The hotter stars pose more difficult problems, since Earth's atmosphere extinguishes all radiation at wavelengths shorter than 2900 Å. A star whose surface temperature is 20,000 K or higher radiates most of its energy in the inaccessible ultraviolet part of the electromagnetic spectrum. Measurements made with detectors flown in rockets or spacecraft extend the observable wavelength region down to 1000 Å or lower, though most radiation of distant stars is extinguished below 912 Å—a region in which absorption by neutral hydrogen atoms in intervening space becomes effective.

To compare the true luminosities of two stars, the appropriate bolometric corrections must first be added to each of their absolute magnitudes. The ratio of the luminosities can then be calculated.

STELLAR SPECTRA

A star's spectrum contains information about its temperature, chemical composition, and intrinsic luminosity. Spectrograms secured with a slit spectrograph consist of a sequence of images of the slit in the light of the star at successive wavelengths. Adequate spectral resolution (or dispersion) might show the star to be a member of a close binary system, in rapid rotation, or to have an extended atmosphere. Quantitative determination of its chemical composition then becomes possible. Inspection of a high-resolution spectrum of the star may reveal evidence of a strong magnetic field.

Line Spectrum

Spectral lines are produced by transitions of electrons within atoms or ions. As the electrons move closer to or farther from the nucleus of an atom (or of an ion), energy in the form of light (or other radiation) is emitted or absorbed. The yellow "D" lines of sodium or the "H" and "K" lines of ionized calcium (seen as dark absorption lines) are produced by discrete quantum jumps from the lowest energy levels (ground states) of these atoms. The visible hydrogen lines (the so-called Balmer series), however, are produced by electron transitions within atoms in the second energy level (or first excited state), which lies well above the ground level in energy. Only at high temperatures are sufficient numbers of atoms maintained in this state by collisions, radiations, and so forth to permit an appreciable number of absorptions to occur. At the low surface temperatures of a red dwarf star, few electrons populate the second level of hydrogen, and thus the hydrogen lines are dim. By contrast, at very high temperatures—for instance, that of the surface of a blue giant star—the hydrogen atoms are nearly all ionized and therefore cannot absorb or emit any line radiation. Consequently, only faint dark hydrogen lines are observed. The characteristic features of ionized metals such as iron are often weak in such hotter stars because the appropriate electron transitions involve higher energy levels that tend to be more sparsely populated than the lower levels. Another factor is that the general "fogginess," or opacity, of the atmospheres of these hotter stars is greatly increased, resulting in fewer atoms in the visible stellar layers capable of producing the observed lines.

The continuous (as distinct from the line) spectrum of the Sun is produced primarily by the photodissociation of negatively charged hydrogen ions (H^-)—i.e., atoms of hydrogen to which an extra electron is loosely attached. In the Sun's atmosphere, when H^- is subsequently destroyed by photodissociation, it can absorb energy at any of a whole range of wavelengths and thus produce a continuous range of absorption of radiation. The main source of light absorption in the hotter stars is the photoionization of hydrogen atoms, both from ground level and from higher levels.

Spectral Analysis

The physical processes behind the formation of stellar spectra are well enough understood to permit determinations of temperatures, densities, and chemical compositions of stellar atmospheres. The star studied most extensively is, of course, the Sun, but many others also have been investigated in detail.

The general characteristics of the spectra of stars depend more on temperature variations among the stars than on their chemical differences. Spectral features also depend on the density of the absorbing atmospheric matter, and density in turn is related to a star's surface gravity. Dwarf stars, with great surface gravities, tend to have high atmospheric densities; giants and supergiants, with low surface gravities, have relatively low densities. Hydrogen absorption lines provide a case in point. Normally, an undisturbed atom radiates a very narrow line. If its energy levels are perturbed by charged particles passing nearby, it radiates at a wavelength near its characteristic wavelength. In a hot gas, the range of disturbance of the hydrogen lines is very high, so that the spectral line radiated by the whole mass of gas is spread out considerably; the amount of blurring depends on the density of the gas in a known fashion. Dwarf stars such as Sirius show broad hydrogen features with extensive "wings" where the line fades slowly out into the background, while supergiant stars, with less-dense atmospheres, display relatively narrow hydrogen lines.

CLASSIFICATION OF SPECTRAL TYPES

Most stars are grouped into a small number of spectral types. The *Henry Draper Catalogue* and the *Bright Star Catalogue* list spectral types from the hottest to the coolest stars. These types are designated, in order of decreasing temperature, by the letters O, B, A, F, G, K, and M. This group is supplemented by R- and N-type stars (today often referred to as carbon, or C-type, stars) and S-type stars. The R-, N-, and S-type stars differ from the others in chemical composition; also, they are invariably giant or supergiant stars. With the discovery of brown dwarfs, objects that form like stars but do not shine through thermonuclear fusion, the system of stellar classification has been expanded to include spectral types L and T.

The spectral sequence O through M represents stars of essentially the same chemical composition but of different temperatures and atmospheric pressures. This simple interpretation, put forward in the 1920s by the Indian astrophysicist Meghnad N. Saha, has provided the physical basis for all subsequent interpretations of stellar spectra. The spectral sequence is also a colour sequence: the O- and B-type stars are intrinsically the bluest and hottest; the M-, R-, N-, and S-type stars are the reddest and coolest.

In the case of cool stars of type M, the spectra indicate the presence of familiar metals, including iron, calcium, magnesium, and also titanium oxide molecules (TiO), particularly in the red and green parts of the spectrum. In the somewhat hotter K-type stars, the TiO features disappear, and the spectrum exhibits a wealth of metallic lines. A few especially stable fragments of molecules such as cyanogen (CN) and the hydroxyl radical (OH) persist in these stars and even in G-type stars such as the Sun. The spectra of G-type stars are dominated by the characteristic lines of metals, particularly those of iron, calcium, sodium, magnesium, and titanium.

The behaviour of calcium illustrates the phenomenon of thermal ionization. At low temperatures a calcium atom retains all of its electrons and radiates a spectrum characteristic of the neutral, or normal, atom; at higher temperatures collisions between atoms and electrons and the absorption of radiation both tend to detach electrons and to produce singly ionized calcium atoms. At the same time, these ions can recombine with electrons to produce neutral calcium atoms. At high temperatures or low electron pressures, or both, most of the atoms are ionized. At low temperatures and high densities, the equilibrium favours the neutral state. The concentrations of ions and neutral atoms can be computed from the temperature, the density, and the ionization potential (namely, the energy required to detach an electron from the atom).

The absorption line of neutral calcium at 4227 Å is thus strong in cool M-type dwarf stars, in which the pressure is high and the temperature is low. In the hotter G-type stars, however, the lines of ionized calcium at 3968 and 3933 Å (the "H" and "K" lines) become much stronger than any other feature in the spectrum.

In stars of spectral type F, the lines of neutral atoms are weak relative to those of ionized atoms. The hydrogen lines are stronger, attaining their maximum intensities in A-type stars, in which the surface temperature is about 9,000 K. Thereafter, these absorption lines gradually fade as the hydrogen becomes ionized.

The hot B-type stars, such as Epsilon Orionis, are characterized by lines of helium and of singly ionized oxygen, nitrogen, and neon. In very hot O-type stars, lines of ionized helium appear. Other prominent features include lines of doubly ionized nitrogen, oxygen, and carbon and of trebly ionized silicon, all of which require more energy to produce.

In the more modern system of spectral classification, called the MK system (after the American astronomers William W. Morgan and Philip C. Keenan, who introduced it), luminosity class is assigned to the star along with the Draper spectral type. For example, the star Alpha Persei is classified as F5 Ib, which means that it falls about halfway between the beginning of type F (i.e., F0) and of type G (i.e., G0). The Ib suffix means that it is a moderately luminous supergiant. The star Pi Cephei, classified as G2 III, is a giant falling between G0 and K0 but much closer to G0. The Sun, a dwarf star of type G2, is classified as G2 V. A star of luminosity class II falls between giants and supergiants; one of class IV is called a subgiant.

BULK STELLAR PROPERTIES

When a star is considered as a whole, its properties reveal much of interest. From a star's temperature to how it interacts with a companion star, the consideration of bulk stellar properties has been and will continue to be a major part of astronomical studies.

STELLAR TEMPERATURES

Temperatures of stars can be defined in a number of ways. From the character of the spectrum and the various degrees of ionization and excitation found from its analysis, an ionization or excitation temperature can be determined.

A comparison of the V and B magnitudes yields a $B - V$ colour index, which is related to the colour temperature of the star. The colour temperature is therefore a measure of the relative amounts of radiation in two more or less broad wavelength regions, while the ionization and excitation temperatures pertain to the temperatures of strata wherein spectral lines are formed.

Provided that the angular size of a star can be measured and that the total energy flux received at Earth (corrected for atmospheric extinction) is known, the so-called brightness temperature can be found.

The effective temperature, T_{eff}, of a star is defined in terms of its total energy output and radius. Thus, since σT^4_{eff} is the rate of radiation per unit area for a perfectly radiating sphere and if L is the total radiation (i.e., luminosity) of a star considered to be a sphere of radius R, such a sphere (called a blackbody) would emit a total amount of energy equal to its surface area, $4\pi R^2$, multiplied by its energy per unit area. In symbols,

$$L = 4\pi R^2 \sigma T^4_{eff}.$$

This relation defines the star's equivalent blackbody, or effective, temperature.

Since the total energy radiated by a star cannot be directly observed (except in the case of the Sun), the effective temperature is a derived quantity rather than an observed one. Yet, theoretically, it is the fundamental temperature. If the bolometric corrections are known, the effective temperature can be found for any star whose absolute visual magnitude and radius are known. Effective temperatures are closely related to spectral type and range from about 40,000 K for hot O-type stars, through 5,800 K for stars like the Sun, to about 800 K for brown dwarfs.

STELLAR MASSES

The mass of most stars lies within the range of 0.3 to 3 solar masses. One of the most massive stars determined to date is the O3-type star HD 93250, a giant that has perhaps 120 solar masses. There is a theoretical upper limit to the masses of nuclear-burning stars (the Eddington limit), which limits stars to no more than a few hundred solar masses. The physics of instability and fragmentation probably prohibits the formation of stars much more than 100 times the mass of the Sun. On the low mass side, most stars seem to have at least 0.1 solar mass. The theoretical lower mass limit for an ordinary star is about 0.075 solar mass, for below this value an object cannot attain a central temperature high enough to enable it to shine by nuclear energy. Instead, it may produce a much lower level of energy by gravitational shrinkage. If its mass is not much below the critical 0.075 solar mass value, it will appear as a very cool, dim star known as a brown dwarf. Its evolution is simply to continue cooling toward eventual extinction. At still somewhat lower masses, the object would be a giant planet. Jupiter, with a mass roughly 0.001 that of the Sun, is just such an object, emitting a very low level of energy (apart from reflected sunlight) that is derived from gravitational shrinkage.

Brown dwarfs were late to be discovered, the first unambiguous identification having been made in 1995. It is estimated, however, that hundreds must exist in the solar neighbourhood. An extension of the spectral sequence for objects cooler than M-type stars has been constructed, using L for warmer brown dwarfs and T for cooler ones. A major observational difference between the two types is the absence (in L-type dwarfs) or presence (in T-type dwarfs) of methane in their spectra. The presence of methane in the cooler brown dwarfs emphasizes their similarity to giant planets. The class Y has been proposed for objects even cooler than those of class T.

Masses of stars can be found only from binary systems and only if the scale of the orbits of the stars around each other is known. Binary stars are divided into three categories, depending on the mode of observation employed: visual binaries, spectroscopic binaries, and eclipsing binaries.

VISUAL BINARIES

Visual binaries can be seen as double stars with the telescope. True doubles, as distinguished from apparent doubles caused by line-of-sight effects, move through space together and display a common space motion. Sometimes a common orbital motion can be measured as well. Provided that the distance to the binary is known, such systems permit a determination of stellar masses, m_1 and m_2, of the two members. The angular radius, a'', of the orbit (more accurately, its semimajor axis) can be measured directly, and, with the distance known, the true dimensions of the semimajor axis, a, can be found. If a is expressed in astronomical units, which is given by a (measured in seconds of arc) multiplied by the distance in parsecs, and the period, P, also measured directly, is expressed in years, then the sum of the masses of the two orbiting stars can be found from an application of Kepler's third law. (An astronomical unit is the average distance from Earth to the Sun, approximately 149,597,870 km [92,955,808 miles].) In symbols,

$$(m_1 + m_2) = a^3/P^2$$

in units of the Sun's mass.

For example, for the binary system 70 Ophiuchi, P is 87.8 years, and the distance is 5.0 parsecs; thus, a is 22.8 astronomical units, and

$$m_1 + m_2 = 1.56$$

solar masses. From a measurement of the motions of the two members relative to the background stars, the orbit of each star has been determined with respect to their common centre of gravity. The mass ratio, $m_2/(m_1 + m_2)$, is 0.42; the individual masses for m_1 and m_2, respectively, are then 0.90 and 0.66 solar mass.

The star known as 61 Cygni was the first whose distance was measured (via parallax by the German astronomer Friedrich W. Bessel in the mid-19th century). Visually, 61 Cygni is a double star separated by 83.2 astronomical units. Its members move around one another with a period of 653 years. It was among the first stellar systems thought to contain a potential planet, although this has not been confirmed and is now considered unlikely. Nevertheless, since the 1990s a variety of discovery techniques have confirmed the existence of more than 300 planets orbiting other stars.

SPECTROSCOPIC BINARIES

Spectroscopic binary stars are found from observations of radial velocity. At least the brighter member of such a binary can be seen to have a continuously changing periodic velocity that alters the wavelengths of its spectral lines in a rhythmic way. The velocity curve repeats itself exactly from one cycle to the next, and the motion can be interpreted as orbital motion. In some cases, rhythmic changes in the lines of both members can be measured. Unlike visual binaries, the semimajor axes or the individual masses cannot be found for most spectroscopic binaries, since the angle between the orbit plane and the plane of the sky cannot be determined. If spectra from both members are observed, mass ratios can be found. If one spectrum alone is observed, only a quantity called the mass function can be derived, from which is calculated a lower limit to the stellar masses. If a spectroscopic binary is also observed to be an eclipsing system, the inclination of the orbit and often the values of the individual masses can be ascertained.

ECLIPSING BINARIES

An eclipsing binary consists of two close stars moving in an orbit so placed in space in relation to Earth that the light of one can at times be hidden behind the other. Depending on the orientation of the orbit and sizes of the stars, the eclipses can be total or annular (in the latter, a ring of one star shows behind the other at the maximum of the eclipse) or both eclipses can be partial. The best known example of an eclipsing binary is Algol (Beta Persei), which has a period (interval between eclipses) of 2.9 days. The brighter (B8-type) star contributes about 92 percent of the light of the system, and the eclipsed star provides less than 8 percent. The system contains a third star that is not eclipsed. Some 20 eclipsing binaries are visible to the naked eye.

The light curve for an eclipsing binary displays magnitude measurements for the system over a complete light cycle. The light of the variable star is usually compared with that of a nearby (comparison) star thought to be fixed in brightness. Often, a deep, or primary, minimum is produced when the component having the higher surface brightness is eclipsed. It represents the total eclipse and is characterized by a flat bottom. A shallower secondary eclipse occurs when the brighter component passes in front of the other; it corresponds to an annular eclipse (or transit). In a partial eclipse neither star is ever completely hidden, and the light changes continuously during an eclipse.

The shape of the light curve during an eclipse gives the ratio of the radii of the two stars and also one radius in terms of the size of the orbit, the ratio of luminosities, and the inclination of the orbital plane to the plane of the sky.

If radial-velocity curves are also available—i.e., if the binary is spectroscopic as well as eclipsing—additional information can be obtained. When both velocity curves are observable, the size of the orbit as well as the sizes, masses, and densities of the stars can be calculated. Furthermore, if the distance of the system is measurable, the brightness temperatures of the individual stars can be estimated from their luminosities and radii. All of these procedures have been carried out for the faint binary Castor C (two red-dwarf components of the six-member Castor multiple star system) and for the bright B-type star Mu Scorpii.

Close stars may reflect each other's light noticeably. If a small, high-temperature star is paired with a larger object of low surface brightness and if the distance between the stars is small, the part of the cool star facing the hotter one is substantially brightened by it. Just before (and just after) secondary eclipse, this illuminated hemisphere is pointed toward the observer, and the total light of the system is at a maximum.

The properties of stars derived from eclipsing binary systems are not necessarily applicable to isolated single stars. Systems in which a smaller, hotter star is accompanied by a larger, cooler object are easier to detect than are systems that contain, for example, two main-sequence stars. In such an unequal system, at least the cooler star has certainly been affected by evolutionary changes and probably so has the brighter one. The evolutionary development of two stars near one another does not exactly parallel that of two well-separated or isolated ones.

Eclipsing binaries include combinations of a variety of stars ranging from white dwarfs to huge supergiants (e.g., VV Cephei), which would engulf Jupiter and all the inner planets of the solar system if placed at the position of the Sun.

Some members of eclipsing binaries are intrinsic variables, stars whose energy output fluctuates with time. In many such systems, large clouds of ionized gas swirl between the stellar members. In others, such as Castor C, at least one of the faint M-type dwarf components might be a flare star, one in which the brightness can unpredictably and suddenly increase to many times its normal value.

BINARIES AND EXTRASOLAR PLANETARY SYSTEMS

Near the Sun, most stars are members of binaries, and many of the nearest single stars are suspected of having companions. Although some binary members are separated by hundreds of astronomical units and others are contact binaries (stars close enough for material to pass between them), binary systems are most frequently built on the same scale as that of the solar system—namely, on the order of about 10 astronomical units. The division in mass between two components of a binary seems to be nearly random. A mass ratio as small as about 1:20 could occur about 5 percent of the time, and under these circumstances a planetary system comparable to the solar system is able to form.

The formation of double and multiple stars on the one hand and that of planetary systems on the other seem to be different facets of the same process. Planets are probably produced as a natural by-product of star formation. Only a small fraction of the original nebula matter is likely to be retained in planets, since much of the mass and angular momentum is swept out of the system. Conceivably, as many as 100 million stars could have bona fide planets in the Milky Way Galaxy.

Because planets are much fainter than the stars they orbit, extrasolar planets are extremely difficult to detect directly. Jupiter, for example, would be only one-billionth as bright as the Sun and appear so close to it as to be undetectable from even the nearest star. If candidate stars are treated as possible spectroscopic binaries, however, then one may look for a periodic change in the star's radial velocity caused by a planet swinging around it. The effect is very small—even Jupiter would cause a change in the apparent radial velocity of the Sun of only about 10 metres (33 feet) per second spread over Jupiter's orbital period of about 12 years at best.

Current techniques using very large telescopes to study fairly bright stars can measure radial velocities with a precision of a few metres per second, provided that the star has very sharp spectral lines, such as is observed for Sun-like stars and stars of types K and M. This means that at present the radial-velocity method normally can detect only massive extrasolar planets. Planets like Earth, 300 times less massive, would cause too small a change in radial velocity to be detectable presently. Moreover, the closer the planet is to its parent star, the greater and quicker the velocity swing, so that detection of giant planets close to a star is favoured over planets farther out.

Even when a planet is detected, the usual spectroscopic binary problem of not knowing the angle between the orbit plane and that of the sky allows only a minimum mass to be assigned to the planet. The first planet discovered with this technique was 51 Pegasi in 1995.

One exception to this last problem is HD 209458, a seventh-magnitude G0 V star about 150 light-years away with a

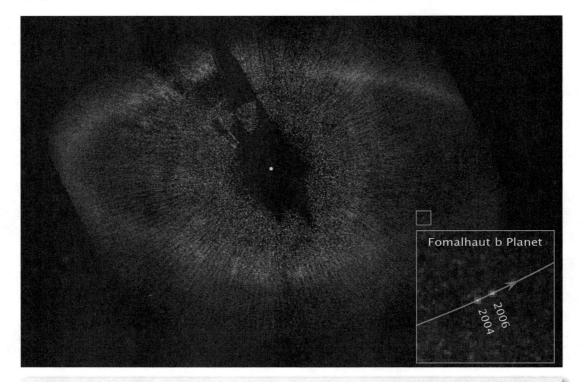

The extrasolar planet Fomalhaut b in images taken by the Hubble Space Telescope in 2004 and 2006. The black spot at the centre of the image is a coronagraph used to block the light from Fomalhaut, which is located at the white dot. The oval ring is Fomalhaut's dust belt, and the lines radiating from the centre of the image are scattered starlight. NASA; ESA; P. Kalas; J. Graham, E. Chiang; E. Kite, University of California, Berkeley; M. Clampin, NASA Goddard Space Flight Center; M. Fitzgerald, Lawrence Livermore National Laboratory; and K. Stapelfeldt and J. Krist, NASA/JPL

planetary object orbiting it every 3.5 days. Soon after the companion was discovered in 1999 by its effect on the star's radial velocity, it also was found to be eclipsing the star, meaning that its orbit is oriented almost edge-on toward Earth. This fortunate circumstance allowed determination of the planet's mass and radius—0.69 and 1.42 times those of Jupiter, respectively. These numbers imply that the planet is even more of a giant than Jupiter itself. What was unexpected is its proximity to the parent star—more than 100 times closer than Jupiter is to the Sun, raising the question of how a giant gaseous planet that close can survive the star's radiation. The fact that many other extrasolar planets have been found to have orbital periods measured in days rather than years, and thus to be very close to their parent stars, suggests that the HD 209458 case is not unusual. There are also some confirmed cases of planets around supernova remnants called pulsars, although whether the planets preceded the supernova explosions that produced the pulsars or were acquired afterward remains to be determined.

The first extrasolar planets were discovered in 1992. More than 300 extrasolar planets were known by the early years of the 21st century, with more such discoveries being added regularly. Some of those studied have minimum masses of 40 or even 60 Jupiters, which means they are likely brown dwarfs.

Between 5 and 10 percent of stars surveyed have planets at least 100 times as massive as Earth with orbital periods of a few Earth years or less. Almost 1 percent of stars have such giant planets in very close orbits, with orbital periods of less than one week. In contrast, Jupiter, which has the shortest orbital period of any large planet (i.e., any planet more massive than Earth) in the solar system, takes nearly 12 years to travel around the Sun. Even the closest planet to the Sun, tiny Mercury, requires 88 days to complete an orbit. Models of planetary formation suggest that giant extrasolar planets detected very near their stars were formed at greater distances and migrated inward as a result of gravitational interactions with remnants of the circumstellar disks from which they accumulated.

The most massive planets that transit their stars are made primarily of the two lightest elements, hydrogen and helium, as are the Sun and its two largest planets, Jupiter and Saturn. Some of these planets seem to be distended in size as a result of heating by their stars. The lowest mass transiting planets contain larger fractions of heavier elements, as do the smaller planets within the solar system.

The majority of extrasolar planets with orbital periods longer than two weeks have quite eccentric (elongated) orbits. Within the solar system, the planets, especially the larger ones, travel on nearly circular paths about the Sun.

Stars that contain a larger fraction of heavy elements (i.e., any element aside from hydrogen and helium) are more likely to possess detectable planets. More massive stars are more likely to host planets more massive than Saturn, but this correlation may not exist for smaller planets. Many extrasolar planets orbit stars that are members of binary star systems, and it is common for stars with one detectable planet to have others. The planets detected so far around stars other than the Sun have masses from nearly twice to thousands of times that of Earth. Most, if not all, appear to be too massive to support life, but this too is the result of detection biases and does not indicate that planets like Earth are uncommon.

Research in the field of extrasolar planets is advancing rapidly, as new technologies enable the detection of smaller and more distant planets as well as the characterization of previously detected planets. Almost all the extrasolar planetary systems known appear very different from the solar system, but planets like those

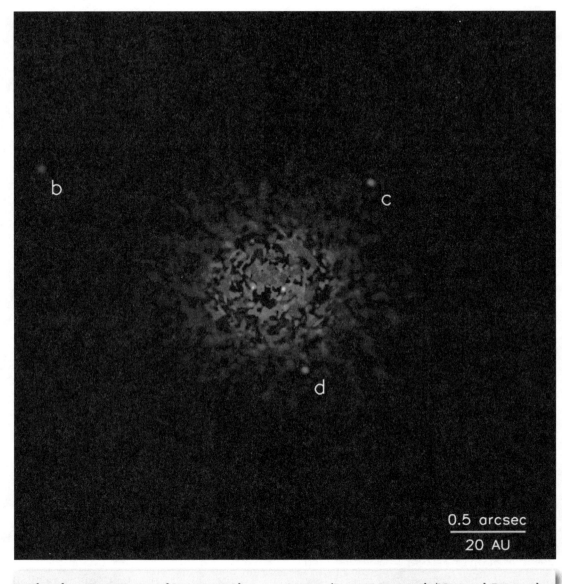

The planetary system of HR 8799. Christian Marois/Bruce Macintosh/National Research Council Canada(NRC)/Keck Observatory

within the solar system would be very difficult to find around other stars with current technology. Thus, as more than 90 percent of those stars surveyed do not have detectable planets, it is still not known whether the solar system is normal or unusual. The U.S. National Aeronautics and Space Administration's

Kepler mission was launched in 2009 and—using transit photometry from space, optimized to achieve unprecedented sensitivity for small planets with orbital periods of up to two years—aims to discover whether planets analogous to Earth are common or rare.

In addition to the growing evidence for existence of extrasolar planets, space-based observatories designed to detect infrared radiation have found more than 100 young nearby stars (including Vega, Fomalhaut and Beta Pictoris) to have disks of warm matter orbiting them. This matter is composed of myriad particles mostly about the size of sand grains and might be taking part in the first stage of planetary formation.

STELLAR RADII

Angular sizes of bright red giant and supergiant stars were first measured directly during the 1920s, using the principle of interference of light. Only bright stars with large angular size can be measured by this method. Provided the distance to the star is known, the physical radius can be determined.

Eclipsing binaries also provide extensive data on stellar dimensions. The timing of eclipses provides the angular size of any occulting object, and so analyzing the light curves of eclipsing binaries can be a useful means of determining the dimensions of either dwarf or giant stars. Members of close binary systems, however, are sometimes subject to evolutionary effects, mass exchange,

and other disturbances that change the details of their spectra.

A more recent method, called speckle interferometry, has been developed to reproduce the true disks of red supergiant stars and to resolve spectroscopic binaries such as Capella. The speckle phenomenon is a rapidly changing interference-diffraction effect seen in a highly magnified diffraction image of a star observed with a large telescope.

If the absolute magnitude of a star and its temperature are known, its size can be computed. The temperature determines the rate at which energy is emitted by each unit of area, and the total luminosity gives the total power output. Thus, the surface area of the star and, from it, the radius of the object can be estimated. This is the only way available for estimating the dimensions of white dwarf stars. The chief uncertainty lies in choosing the temperature that represents the rate of energy emission.

AVERAGE STELLAR VALUES

Main-sequence stars range from very luminous objects to faint M-type dwarf stars, and they vary considerably in their surface temperatures, their bolometric (total) luminosities, and their radii. Moreover, for stars of a given mass, a fair spread in radius, luminosity, surface temperature, and spectral type may exist. This spread is produced by stellar evolutionary effects and tends to broaden the main sequence. Masses are obtained from visual and eclipsing binary systems observed spectroscopically. Radii are found from eclipsing binary systems, from direct measurements in a few favourable cases, by calculations, and from absolute visual magnitudes and temperatures.

Average values for radius, bolometric luminosity, and mass are meaningful only for dwarf stars. Giant and subgiant stars all show large ranges in radius for a given mass. Conversely, giant stars of very nearly the same radius, surface temperature, and luminosity can have appreciably different masses.

Stellar Statistics

Some of the most important generalizations concerning the nature and evolution of stars can be derived from correlations between observable properties and certain statistical results. One of the most important of these correlations concerns temperature and luminosity—or, equivalently, colour and magnitude.

Hertzsprung-Russell Diagram

When the absolute magnitudes of stars (or their intrinsic luminosities on a logarithmic scale) are plotted in a diagram against temperature or, equivalently, against the spectral types, the stars do not fall at random on the diagram but tend to congregate in certain restricted domains. Such a plot is usually called a Hertzsprung-Russell diagram, named for the early 20th-century astronomers Ejnar Hertzsprung of Denmark and Henry Norris Russell of the United States, who independently discovered the relations shown in it.

As is seen in the diagram, most of the congregated stars are dwarfs lying closely around a diagonal line called the main sequence. These stars range from hot, O- and B-type, blue objects at least 10,000 times brighter than the Sun down through white A-type stars such as Sirius to orange K-type stars such as Epsilon Eridani and finally to M-type red dwarfs thousands of times fainter than the Sun. The sequence is continuous; the luminosities fall off smoothly with decreasing surface temperature; the masses and radii decrease but at a much slower rate; and the stellar densities gradually increase.

The second group of stars to be recognized was a group of giants—such objects as Capella, Arcturus, and Aldebaran—which are yellow, orange, or red stars about 100 times as bright as the Sun and have radii on the order of 10–30 million km (about 6–20 million miles, or 15–40 times as large as the Sun). The giants lie above the main sequence in the upper right portion of the diagram. The category of supergiants includes stars of all spectral types; these stars show a large spread in intrinsic brightness, and some even approach absolute magnitudes of -7 or -8. A few red supergiants, such as the variable star VV Cephei, exceed in size the orbit of Jupiter or even that of Saturn, although most of them are smaller. Supergiants are short-lived and rare objects, but they can be seen at great distances because of their tremendous luminosity.

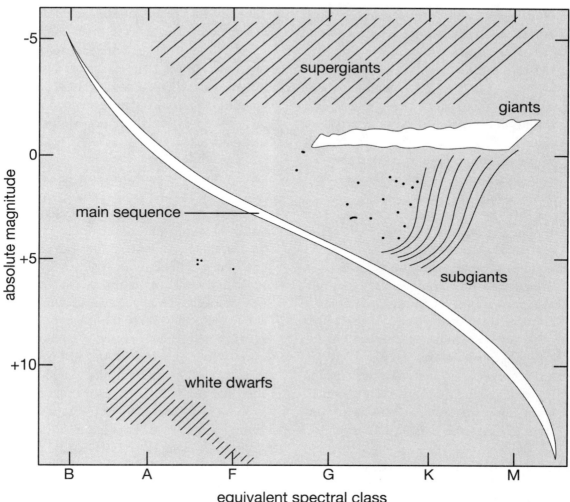

Schematic spectrum–luminosity correlation (Hertzsprung–Russell diagram) of spiral-arm stars in the neighbourhood of the Sun. From *Astrophysical Journal,* reproduced by permission of the American Astronomical Society

Subgiants are stars that are redder and larger than main-sequence stars of the same luminosity. Many of the best known examples are found in close binary systems where conditions favour their detection.

The white dwarf domain lies about 10 magnitudes below the main sequence. These stars are in the last stages of their evolution.

The spectrum-luminosity diagram has numerous gaps. Few stars exist above the white dwarfs and to the left of the main sequence. The giants are separated from the main sequence by a gap named for Hertzsprung, who in 1911 became the first to recognize the difference between main-sequence and giant stars. The actual concentration of stars differs considerably in different parts of the diagram. Highly luminous stars are rare, whereas those of low luminosity are very numerous.

The spectrum-luminosity diagram applies to the stars in the galactic spiral arm in the neighbourhood of the Sun and represents what would be obtained if a composite Hertzsprung-Russell diagram was constructed combining data for a large number of the star groups called open (or galactic) star clusters, as, for example, the double cluster h and χ Persei, the Pleiades, the Coma cluster, and the Hyades. It includes very young stars, a few million years old, as well as ancient stars, perhaps as old as 10 billion years.

By contrast, the second diagram exhibits the type of temperature-luminosity (or colour-magnitude) relation characteristic of stars in globular clusters, in the central bulge of the Galaxy, and in elliptical external galaxies—namely, of the so-called stellar Population II. (In addition to these oldest objects, Population II includes other very old stars that occur between the spiral arms of the Galaxy and at some distance above and below the galactic plane.) Because these systems are very remote from the observer, the stars are faint, and their spectra can be observed only with

difficulty. As a consequence, their colours rather than their spectra must be measured. Since the colours are closely related to surface temperature and therefore to spectral types, equivalent spectral types may be used; but it is stellar colours, not spectral types, that are observed in this instance.

The differences between the two Hertzsprung-Russell diagrams are striking. In the second figure, there are no supergiants, and, instead of a domain at an absolute magnitude of about 0, the giant stars form a branch that starts high and to the right at about -3.5 for very red stars and flows in a continuous sequence until it reaches an absolute magnitude of about 0. At that point the giant branch splits—a main band of stars, all about the same colour, proceeds downward (i.e., to fainter stars) to a magnitude of about +3 and then connects to the main sequence at about +4 by way of a narrow band. The main sequence of Population II stars extends downward to fainter, redder stars in much the same way as in the spiral-arm Population I stars. The main sequence ends at about spectral type G, however, and does not extend up through the A, B, and O spectral types, though occasionally a few such stars are found in the region normally occupied by the main sequence.

The other band of stars formed from the split of the giant branch is the "horizontal branch," which falls near magnitude +0.6 and fills the aforementioned Hertzsprung gap, extending to increasingly blue stars beyond the RR Lyrae stars, which are indicated by the cross-hatched area in the diagram. Among these blue hot stars are found novae and the nuclei of planetary nebulae, the latter so called because their photographic image resembles that of a distant planet. Not all globular clusters show identical colour-magnitude diagrams, which may be due to differences in the cluster ages or other factors.

ESTIMATES OF STELLAR AGES

The shapes of the colour-magnitude diagrams permit estimates of globular-cluster ages. Stars more massive than about 1.3 solar masses have evolved away from the main sequence at a point just above the position occupied by the Sun. The time required for such a star to exhaust the hydrogen in its core is about 5–6 billion years, and the cluster must be at least as old. More ancient clusters have been identified. In the Galaxy, globular clusters are all very ancient objects, having ages within a few billion years of the average of 14 billion years. In the Magellanic Clouds, however, clusters exist that resemble globular ones, but they contain numerous blue stars and therefore must be relatively young.

Open clusters in the spiral arms of the Galaxy—extreme Population I—tell a somewhat different story. A colour-magnitude diagram can be plotted for a number of different open clusters—for example, the double cluster h and χ Persei, the Pleiades, Praesepe, and M67—with the main feature distinguishing the clusters

being their ages. The young cluster h and χ Persei, which is a few million years old, contains stars ranging widely in luminosity. Some stars have already evolved into the supergiant stage (in such a diagram the top of the main sequence is bent over). The stars of luminosity 10,000 times greater than that of the Sun have already largely depleted the hydrogen in their cores and are leaving the main sequence.

The brightest stars of the Pleiades cluster, aged about 100 million years, have begun to leave the main sequence and are approaching the critical phase when they will have exhausted all the hydrogen in their cores. There are no giants in the Pleiades. Presumably, the cluster contained no stars as massive as some of those found in h and χ Persei.

The cluster known as Praesepe, or the Beehive, at an age of 790 million years, is older than the Pleiades. All stars much more luminous than the first magnitude have begun to leave the main sequence; there are some giants. The Hyades, about 620 million years old, displays a similar colour-magnitude array. These clusters contain a number of white dwarfs, indicating that the initially most luminous stars have already run the gamut of evolution. In a very old cluster such as M67, which is 4.5 billion years old, all of the bright main-sequence stars have disappeared.

The colour-magnitude diagrams for globular and open clusters differ quantitatively because the latter show a wider range of ages and differ in chemical composition. Most globular clusters have smaller metal-to-hydrogen ratios than do open clusters or the Sun. The gaps between the red giants and blue main-sequence stars of the open clusters (Population I) often contain unstable stars such as variables. The Cepheid variable stars, for instance, fall in these gaps.

The giant stars of the Praesepe cluster are comparable to the brightest stars in M67. The M67 giants have evolved from the main sequence near an absolute magnitude of +3.5, whereas the Praesepe giants must have masses about twice as great as those of the M67 giants. Giant stars of the same luminosity may therefore have appreciably different masses.

NUMBERS OF STARS VERSUS LUMINOSITY

Of great statistical interest is the relationship between the luminosities of the stars and their frequency of occurrence. The naked-eye stars are nearly all intrinsically brighter than the Sun, but the opposite is true for the known stars within 20 light-years of the Sun. The bright stars are easily seen at great distances; the faint ones can be detected only if they are close. Only if stars of magnitude +11 were a billion times more abundant than stars of magnitude –4 could they be observed to some fixed limit of apparent brightness.

The luminosity function depends on population type. The luminosity function for pure Population II differs substantially from that for pure Population I. There is a small peak near absolute magnitude +0.6, corresponding to the horizontal branch for Population II, and no stars as bright as absolute magnitude –5. The luminosity function for pure Population I is evaluated best from open star clusters, the stars in such a cluster being at about the same distance. The neighbourhood of the Sun includes examples of both Populations I and II.

MASS-LUMINOSITY CORRELATIONS

A plot of mass against bolometric luminosity for visual binaries for which good parallaxes and masses are available shows that for stars with masses comparable to that of the Sun the luminosity, L, varies as a power, $3 + \beta$, of the mass M. This relation can be expressed as

$$L = (M)^{3+\beta}.$$

The power differs for substantially fainter or much brighter stars.

This mass-luminosity correlation applies only to unevolved main-sequence stars. It fails for giants and supergiants and for the subgiant (dimmer) components of eclipsing binaries, all of which have changed considerably during their lifetimes. It does not apply to any stars in a globular cluster not on the main sequence, or to white dwarfs that are abnormally faint for their masses.

The mass-luminosity correlation, predicted theoretically in the early 20th century by the English astronomer Arthur Eddington, is a general relationship that holds for all stars having essentially the same internal density and temperature distributions—i.e., for what are termed the same stellar models.

VARIABLE STARS

Many stars are variable. Some are geometric variables, as in the eclipsing binaries considered earlier. Others are intrinsically variable—i.e., their total energy output fluctuates with time. Such intrinsic variable stars are dealt with in this section.

A fair number of stars are intrinsically variable. Some objects of this type were found by accident, but many were detected as a result of carefully planned searches. Variable stars are important in astronomy for several reasons. They usually appear to be stars at critical or short-lived phases of their evolution; detailed studies of their light and spectral characteristics, spatial distribution, and association with other types of stars may provide valuable clues to the life histories of various classes of stars. Certain kinds of variable stars, such as Cepheids (periodic variables) and novae and supernovae (explosive variables), are extremely important in that they make it possible to establish the distances of remote stellar systems beyond the Galaxy. If the intrinsic luminosity of a recognizable variable is known and this kind of variable star can be found in a distant stellar system, the distance of the latter can be estimated from a measurement of apparent and absolute magnitudes, provided the interstellar absorption is also known.

CLASSIFICATION

Variables are often classified as behaving like a prototype star, and the entire class is then named for this star—e.g., RR Lyrae stars are those whose variability follows the pattern of the star RR Lyrae. The most important classes of intrinsically variable stars are

(1) Pulsating variables—stars whose variations in light and colour are thought to arise primarily from stellar pulsations. These include Beta Canis Majoris stars, RR Lyrae stars, and Delta Scuti stars, all with short regular periods of less than a day; Cepheids, with periods between 1 and 100 days; and long-period variables, semiregular variables, and irregular red variables, usually with unstable periods of hundreds of days.

(2) Explosive, or catastrophic, variables—stars in which the variations are produced by the wrenching away of part of the star, usually the outer layers, in some explosive process. They include SS Cygni or U Geminorum stars, novae, and supernovae (the last of which are usually regarded as representing an enormous explosion involving most of the matter in a star).

(3) Miscellaneous and special types of variables—R Coronae Borealis stars, T Tauri stars, flare stars, pulsars (neutron stars), spectrum and magnetic variables, X-ray variable stars, and radio variable stars.

Pulsating Stars

An impressive body of evidence indicates that stellar pulsations can account for the variability of Cepheids, long-period variables, semiregular variables, Beta Canis Majoris stars, and even the irregular red variables. Of this group, the Cepheid variables have been studied in greatest detail, both theoretically and observationally. These stars are regular in their behaviour; some repeat their light curves with great faithfulness from one cycle to the next over periods of many years.

Much confusion existed in the study of Cepheids until it was recognized that different types of Cepheids are associated with different groups, or population types, of stars. Cepheids belonging to the spiral-arm Population I are characterized by regularity in their behaviour. They show continuous velocity curves indicative of regular pulsation. They exhibit a relation between period and luminosity in the sense that the longer the period of the star, the greater is its intrinsic brightness. This period-luminosity relationship has been used to establish the distances of remote stellar systems.

Cepheids with different properties are found in Population II, away from the Milky Way, in globular clusters. They are bluer than classic Population I Cepheids having the same period, and their light curves have different shapes. Studies of the light and velocity curves indicate that shells of gas are ejected from the stars as discontinuous layers that later fall back toward the surface. These stars exhibit a relation between period and luminosity different from that for Population I Cepheids, and thus the distance of a Cepheid in a remote stellar system can be determined only if its population type is known.

Closely associated with Population II Cepheids are the cluster-type, or RR Lyrae, variables. Many of these stars are found in clusters, but some, such as the prototype RR Lyrae, occur far from any cluster or the central galactic bulge. Their periods are less than a day, and there is no correlation between period and luminosity. Their absolute magnitudes are about 0.6 but somewhat dependent on metal abundance. They are thus about 50 times as bright as the Sun and so are useful for determining the distance of star clusters and some of the nearer external galaxies, their short periods permitting them to be detected readily.

Long-period variable stars also probably owe their variations to pulsations. Here the situation is complicated by the vast extent of their atmospheres, so that radiation originating at very different depths in the star is observed at the same time. At certain phases of the variations, bright hydrogen lines are observed, overlaid with titanium oxide absorption. The explanation is an outward-moving layer of hot, recombining gas, whose radiation is absorbed by strata of cool gases. These stars are all cool red giants and supergiants of spectral types M (normal composition), R and N (carbon-rich), or S (heavy-metal-rich). The range in visual brightness during a pulsation can be 100-fold, but the range in total energy output is much less, because at very low stellar temperatures (1,500–3,000 K) most of the energy is radiated in the infrared as heat rather than as light.

Unlike the light curves of classic Cepheids, the light curves of these red variables show considerable variations from one cycle to another. The visual magnitude of the variable star Mira Ceti (Omicron Ceti) is normally about 9–9.5 at minimum light, but at maximum it may lie between 5 and 2. Time intervals between maxima often vary considerably. In such cool objects, a very small change in temperature can produce a huge change in the output of visible radiation. At the low temperatures of the red variables, compounds and probably solid particles are formed copiously, so that the visible light may be profoundly affected by a slight change in physical conditions. Random fluctuations from cycle to cycle, which would produce negligible effects in a hotter star, produce marked light changes in a long-period variable.

Long-period variables appear to fall into two groups; those with periods of roughly 200 days tend to be associated with Population II, and those of periods of about a year belong to Population I.

Red semiregular variables such as the RV Tauri stars show complex light and spectral changes. They do not repeat themselves from one cycle to the next; their behaviour suggests a simultaneous operation of two or more modes of oscillation. Betelgeuse is an example of an irregular red variable. In these stars the free period of oscillation does not coincide with the periodicity of the driving mechanism.

Finally, among the various types of pulsating variable stars, the Beta Canis Majoris variables are high-temperature stars (spectral type B) that often show complicated variations in spectral-line shapes and intensities, velocity curves, and light. In many cases, they have two periods of variation so similar in duration that complex interference or beat phenomena are observed, both in radial velocities and in the shapes of spectral lines.

A large body of evidence suggests that all members of this first class of variable stars owe their variability to pulsation. The pulsation theory was first proposed as a possible explanation as early as 1879, was applied to Cepheids in 1914, and was further developed by Arthur Eddington in 1917–18. Eddington found that if stars have roughly the same kind of internal structure, then the period multiplied by the square root of the density equals a constant that depends on the internal structure.

The Eddington theory, though a good approximation, encountered some severe difficulties that have been met through modifications. If the entire star pulsated in synchronism, it should be brightest when compressed and smaller while faintest when expanded and at its largest. The radial velocity should be zero at both maximum and minimum light. Observations contradict these predictions. When the star pulsates, all parts of the main body move in synchronism, but the outer observable strata fall out of step or lag behind the pulsation of the inner regions. Pulsations involve only the outer part of a star; the core, where energy is generated by thermonuclear reactions, is unaffected.

Many years ago, careful measurements of the average magnitudes and colours of RR Lyrae stars in the globular cluster M3 showed that all these stars fell within a narrow range of luminosity and colour (or surface temperature) or, equivalently, luminosity and radius. Also, every star falling in this narrow range of brightness and size was an RR Lyrae variable. Subsequent work has indicated that similar considerations apply to most classic Cepheids. Variability is thus a characteristic of any star whose evolution carries it to a certain size and luminosity, although the amplitude of the variability can vary dramatically.

In the pulsation theory as now developed, the light and velocity changes of Cepheids can be interpreted not only qualitatively but also quantitatively. The light curves of Cepheids, for example, have been precisely predicted by the theory. Stellar pulsation, like other rhythmic actions, may give rise to harmonic phenomena wherein beats reinforce or interfere with one another. Beat and interference phenomena then complicate the light and velocity changes. The RR Lyrae stars supply some of the best examples, but semiregular variables such as the RV Tauri stars or most Delta Scuti stars evidently vibrate simultaneously with two or more periods.

EXPLOSIVE VARIABLES

The evolution of a member of a close double-star system can be markedly affected by the presence of its companion. As the stars age, the more massive one swells up more quickly as it moves away from the main sequence. It becomes so large that its outer envelope falls under the gravitational influence of the smaller star. Matter is continuously fed from the more rapidly evolving star to the less massive one, which still remains on the main sequence. U Cephei is a classic example of such a system for which spectroscopic evidence shows streams of gas flowing from the more highly evolved star to the hotter companion, which is now the more massive of the two. Eventually, the latter will also leave the main sequence and become a giant star, only to lose its outer envelope to the companion, which by that time may have reached the white dwarf stage.

Novae appear to be binary stars that have evolved from contact binaries of the

W Ursae Majoris type, which are pairs of stars apparently similar to the Sun in size but revolving around one another while almost touching. One member may have reached the white dwarf stage. Matter fed to it from its distended companion appears to produce instabilities that result in violent explosions or nova outbursts. The time interval between outbursts can range from a few score years to hundreds of thousands of years.

In ordinary novae the explosion seems to involve only the outer layers, as the star later returns to its former brightness; in supernovae the explosion is catastrophic. Normally, novae are small blue stars much fainter than the Sun, though very much hotter. When an outburst occurs, the star can brighten very rapidly, by 10 magnitudes or more in a few hours. Thereafter it fades; the rate of fading is connected with the brightness of the nova. The brightest novae, which reach absolute magnitudes of about -10, fade most rapidly, whereas a typical slow nova, which reaches an absolute magnitude of -5, can take 10 or 20 times as long to decline in brightness. This property, when calibrated as the absolute magnitude at maximum brightness versus the time taken to decline by two magnitudes, allows novae to be used as distance indicators for nearby galaxies. The changes in light are accompanied by pronounced spectroscopic changes that can be interpreted as arising from alterations in an ejected shell that dissipates slowly in space. In its earliest phases, the expanding shell is opaque. As its area grows, with a surface temperature near 7,000 K, the nova brightens rapidly. Then, near maximum light, the shell becomes transparent, and its total brightness plummets rapidly, causing the nova to dim.

The mass of the shell is thought to be rather small, about 10–100 times the mass of Earth. Only the outer layers of the star seem to be affected; the main mass settles down after the outburst into a state much as before until a new outburst occurs. The existence of repeating novae, such as the star T Coronae Borealis, suggests that perhaps all novae repeat at intervals ranging up to thousands or perhaps millions of years; and probably, the larger the explosion, the longer the interval. There is strong evidence that novae are components of close double stars and, in particular, that they have evolved from the most common kind of eclipsing binaries, those of the W Ursae Majoris type.

Stars of the SS Cygni type, also known as dwarf novae, undergo novalike outbursts but of a much smaller amplitude. The intervals between outbursts are a few months to a year. Such variables are close binaries. The development of this particular type may be possible only in close binary systems.

There are two major types of supernovae, designated type I (or SNe I) and type II (or SNe II). They can be distinguished by the fact that type II have hydrogen features in their spectra, while type I do not. Type II supernovae arise from the collapse of a single star more massive than about eight solar masses, resulting in either a neutron star or black hole. Type I supernovae, on the other hand, are believed to originate in a binary system containing a white dwarf, rather like the case of ordinary novae. Unlike the latter, however, in which only the outer layers of the white dwarf seem to be affected, in a type I supernova the white dwarf is probably completely destroyed, although the details are not yet fully understood. Certainly a supernova's energy output is enormously greater than that of an ordinary nova.

Type I supernovae can be further divided into Ia and Ib, the distinguishing feature being that the spectra of Ia show a strong silicon line, whereas the spectra of Ib show a weak one. Empirical evidence indicates that in a type Ia supernova the absolute magnitude at maximum light can be determined by a combination of data derived from the rate of dimming after maximum, the shape of the light curve, and certain colour measurements. A comparison of the absolute and apparent magnitudes of maximum light, in turn, allows the distance of the supernova to be found. This is a matter of great usefulness because type Ia supernovae at maximum light are the most luminous "standard candles" available for determining distances to external galaxies and thus can be observed in more distant galaxies more than any other kind of standard candle. In 1999, application of this technique led to the totally unexpected discovery that the expansion of the universe appears to be accelerating rather than slowing down due to the presence of dark energy.

Probably all variable stars represent more or less ephemeral phases in the evolution of a star. Aside from catastrophic events of the kind that produce a supernova, some phases of stellar variability might be of such brief duration as to permit recognizable changes during an interval of 50–100 years. Other stages may require many thousands of years. For example, the period of Delta Cephei, the prototype star of the Cepheid variables, has barely changed by a detectable amount since its variability was discovered in 1784.

Peculiar Variables

R Coronae Borealis variables are giant stars of about the Sun's temperature whose atmospheres are characterized by excessive quantities of carbon and very little hydrogen. The brightness of such a star remains constant until the star suddenly dims by several magnitudes and then slowly recovers its original brightness. (The star's colour remains the same during the changes in brightness.) The dimmings occur in a random fashion and seem to be due to the huge concentrations of carbon. At times the carbon vapour literally condenses into soot, and the star is hidden until the smog blanket is evaporated. Similar veiling may sometimes occur in other types of low-temperature stars, particularly in long-period variables.

Flare stars are cool dwarfs (spectral type M) that display flares apparently very much like, but much more intense than, those of the Sun. In fact, the flares are sometimes so bright that they overwhelm the normal light of the star. Solar flares are associated with copious emission of radio waves, and simultaneous optical and radio-wave events appear to have been found in the stars UV Ceti, YZ Canis Minoris, and V371 Orionis.

Spectrum and magnetic variables, mostly of spectral type A, show only small amplitudes of light variation but often pronounced spectroscopic changes. Their spectra typically show strong lines of metals such as manganese, titanium, iron, chromium, and the lanthanides (also called rare earths), which vary periodically in intensity. These stars have strong magnetic fields, typically from a few hundred to a few thousand gauss; one star, HD 215441, has a field on the order of 30,000 gauss. Not all magnetic stars are known to be variable in light; these objects also seem to have variable magnetic fields. The best interpretation is that these stars are rotating about an inclined axis. As with Earth, the magnetic and rotation axes do not coincide. Different ions are concentrated in different areas (e.g., chromium in one area and the lanthanides in another).

The Sun is an emitter of radio waves, but with present techniques its radio emission could only just be detected— even in its most active phases—at the distance of the nearest star, about four light-years away. Most discrete radio-frequency sources have turned out to be objects such as old supernovae, radio galaxies, and quasars, though well-recognized

radio stars also have been recorded on occasion. These probably include flare stars, possibly red supergiants such as Betelgeuse, the high-temperature dwarf companion to the red supergiant Antares, and the shells ejected from Nova Serpentis 1970 and Nova Delphini. The radio emission from the latter objects is consistent with that expected from an expanding shell of ionized gas that fades away as the gas becomes attenuated. The central star of the Crab Nebula has been detected as a radio (and optical) pulsar.

Measurements from rockets, balloons, and spacecraft have revealed distinct X-ray sources outside the solar system. The strongest galactic source, Scorpius X-1, appears to be associated with a hot variable star resembling an old nova. In all likelihood this is a binary star system containing a low-mass normal star and a nonluminous companion.

A number of globular clusters are sources of cosmic X-rays. Some of this X-ray emission appears as intense fluctuations of radiation lasting only a few seconds but changing in strength by as much as 25 times. These X-ray sources have become known as bursters, and several such objects have been discovered outside of globular clusters as well. Some bursters vary on a regular basis, while others seem to turn on and off randomly. The most popular interpretation holds that bursters are the result of binary systems in which one of the objects—a compact neutron star or black hole—pulls matter from the companion, a normal star. This matter is violently heated in the process, giving rise to X-rays. That the emission is often in the form of a burst is probably caused by something interrupting the flow of matter onto (or into) the compact object or by an eclipsing orbit of the binary system.

STELLAR ATMOSPHERES

To interpret a stellar spectrum quantitatively, knowledge of the variation in temperature and density with depth in the star's atmosphere is needed. Some general theoretical principles are outlined here.

The gradient of temperature in a star's atmosphere depends on the method of energy transport to the surface. One way to move energy from the interior of a star to its surface is via radiation; photons produced in the core are repeatedly absorbed and reemitted by stellar atoms, gradually propagating to the surface. A second way is via convection, which is a nonradiative mechanism involving a physical upwelling of matter much as in a pot of boiling water. For the Sun, at least, there are ways of distinguishing the mechanism of energy transport.

High-speed photographs of the Sun's disk show that the centre of the disk is brighter than the limb. The difference in brightness depends on the wavelength of the radiation detected; it is large in violet light, is small in red light, and nearly vanishes when the Sun is imaged in infrared radiation. This limb darkening arises because the Sun becomes hotter toward its core. At the centre of the disk, radiation is received from deeper and hotter

layers (on average) instead of from the limb, and the dependence of temperature on depth can be shown to correspond to the transport of energy by radiation, not by convection, at least in the outer layers of the Sun's atmosphere.

The amount of limb darkening in any star depends on the effective temperature of the star and on the variation in temperature with depth. Limb darkening is occasionally an important factor in the analysis of stellar observations. For example, it must be taken into account to interpret properly the observed light curves of eclipsing binaries, and here again the results suggest transport of energy via radiation.

The layers of a normal star are assumed to be in mechanical, or hydrostatic, equilibrium. This means that at each point in the atmosphere, the pressure supports the weight of the overlying layers. In this way, a relation between pressure and density can be found for any given depth.

In addition to the temperature and density gradients, the chemical composition of the atmospheric layers as well as the absorptivity, or opacity, of the material must be known. In the Sun the principal source of opacity is the negative hydrogen ion (H^-), a hydrogen atom with one extra electron loosely bound to it. In the atmospheres of many stars, the extra electrons break loose and recombine with other ions, thereby causing a reemission of energy in the form of light. At visible wavelengths the main contribution to the opacity comes from the destruction of this ion by interaction with a photon (the above-cited process is termed *photodissociation*). In hotter stars, such as Sirius A (the temperature of which is about 10,000 K), atomic hydrogen is the main source of opacity, whereas in cooler stars much of the outgoing energy is often absorbed by molecular bands of titanium oxide, water vapour, and carbon monoxide. Additional sources of opacity are absorption by helium atoms and electron scattering in hotter stars, absorption by hydrogen molecules and molecular ions, absorption by certain abundant metals such as magnesium, and Rayleigh scattering (a type of wavelength-dependent scattering of radiation by particles named for the British physicist Lord Rayleigh) in cool supergiant stars.

At considerable depths in the Sun and similar stars, convection sets in. Though most models of stellar atmospheres (particularly the outer layers) assume plane-parallel stratified layers, photographs of granulation on the Sun's visible surface belie this simple picture. Realistic models must allow for rising columns of heated gases in some areas and descent of cooler gases in others. The motions of the radiating gases are especially important when the model is to be used to calculate the anticipated line spectrum of the star. Typical gas velocities are on the order of 2 km (1.4 miles) per second in the Sun; in other stars they can be much larger.

Temperature, density, and pressure all increase steadily inward in the Sun's atmosphere. The Sun has no distinct solid surface, so the point from which the depth or height is measured is arbitrary. The temperature of the visible layers ranges from 4,700 to 6,200 K, the density from about 10^{-7} to 4×10^{-7} gram per cubic cm (1 cubic cm = .06 cubic inch), and the gas pressure from 0.002 to 0.14 atmosphere. The visible layers of stars such as the Sun have very low densities and pressures compared with Earth's atmosphere, even though the temperature is much higher. The strata of the solar atmosphere are very opaque compared with the terrestrial atmosphere.

For stars other than the Sun, the dependence of temperature on depth cannot be directly determined. Calculations must proceed by a process of successive approximations, during which the flux of energy is taken to be constant with depth. Computations have been undertaken for atmospheres of a variety of stars ranging from dwarfs to supergiants, from cool to hot stars. Their validity can be evaluated only by examining how well they predict the observed features of a star's continuous and line spectrum, including the detailed shapes of spectral-line features. Considering the known complexities of stellar atmospheres, the results fit the observations remarkably well.

Severe deviations exist for stars with extended and expanding atmospheres. Matter flowing outward from a star produces a stellar wind analogous to the solar wind, but one that is often much more extensive and violent. In the spectrum of certain very hot O-type stars (e.g., Zeta Puppis), strong, relatively narrow emission lines can be seen; however, in the ultraviolet, observations from rockets and spacecraft show strong emission lines with distinct absorption components on the shorter wavelength side. These absorption features are produced by rapidly outflowing atoms that absorb the radiation from the underlying stellar surface. The observed shifts in frequency correspond to ejection velocities of about 100 km (60 miles) per second. Much gentler stellar winds are found in cool M-type supergiants.

Rapid stellar rotation also can modify the structure of a star's atmosphere. Since effective gravity is much reduced near the equator, the appropriate description of the atmosphere varies with latitude. Should the star be spinning at speeds near the breakup point, rings or shells may be shed from the equator.

Some of the most extreme and interesting cases of rotational effects are found in close binary systems. Interpretations of the light and velocity curves of these objects suggest that the spectroscopic observations cannot be reconciled with simple, orderly rotating stars. Instead, emission and absorption lines sometimes overlap in such a way as to suggest streams of gas moving between the stars. For example, Beta Lyrae, an eclipsing binary system, has a period of 12.9 days and displays very large shifts in orbital velocity. The brighter member at visible wavelengths is a B9-type star; the other member appears to be a hot, abnormal object whose spectral lines have not been observed. The spectrum of the B9-type component shows the regular velocity changes expected of a binary star but with an absorption (and associated emission) spectrum corresponding to a higher temperature (near spectral type B5) and a blue continuum corresponding to a very-high-temperature star. The anomalous B5-type spectrum is evidently excited principally by the hotter source; it envelopes the entire system and shows few changes in velocity with time.

Supergiant stars have very extended atmospheres that are probably not even approximately in hydrostatic equilibrium. The atmospheres of M-type supergiant stars appear to be slowly expanding outward. Observations of the eclipsing binary 31 Cygni show that the K-type supergiant component has an extremely inhomogeneous, extended atmosphere composed of numerous blobs and filaments. As the secondary member of this system slowly moves behind the larger star, its light shines through larger masses of the K-type star's atmosphere. If the atmosphere were in orderly layers, the lines of ionized calcium, for example, produced by absorption of the light of the B-type star by the K-type star's atmosphere, would grow stronger uniformly as the eclipse proceeds. They do not, however.

STELLAR INTERIORS

Models of the internal structure of stars—particularly their temperature, density, and pressure gradients below the surface—depend on basic principles explained in this section. It is especially important that model calculations take account of the change in the star's structure with time as its hydrogen supply is gradually converted into helium. Fortunately, given that most stars can be said to be examples of an "ideal gas", the relations between temperature, density, and pressure have a basic simplicity.

DISTRIBUTION OF MATTER

Several mathematical relations can be derived from basic physical laws, assuming that the gas is "ideal" and that a star has spherical symmetry; both these assumptions are met with a high degree of validity. Another common assumption is that the interior of a star is in hydrostatic equilibrium. This balance is often expressed as a simple relation between pressure gradient and density. A second relation expresses the continuity of mass—i.e., if M is the mass of matter within a sphere of radius r, the mass added, ΔM, when encountering an increase in distance Δr through a shell of volume $4\pi r^2 \Delta r$, equals the volume of the shell multiplied by the density, ρ. In symbols,

$$\Delta M = 4\pi r^2 \rho \Delta r.$$

A third relation, termed the equation of state, expresses an explicit relation between the temperature, density, and pressure of a star's internal matter. Throughout the star the matter is entirely gaseous, and, except in certain highly evolved objects, it obeys closely the perfect gas law. In such neutral gases the molecular weight is 2 for molecular hydrogen, 4 for helium, 56 for iron, and so on. In the interior of a typical star, however, the high temperatures and densities virtually guarantee that nearly all the matter is completely ionized; the gas is said to be a plasma, the fourth state of matter. Under these conditions not only are the hydrogen molecules dissociated into individual atoms, but also the atoms themselves are broken apart (ionized) into their constituent protons and electrons. Hence, the molecular weight of ionized hydrogen is the average mass of a proton and an electron—namely, ½ on the atom-mass scale noted above. By contrast, a completely ionized helium atom contributes a mass of 4 with a helium nucleus (alpha particle) plus two electrons of negligible mass; hence, its average molecular weight is ⁴⁄₃. As another example, a totally ionized nickel atom contributes a nucleus of mass 58.7 plus 28 electrons; its molecular weight is then 58.7/29 = 2.02. Since stars contain a preponderance of hydrogen and helium that are completely ionized throughout the interior, the average particle mass, μ, is the (unit) mass of a proton, divided by a factor taking into account the concentrations by weight of hydrogen, helium, and heavier ions. Accordingly, the molecular weight depends critically on the star's chemical composition, particularly on the ratio of helium to hydrogen as well as on the total content of heavier matter.

If the temperature is sufficiently high, the radiation pressure, P_r, must be taken into account in addition to the perfect gas pressure, P_g. The total equation of state then becomes

$$P = P_g + P_r.$$

Here P_g depends on temperature, density, and molecular weight, whereas P_r depends on temperature and on the radiation density constant,

$$a = 7.5 \times 10^{-15}$$

ergs per cubic cm per degree to the fourth power. With $\mu = 2$ (as an upper limit) and $\rho = 1.4$ grams per cubic cm (the mean density of the Sun), the temperature at which the radiation pressure would equal the gas pressure can be calculated. The answer is 28 million K, much hotter than the core of the Sun. Consequently, radiation pressure may be neglected for the Sun, but it cannot be ignored for hotter, more massive stars. Radiation pressure may then set an upper limit to stellar luminosity.

Certain stars, notably white dwarfs, do not obey the perfect gas law. Instead, the pressure is almost entirely contributed by the electrons, which are said to be particulate members of a degenerate gas. If μ' is the average mass per free electron of the totally ionized gas, the pressure, P, and density, ρ, are such that P is proportional to a $5/3$ power of the density divided by the average mass per free electron; i.e.,

$$P = 10^{13}(\rho/\mu')^{5/3}.$$

The temperature does not enter at all. At still higher densities the equation of state becomes more intricate, but it can be shown that even this complicated equation of state is adequate to calculate the internal structure of the white dwarf stars. As a result, white dwarfs are probably better understood than most other celestial objects.

For normal stars such as the Sun, the energy-transport method for the interior must be known. Except in white dwarfs or in the dense cores of evolved stars, thermal conduction is unimportant because the heat conductivity is very low. One significant mode of transport is an actual flow of radiation outward through the star. Starting as gamma rays near the core, the radiation is gradually "softened" (becomes longer in wavelength) as it works its way to the surface (typically, in the Sun, over the course of about a million years) to emerge as ordinary light and heat. The rate of flow of radiation is proportional to the thermal gradient—namely, the rate of change of temperature with interior distance. Providing yet another relation of stellar structure, this equation uses the following important quantities: a, the radiation constant noted above; c, the velocity of light; ρ, the density; and κ, a measure of the opacity of the matter. The larger the value of κ, the lower the transparency of the material and the steeper the temperature fall required to push the energy outward at the required rate. The opacity, κ, can be calculated for any temperature, density, and chemical composition and is found to depend in a complex manner largely on the two former quantities.

In the Sun's outermost (though still interior) layers and especially in certain giant stars, energy transport takes place by quite another mechanism: large-scale mass motions of gases—namely, convection. Huge volumes of gas deep within the star become heated, rise to higher layers, and mix with their surroundings, thus releasing great quantities of energy. The extraordinarily complex flow patterns cannot be followed in detail, but when convection occurs, a relatively simple mathematical relation connects density and pressure. Wherever convection does occur, it moves energy much more efficiently than radiative transport.

SOURCE OF STELLAR ENERGY

The most basic property of stars is that their radiant energy must derive from internal sources. Given the great length of time that stars endure (some 10 billion years in the case of the Sun), it can be shown that neither chemical nor gravitational effects could possibly yield the required energies. Instead, the cause must be nuclear events wherein lighter nuclei are fused to create heavier nuclei, an inevitable by-product being energy.

In the interior of a star, the particles move rapidly in every direction because of the high temperatures present. Every so often a proton moves close enough to a nucleus to be captured, and a nuclear reaction takes place. Only protons of extremely high energy (many times the average energy in a star such as the Sun) are capable of producing nuclear events of this kind. A minimum temperature required for fusion is roughly 10 million K. Since the energies of protons are proportional to temperature, the rate of energy production rises steeply as temperature increases.

For the Sun and other normal main-sequence stars, the source of energy lies in the conversion of hydrogen to helium. The nuclear reaction thought to occur in the Sun is called the proton-proton cycle. In this fusion reaction, two protons (^{1}H) collide to form a deuteron (a nucleus of deuterium, ^{2}H), with the liberation of a positron (the electron's positively charged antimatter counterpart, denoted e^+). Also emitted is a neutral particle of very small (or possibly zero) mass called a neutrino, v. While the helium "ash" remains in the core where it was produced, the neutrino escapes from the solar interior within seconds. The positron encounters an ordinary negatively charged electron, and the two annihilate each other, with much energy being released. This annihilation energy amounts to 1.02 megaelectron volts (MeV), which accords well with Einstein's equation

$$E = mc^2$$

(where m is the mass of the two particles, c the velocity of light, and E the liberated energy).

Next, a proton collides with the deuteron to form the nucleus of a light helium atom of atomic weight 3, ^{3}He. A "hard"

X-ray (one of higher energy) or gamma-ray (γ) photon also is emitted. The most likely event to follow in the chain is a collision of this ^{3}He nucleus with a normal ^{4}He nucleus to form the nucleus of a beryllium atom of weight 7, ^{7}Be, with the emission of another gamma-ray photon. The ^{7}Be nucleus in turn captures a proton to form a boron nucleus of atomic weight 8, ^{8}B, with the liberation of yet another gamma ray.

The ^{8}B nucleus, however, is very unstable. It decays almost immediately into beryllium of atomic weight 8, ^{8}Be, with the emission of another positron and a neutrino. The nucleus itself thereafter decays into two helium nuclei, ^{4}He. These nuclear events can be represented by the following equations:

$$^3\text{He} + {}^4\text{He} \rightarrow {}^7\text{Be} + \gamma \quad \text{(rather slow reaction)}$$
$$^7\text{Be} + {}^1\text{H} \rightarrow {}^8\text{B} + \gamma \quad \text{(rapid reaction)}$$
$$\left.\begin{array}{l} ^8\text{B} \rightarrow {}^8\text{Be} + e^+ + \nu \\ ^8\text{Be} \rightarrow 2\,{}^4\text{He} \end{array}\right\} \text{(instantaneous reactions)}$$

In the course of these reactions, four protons are consumed to form one helium nucleus, while two electrons perish.

The mass of four hydrogen atoms is 4 × 1.00797, or 4.03188, atomic mass units; that of a helium atom is 4.0026. Hence, 0.02928 atomic mass unit, or 0.7 percent of the original mass, has disappeared. Some of this has been carried away by the elusive neutrinos, but most of it has been converted to radiant energy. In order to keep shining at its present rate, a typical star (e.g., the Sun) needs to convert 674 million tons of hydrogen to 670 million tons of helium every second. According to the formula

$$E = mc^2,$$

more than four million tons of matter literally disappear into radiation each second.

This theory provides a good understanding of solar-energy generation, although for decades it has suffered from one potential problem. For the past several decades the neutrino flux from the Sun has been measured by different experimenters, and only one-third of flux of electron neutrinos predicted by the theory have been detected. Over that time, however, the consensus has grown that the problem and its solution lie not with the astrophysical model of the Sun but with the physical nature of neutrinos themselves. In late 1990s and early 21st century, scientists collected evidence that neutrinos oscillate between the state in which they were created in the Sun and a state that is more difficult to detect when they reach Earth.

The main source of energy in hotter stars is the carbon cycle (also called the CNO cycle for carbon, nitrogen, and oxygen), in which hydrogen is transformed into helium, with carbon serving as a catalyst. The reactions proceed as follows: first, a carbon nucleus, ^{12}C, captures a proton (hydrogen nucleus), ^{1}H, to form a nucleus of nitrogen, ^{13}N, a gamma-ray photon being emitted in the process; thus,

$$^{12}C + {}^{1}H \rightarrow {}^{13}N + \gamma.$$

The light ^{13}N nucleus is unstable, however. It emits a positron, e^+, which encounters an ordinary electron, e^-, and the two annihilate one another. A neutrino also is released, and the resulting ^{13}C nucleus is stable. Eventually the ^{13}C nucleus captures another proton, forms ^{14}N, and emits another gamma-ray photon. In symbols the reaction is represented by the equations

$$^{13}N \rightarrow {}^{13}C + e^+ + \nu;$$
$$\text{then } {}^{13}C + {}^{1}H \rightarrow {}^{14}N + \gamma.$$

Ordinary nitrogen, ^{14}N, is stable, but when it captures a proton to form a nucleus of light oxygen-15, ^{15}O, the resulting nucleus is unstable against beta decay. It therefore emits a positron and a neutrino, a sequence of events expressed by the equations

$$^{14}N + {}^{1}H \rightarrow {}^{15}O + \gamma;$$
$$\text{then } {}^{15}O \rightarrow {}^{15}N + e^+ + \nu.$$

Again, the positron meets an electron, and the two annihilate each other while the neutrino escapes. Eventually the ^{15}N nucleus encounters a fast-moving proton, ^{1}H, and captures it, but the formation of an ordinary ^{16}O nucleus by this process occurs only rarely. The most likely effect of this proton capture is a breakdown of ^{15}N and a return to the ^{12}C nucleus—that is,

$$^{15}N + {}^{1}H \rightarrow {}^{12}C + {}^{4}He + \gamma.$$

Thus, the original ^{12}C nucleus reappears, and the four protons that have been added permit the formation of a helium nucleus. The same amount of mass has disappeared, though a different fraction of it may have been carried off by the neutrinos.

Only the hottest stars that lie on the main sequence shine with energy produced by the carbon cycle. The faint red dwarfs use the proton-proton cycle exclusively, whereas stars such as the Sun shine mostly by the proton-proton reaction but derive some contribution from the carbon cycle as well.

The aforementioned mathematical relationships permit the problem of stellar structure to be addressed notwithstanding the complexity of the problem. An early assumption that stars have a uniform chemical composition throughout their interiors simplified the calculations considerably, but it had to be abandoned when studies in stellar evolution proved that the compositions of stars change with age. Computations need to be carried out by a step-by-step process known as numerical integration. They must take into account that the density and pressure of a star vanish at the surface, whereas these quantities and the temperature remain finite at the core.

Resulting models of a star's interior, including the relation between mass, luminosity, and radius, are determined largely by the mode of energy transport. In the Sun and the fainter main-sequence stars, energy is transported throughout the outer layers by convective currents, whereas in the deep interior, energy is transported by radiation. Among the hotter stars of the main sequence, the reverse appears to be true. The deep interiors of the stars that derive their energy primarily from the carbon cycle are in convective equilibrium, whereas in the outer parts the energy is carried by radiation. The observed masses, luminosities, and radii of most main-sequence stars can be reproduced with reasonable and uniform chemical composition.

Chemically homogeneous models of giant and supergiant stars cannot be constructed. If a yellow giant such as Capella is assumed to be built like a main-sequence star, its central temperature turns out to be so low that no known nuclear process can possibly supply the observed energy output. Progress has been made only by assuming that these stars were once main-sequence objects that, in the course of their development, exhausted the hydrogen in their deep interiors. Inert cores consequently formed, composed mainly of the helium ash left from the hydrogen-fusion process. Since no helium nuclear reactions are known to occur at the few tens of millions of kelvins likely to prevail in these interiors, no thermonuclear energy could be released from such depleted cores. Instead, energy is assumed to be generated in a thin shell surrounding the inert core where some fuel remains, and it is presumably produced by the carbon cycle. Such models are called shell-source models. As a star uses up increasing amounts of its hydrogen supply, its core grows in mass, all the while the outer envelope of the star continues to expand. These shell-source models explain the observed luminosities, masses, and radii of giants and supergiants.

The depletion of hydrogen fuel is appreciable even for a dwarf, middle-aged star such as the Sun. The Sun seems to have been shining at its present rate for about the last 20 percent of its current age of five billion years. For its observed luminosity to be maintained, the Sun's central temperature must have increased considerably since the formation of the solar system, largely as a consequence of the depletion of the hydrogen in its interior along with an accompanying increase in molecular weight and temperature. During the past five billion years, the Sun probably brightened by about half a magnitude; in early Precambrian time (about two billion years ago), the solar luminosity must have been some 20 percent less than it is today.

CHAPTER 3

STAR FORMATION AND EVOLUTION

Throughout the Milky Way Galaxy (and even near the Sun itself), astronomers have discovered stars that are well evolved or even approaching extinction, or both, as well as occasional stars that must be very young or still in the process of formation. Evolutionary effects on these stars are not negligible, even for a middle-aged star such as the Sun. More massive stars must display more spectacular effects because the rate of conversion of mass into energy is higher. While the Sun produces energy at the rate of about two ergs per gram per second, a more luminous main-sequence star can release energy at a rate some 1,000 times greater. Consequently, effects that require billions of years to be easily recognized in the Sun might occur within a few million years in highly luminous and massive stars. A supergiant star such as Antares, a bright main-sequence star such as Rigel, or even a more modest star such as Sirius cannot have endured as long as the Sun has endured. These stars must have been formed relatively recently.

BIRTH OF STARS AND EVOLUTION TO THE MAIN SEQUENCE

Detailed radio maps of nearby molecular clouds reveal that they are clumpy, with regions containing a wide range of densities—from a few tens of molecules (mostly hydrogen) per cubic centimetre to more than one million. Stars form only from the densest regions, termed cloud cores, though they need not lie at the geometric centre of the cloud. Large cores (which probably contain subcondensations) up to a few light-years in size seem to give rise to unbound associations of very massive stars (called OB associations after the spectral type of their most prominent members, O and B stars) or to bound clusters of less massive stars. Whether a stellar group materializes as an association or a cluster seems to depend on the efficiency of star formation.

If only a small fraction of the matter goes into making stars, the rest being blown away in winds or expanding H II regions, then the remaining stars end up in a gravitationally unbound association, dispersed in a single crossing time (diameter divided by velocity) by the random motions of the formed stars. On the other hand, if 30 percent or more of the mass of the cloud core goes into making stars, then the formed stars will remain bound to one another, and the ejection of stars by random gravitational encounters between cluster members will take many crossing times.

Low-mass stars also are formed in associations called T associations after the prototypical stars found in such groups, T Tauri stars. The stars of a T association form from loose aggregates of small molecular cloud cores a few tenths of a light-year in size that are randomly distributed through a larger region of lower average density. The formation of stars in associations is the most common outcome; bound clusters account for only about 1 to 10 percent of all star births. The overall efficiency of star formation in associations is quite small. Typically less than 1 percent of the mass of a molecular cloud becomes stars in one crossing time of the molecular cloud (about $5 \cdot 10^6$ years). Low efficiency of star formation presumably explains why any interstellar gas remains in the Galaxy after 10^{10} years of evolution. Star formation at the present time must be a mere trickle of the torrent that occurred when the Galaxy was young.

A typical cloud core rotates fairly slowly, and its distribution of mass is strongly concentrated toward the centre. The slow rotation rate is probably attributable to the braking action of magnetic fields that thread through the core and its envelope. This magnetic braking forces the core to rotate at nearly the same angular speed as the envelope as long as the core does not go into dynamic collapse. Such braking is an important process because it assures a source of matter of relatively low angular momentum (by the standards of the interstellar medium) for the formation of stars and planetary systems.

It also has been proposed that magnetic fields play an important role in the very separation of the cores from their envelopes. The proposal involves the slippage of the neutral component of a lightly ionized gas under the action of the self-gravity of the matter past the charged particles suspended in a background magnetic field. This slow slippage would provide the theoretical explanation for the observed low overall efficiency of star formation in molecular clouds.

At some point in the course of the evolution of a molecular cloud, one or more of its cores become unstable and subject to gravitational collapse. Good arguments exist that the central regions should collapse first, producing a condensed protostar whose contraction is halted by the large buildup of thermal pressure when radiation can no longer escape from the interior to keep the (now opaque) body relatively cool. The protostar, which initially has a mass not much larger than Jupiter, continues to grow by accretion as more and more overlying material falls on top of it. The infall shock, at the surfaces of the protostar and the swirling nebular disk surrounding it, arrests the inflow, creating an intense radiation field that tries to work its way out of the infalling envelope of gas and dust. The photons, having optical wavelengths, are degraded into longer wavelengths by dust absorption and reemission, so that the protostar is apparent to a distant observer only as an infrared object. Provided that proper account is taken of the effects of rotation and magnetic field, this theoretical picture correlates with the radiative spectra emitted by many candidate protostars discovered near the centres of molecular cloud cores.

An interesting speculation concerning the mechanism that ends the infall phase exists: it notes that the inflow process cannot run to completion. Since molecular clouds as a whole contain much more mass than what goes into each generation of stars, the depletion of the available raw material is not what stops the accretion flow. A rather different picture is revealed by observations at radio, optical, and X-ray wavelengths. All newly born stars are highly active, blowing powerful winds that clear the surrounding regions of the infalling gas and dust. It is apparently this wind that reverses the accretion flow.

The geometric form taken by the outflow is intriguing. Jets of matter seem to squirt in opposite directions along the rotational poles of the star (or disk) that sweep up the ambient matter in two lobes of outwardly moving molecular gas—the so-called bipolar flows. Such jets and bipolar flows are doubly interesting because their counterparts were discovered some time earlier on a fantastically larger scale in the double-lobed forms of extragalactic radio sources, such as quasars.

The underlying energy source that drives the outflow is unknown. Promising mechanisms invoke tapping the rotational energy stored in either the newly formed star or the inner parts of its nebular disk. There exist theories suggesting that strong magnetic fields coupled with rapid rotation act as whirling rotary blades to fling out the nearby gas. Eventual collimation of the outflow toward the rotation axes appears to be a generic feature of many proposed models.

Pre-main-sequence stars of low mass first appear as visible objects, T Tauri stars, with sizes that are several times their ultimate main-sequence sizes. They subsequently contract on a timescale of tens of millions of years, the main source of radiant energy in this phase being the release of gravitational energy. As the internal temperature rises to a few million kelvins, deuterium (heavy hydrogen) is first destroyed. Then lithium, beryllium, and boron are broken down into helium as their nuclei are bombarded by protons moving at increasingly high speeds. When their central temperatures reach values comparable to 10^7 K, hydrogen fusion ignites in their cores, and they settle down to long stable lives on the main sequence. The early evolution of high-mass stars is similar. The only difference is that their faster overall evolution may allow them to reach the main sequence while they are still enshrouded in the cocoon of gas and dust from which they formed.

Detailed calculations show that a protostar first appears on the Hertzsprung-Russell diagram well above the main sequence because it is too bright for its colour. As it continues to contract, it moves downward and to the left toward the main sequence.

SUBSEQUENT DEVELOPMENT ON THE MAIN SEQUENCE

As the central temperature and density continue to rise, the proton-proton and carbon cycles become active, and the development of the (now genuine) star is stabilized. The star then reaches the main sequence, where it remains for most of its active life. The time required for the contraction phase depends on the mass of the star. A star of the Sun's mass generally requires tens of millions of years to reach the main sequence, whereas one of much greater mass might take a few hundred thousand years.

By the time the star reaches the main sequence, it is still chemically homogeneous. With additional time, the hydrogen fuel in the core is converted to helium, and the temperature slowly rises. If the star is sufficiently massive to have a convective core, the matter in this region has a chance to be thoroughly mixed, but the outer region does not mix with the core. The Sun, by contrast, has no convective core, and the helium-to-hydrogen ratio is maximum at the centre and decreases outward. Throughout the life of the Sun, there has been a steady depletion of hydrogen, so that the concentration of hydrogen at the centre today is probably only about one-third of the original amount. The rest has been transformed into helium. Like the rate of formation of a star, the subsequent rate of evolution on the main sequence is proportional to the mass of the star; the greater the mass, the more rapid the evolution. Whereas the Sun is destined to endure for some 10 billion years, a star of twice the Sun's mass burns its fuel at such a rate that it lasts about 3 billion years, and a star of 10 times the Sun's mass has a lifetime measured in tens of millions of years. By contrast, stars having a fraction of the mass of the Sun seem able to endure for trillions of years, which is much greater than the current age of the universe.

The spread of luminosities and colours of stars within the main sequence can be understood as a consequence of evolution. At the beginning of their lives as hydrogen-burning objects, stars define a nearly unique line in the Hertzsprung-Russell diagram called the zero-age main sequence. Without differences in initial chemical composition or in rotational velocity, all the stars would start exactly from this unique line. As the stars evolve, they adjust to the increase in the helium-to-hydrogen ratio in their cores and gradually move away from the zero-age main sequence. When the core fuel is exhausted, the internal structure of the star changes rapidly; it quickly leaves the main sequence and moves toward the region of giants and supergiants.

As the composition of its interior changes, the star departs the main sequence slowly at first and then more rapidly. When about 10 percent of the star's mass has been converted to helium, the structure of the star changes drastically. All of the hydrogen in the core has been burned out, and this central region is composed almost entirely of inert helium, with trace admixtures of heavier elements. The energy production now occurs in a thin shell where hydrogen is consumed and more helium added to a growing but inert core. The outer parts of the star expand outward because of the increased burning there, and as the star swells up, its luminosity gradually increases. The details of the evolutionary process depend on the metal-to-hydrogen ratio, and the course of evolution differs for stars of different population types.

LATER STAGES OF EVOLUTION

The great spread in luminosities and colours of giant, supergiant, and subgiant stars is also understood to result from evolutionary events. When a star leaves the main sequence, its future evolution is precisely determined by its mass, rate of rotation (or angular momentum), and chemical composition and whether it is a member of a close binary system. Giants and supergiants of nearly the same radius and surface temperature may have evolved from main-sequence stars of different ages and masses.

EVOLUTION OF LOW-MASS STARS

Theoretical calculations suggest that, as the star evolves from the main sequence, the hydrogen-helium core gradually increases in mass but shrinks in size as more and more helium ash is fed in through the outer hydrogen-burning shell. Energy is carried outward from the shell by rapid convection currents. The temperature of the shell rises; the star becomes more luminous; and it finally approaches the top of the giant domain on the Hertzsprung-Russell diagram. By contrast, the core shrinks by gravitational contraction, becoming hotter and denser until it reaches a central temperature of about 120 million K. At that temperature the previously inert helium is consumed in the production of heavier elements.

When two helium nuclei each of mass 4 atomic units (^{4}He) are jammed together, it might be expected that they would form a nucleus of beryllium of mass 8 atomic units (^{8}Be). In symbols,

$$^4He + {}^4He \rightarrow {}^8Be.$$

Actually, however, ^{8}Be is unstable and breaks down into two helium nuclei. If the temperature and density are high enough, though, the short-lived beryllium nucleus can (before it decays) capture another helium nucleus in what is essentially a three-body collision to form a nucleus of carbon-12—namely,

$$^8Be + {}^4He \rightarrow {}^{12}C.$$

This fusion of helium in the core, called the triple alpha process, can begin gradually in some stars, but in stars with masses between about half of and three times the Sun's mass, it switches on with dramatic suddenness, a process known as the helium flash. Outwardly the star shows no discernible effect, but the course of its evolution is changed with this new source of energy. Having only recently become a red giant, it now evolves somewhat down and then to the left in the Hertzsprung-Russell diagram, becoming smaller and hotter. This stage of core helium burning, however, lasts only about a hundredth of the time taken for core hydrogen burning. It continues until the core helium supply is exhausted, after which helium fusion is limited to a shell around the core, just as was the case for hydrogen in an earlier stage. This again sets the star evolving toward the red giant stage along what is called the asymptotic giant branch, located slightly above the main region of giants in the Hertzsprung-Russell diagram.

In more massive stars, this cycle of events can continue, with the stellar core reaching ever-higher temperatures and fusing increasingly heavy nuclei, until the star eventually experiences a supernova explosion. In lower-mass stars like the Sun, however, there is insufficient mass to squeeze the core to the temperatures needed for this chain of fusion processes to proceed, and eventually the outermost layers extend so far from the source of nuclear burning that they cool to a few thousand kelvins. The result is an object having two distinct parts: a well-defined core of mostly carbon ash (a white dwarf star) and a swollen spherical shell of cooler and thinner matter spread over a volume roughly the size of the solar system. Such shells of matter, called planetary nebulae, are actually observed in large numbers in the sky. Of the nearly 3,000 examples known in the Milky Way Galaxy alone, NGC 7027 is the most intensively studied.

Objects called brown dwarfs are intermediate between a planet and a star and so evolve differently from low-mass stars. Brown dwarfs usually have a mass less than 0.075 that of the Sun, or roughly 75 times that of Jupiter. (This maximum mass is a little higher for objects with fewer heavy elements than the Sun.) Many astronomers draw the line between brown dwarfs and planets at the lower fusion boundary of about 13 Jupiter

The brown dwarf 2MASSWJ 1207334-393254 (centre) as seen in a photo taken by the Very Large Telescope at the European Southern Observatory, Cerro Paranal, Chile. Orbiting the brown dwarf at a distance of 69 billion km (43 billion miles) is a planet (lower left) that has a mass four times that of Jupiter. ESO

masses. The difference between brown dwarfs and stars is that, unlike stars, brown dwarfs do not reach stable luminosities by thermonuclear fusion of normal hydrogen. Both stars and brown dwarfs produce energy by fusion of deuterium (a rare isotope of hydrogen) in their first few million years. The cores of stars then continue to contract and get hotter until they fuse hydrogen. However, brown dwarfs prevent further contraction because their cores are dense enough to hold themselves up with electron degeneracy pressure. (Those brown dwarfs above 60 Jupiter masses begin to fuse hydrogen, but they then stabilize, and the fusion stops.)

Brown dwarfs are not actually brown but appear from deep red to magenta depending on their temperature. Objects below about 2,200 K, however, do actually have mineral grains in their atmospheres. The surface temperatures of brown dwarfs depend on both their mass and their age. The most massive and youngest brown dwarfs have temperatures as high as 2,800 K, which overlaps with the temperatures of very low-mass stars, or red dwarfs. (By comparison, the Sun has a surface temperature of 5,800 K.) All brown dwarfs eventually cool below the minimum main-sequence stellar temperature of about 1,800 K. The oldest and smallest can be as cool as about 500 K.

Brown dwarfs were first hypothesized in 1963 by American astronomer Shiv Kumar, who called them "black" dwarfs. American astronomer Jill Tarter proposed the name "brown dwarf" in 1975; although brown dwarfs are not brown, the name stuck because these objects were thought to have dust, and the more accurate "red dwarf" already described a different type of star. Searches for brown dwarfs in the 1980s and 1990s found several candidates; however, none was confirmed as a brown dwarf. In order to distinguish brown dwarfs from stars of the same temperature, one can search their spectra for evidence of lithium (which stars destroy when hydrogen fusion begins). Alternatively, one can look for (fainter) objects below the minimum stellar temperature. In 1995 both methods paid off. Astronomers at the University of California, Berkeley, observed lithium in an object in the Pleiades, but this result was not immediately and widely embraced. This object, however, was later accepted as the first binary brown dwarf. Astronomers at Palomar Observatory and Johns Hopkins University found a companion to a low-mass star called Gliese 229 B. The detection of methane in its spectrum showed that it has a surface temperature less than 1,200 K. Its extremely low luminosity, coupled with the age of its stellar companion, implies that it is about 50 Jupiter masses. Hence, Gliese 229 B was the first object widely accepted as a brown dwarf. Infrared sky surveys and other techniques have now uncovered hundreds of brown dwarfs. Some of them are companions to stars; others are binary brown dwarfs; and many of them are isolated objects. They seem to form in much the same way as stars, and there may be 1–10 percent as many brown dwarfs as stars.

ORIGIN OF THE CHEMICAL ELEMENTS

The relative abundances of the chemical elements provide significant clues regarding their origin. Earth's crust has been affected severely by erosion, fractionation, and other geologic events, so that its present varied composition offers few clues as to its early stages. The composition of the matter from which the solar system formed is deduced from that of stony meteorites called chondrites and from the composition of the Sun's atmosphere, supplemented by data acquired from spectral observations of hot stars and gaseous nebulae. The table lists the most abundant chemical elements; it represents an average pertaining to all cosmic objects in general.

THE MOST ABUNDANT CHEMICAL ELEMENTS (by numbers of atoms per 10^9 atoms of hydrogen)		
ELEMENT	SYMBOL	ABUNDANCE
helium	He	9.8×10^7
carbon	C	501,000
nitrogen	N	100,000
oxygen	O	794,000
fluorine	F	33
neon	Ne	123,000
sodium	Na	2,100
magnesium	Mg	38,000
aluminum	Al	3,000
silicon	Si	35,000
phosphorus	P	320
sulfur	S	17,400
chlorine	Cl	250
argon	Ar	3,600
potassium	K	133
calcium	Ca	2,200
titanium	Ti	91
chromium	Cr	473
manganese	Mn	288
iron	Fe	33,000
nickel	Ni	1,800

The most obvious feature is that the light elements tend to be more abundant than the heavier ones. That is to say, when abundance is plotted against atomic mass, the resulting graph shows a decline with increasing atomic mass up to an atomic mass value of about 100. Thereafter the abundance is more nearly constant. Furthermore, the decline is not smooth. Among the lighter elements, those of even atomic number tend to be more abundant, and those with an atomic number divisible by four are especially favoured. The abundances of lithium, beryllium, and boron are rare compared with those of carbon, nitrogen, and oxygen. There is a pronounced abundance peak for iron and a relatively high peak for lead, the most stable of the heavy elements.

The overwhelming preponderance of hydrogen suggests that all the nuclei were built from this simplest element, a hypothesis first proposed many years ago and widely accepted for a time. According to this now-defunct idea, all matter was initially compressed into one huge ball of neutrons. As the universe began to expand, its density decreased and the neutrons decayed into protons and electrons. The protons then captured neutrons, one after another, underwent beta decay (ejection of electrons), and synthesized the heavy elements. A major difficulty with this hypothesis, among various other problems, is that atomic masses 5 and 8 are unstable, and there is no known way to build heavier nuclei by successive neutron capture.

A large body of evidence now supports the idea that only the nuclei of hydrogen and helium, with trace amounts of other light nuclei such as lithium, beryllium, and boron, were produced in the aftermath of the big bang, the hot explosion from which the universe is thought to have emerged, whereas the heavier nuclei were, and continue to be, produced in stars. The majority of them, however, are fashioned only in the most massive stars and some only for a short period of time after supernova explosions.

The splitting in the spectral sequence among the cooler stars can be understood in terms of composition differences. The M-type stars appear to have a normal (i.e., solar) makeup, with oxygen more abundant than carbon and the zirconium group of elements much less abundant than the titanium group. The R-type and N-type stars often contain more carbon than oxygen, whereas the S-type stars appear to have an enhanced content of zirconium as compared with titanium.

Other abundance anomalies are found in a peculiar class of higher temperature stars, called Wolf-Rayet (or W) stars, in which objects containing predominantly helium, carbon, and oxygen are distinguished from those containing helium and nitrogen, some carbon, and little observed oxygen. These stars are extremely hot white stars that have peculiar spectra thought to indicate either great turbulence within the star or a steady, voluminous ejection of material. A typical Wolf-Rayet star is several times the diameter of the Sun and thousands of times more luminous. Only a few hundred are known, located mostly in the spiral arms of the Milky Way Galaxy. (The type was first distinguished in 1867 by the French astronomers Charles-Joseph-Étienne Wolf and Georges-Antoine-Pons Rayet.) Significantly, all these abundance anomalies are found in stars thought to be well advanced in their evolutionary development. No main-sequence dwarfs display such effects.

A most critical observation is the detection of the unstable element technetium in the S-type stars. This element has been produced synthetically in nuclear laboratories on Earth, and its longest-lived isotope, technetium-99, is known to have a half-life of 200,000 years. The implication is that this element must have been produced within the past few hundred thousand years in the stars where it has been observed, suggesting furthermore that this nucleosynthetic process is at work at least in some stars today. How the star upwells this heavy element from the core (where it is produced) to the surface (near where it is observed) in such a short time without the star's exploding provides an impressive challenge to theoreticians.

Researchers have been able to demonstrate how elements might be created in stars by nuclear processes occurring at very high temperatures and densities. No one mechanism can account for all the elements; rather, several distinct processes occurring at different epochs during the late evolution of a star have been proposed.

After hydrogen, helium is the most abundant element. Most of it was probably produced in the initial big bang. Helium is the normal ash of hydrogen consumption, and in the dense cores of highly evolved stars, helium itself is consumed to form, successively, carbon-12, oxygen-16, neon-20, and magnesium-24. By this time in the core of a sufficiently massive star, the temperature has reached some 700 million K. Under these conditions, particles such as protons, neutrons, and helium-4 nuclei also can interact with the newly created nuclei to produce a variety of other elements such as fluorine and sodium. Because these "uneven" elements are produced in lesser quantities than those divisible by four, both the peaks and troughs in the curve of cosmic abundances can be explained.

As the stellar core continues to shrink and the central temperature and density are forced even higher, a fundamental difficulty is soon reached. A temperature of roughly one billion K is sufficient to create silicon (silicon-28) by the usual method of helium capture. This temperature, however, is also high enough to begin to break apart silicon as well as some of the other newly synthesized nuclei. A "semi-equilibrium" is set up in the star's core—a balance of sorts between the production and destruction (photodisintegration) of silicon. Ironically, though destructive, this situation is suitable for the production of even heavier nuclei up to and including iron (iron-56), again through the successive capture of helium nuclei.

Evolution of High-Mass Stars

If the temperature and the density of the core continue to rise, the iron-group nuclei tend to break down into helium nuclei, but a large amount of energy is suddenly consumed in the process. The star then suffers a violent implosion, or collapse, after which it soon explodes as a supernova.

The term *supernova* is derived from *nova* (Latin: "new"), the name for another type of exploding star. Supernovae resemble novae in several respects. Both are characterized by a tremendous, rapid brightening lasting for a few weeks, followed by a slow dimming. Spectroscopically, they show blue-shifted emission lines, which imply that hot gases are blown outward. But a supernova explosion, unlike a nova outburst, is a cataclysmic event for a star, one that essentially ends its active (i.e., energy-generating) lifetime. When a star "goes supernova," considerable amounts of its matter, equaling the material of several Suns, may be blasted into space with such a burst of energy as to enable the exploding star to outshine its entire home galaxy.

Supernovae explosions release not only tremendous amounts of radio waves and X-rays but also cosmic rays. Some gamma-ray bursts have been associated with supernovae. Supernovae also release many of the heavier elements that make up the components of the solar system, including Earth, into the interstellar medium. Spectral analyses show that abundances of the heavier elements are greater than normal, indicating that these elements do indeed form during the course of the explosion. The shell of a supernova remnant continues to expand until, at a very advanced stage, it dissolves into the interstellar medium.

Historically, only seven supernovae are known to have been recorded before the early 17th century. The most famous of them occurred in 1054 and was seen in one of the horns of the constellation Taurus. The remnants of this explosion are visible today as the Crab Nebula, which is composed of glowing ejecta of gases flying outward in an irregular fashion and a rapidly spinning, pulsating neutron star, called a pulsar, in the centre. The supernova of 1054 was recorded by Chinese and Korean observers; it also may have been seen by southwestern American Indians, as suggested by certain rock paintings discovered in Arizona and New Mexico. It was bright enough to be seen during the day, and its great luminosity lasted for weeks. Other prominent supernovae are known to have been observed from Earth in 185, 393, 1006, 1181, 1572, and 1604.

The closest and most easily observed of the hundreds of supernovae that have been recorded since 1604 was first sighted on the morning of Feb. 24, 1987, by the

Canadian astronomer Ian K. Shelton while working at the Las Campanas Observatory in Chile. Designated SN 1987A, this formerly extremely faint object attained a magnitude of 4.5 within just a few hours, thus becoming visible to the unaided eye. The newly appearing supernova was located in the Large Magellanic Cloud at a distance of about 160,000 light-years. It immediately became the subject of intense observation by astronomers throughout the Southern Hemisphere and was observed by the Hubble Space Telescope. SN 1987A's brightness peaked in May 1987, with a magnitude of about 2.9, and slowly declined in the following months.

Supernovae may be divided into two broad classes, Type I and Type II, according to the way in which they detonate. Type I supernovae may be up to three times brighter than Type II; they also differ from Type II supernovae in that their spectra contain no hydrogen lines and they expand about twice as rapidly.

The so-called classic explosion, associated with Type II supernovae, has as progenitor a very massive star (a Population I star) of at least eight solar masses that is at the end of its active lifetime. (These are seen only in spiral galaxies, most often near the arms.) Until this stage of its evolution, the star has shone by means of the nuclear energy released at and near its core in the process of squeezing and heating lighter elements such as hydrogen or helium into successively heavier elements—i.e., in the process of nuclear fusion. Forming elements heavier than iron absorbs rather than produces energy, however, and, since energy is no longer available, an iron core is built up at the centre of the aging, heavyweight star. When the iron core becomes too massive, its ability to support itself by means of the outward explosive thrust of internal fusion reactions fails to counteract the tremendous pull of its own gravity. Consequently, the core collapses. If the core's mass is less than about three solar masses, the collapse continues until the core reaches a point at which its constituent nuclei and free electrons are crushed together into a hard, rapidly spinning core. This core consists almost entirely of neutrons, which are compressed in a volume only 20 km (12 miles) across but whose combined weight equals that of several Suns. A teaspoonful of this extraordinarily dense material would weigh 50 billion tons on Earth. Such an object is called a neutron star.

The supernova detonation occurs when material falls in from the outer layers of the star and then rebounds off the core, which has stopped collapsing and suddenly presents a hard surface to the infalling gases. The shock wave generated by this collision propagates outward and blows off the star's outer gaseous layers. The amount of material blasted outward depends on the star's original mass.

If the core mass exceeds three solar masses, the core collapse is too great to produce a neutron star; the imploding star is compressed into an even smaller and denser body—namely, a black hole. Infalling material disappears into the black hole, the gravitational field of which is so intense that not even light can escape. The entire star is not taken in by the black hole, since much of the falling envelope of the star either rebounds from the temporary formation of a spinning neutron core or misses passing through the very centre of the core and is spun off instead.

Type I supernovae can be divided into subgroups, Ia, Ib, Ic, on the basis of their spectra. The exact nature of the explosion mechanism in Type I generally is still uncertain, although Ia supernovae, at least, are thought to originate in binary systems consisting of a moderately massive star and a white dwarf, with material flowing to the white dwarf from its larger companion. A thermonuclear explosion results if the flow of material is sufficient to raise the mass of the white dwarf above the Chandrasekhar limit of 1.44 solar masses. Unlike the case of an ordinary nova, for which the mass flow is less and only a superficial explosion results, the white dwarf in a Ia supernova explosion is presumably destroyed completely. Radioactive elements, notably nickel-56, are formed. When nickel-56 decays to cobalt-56 and the latter to iron-56, significant amounts of energy are released, providing perhaps most of the light emitted during the weeks following the explosion.

Type Ia supernovae are useful probes of the structure of the universe, since they all have the same luminosity. By measuring the apparent brightness of these objects, one also measures the expansion rate of the universe and that rate's variation with time. Dark energy, a repulsive force that is the dominant component (73 percent) of the universe, was discovered in 1998 with this method. Type Ia supernovae that exploded when the universe was only two-thirds of its present size were fainter and thus farther away than they would be in a universe without dark energy. This implies that the expansion rate of the universe is faster now than it was in the past, a result of the current dominance of dark energy. (Dark energy was negligible in the early universe.)

In the catastrophic events leading to a supernova explosion and for roughly 1,000 seconds thereafter, a great variety of nuclear reactions can take place. These processes seem to be able to explain the trace abundances of all the known elements heavier than iron.

Two situations have been envisioned, and both involve the capture of neutrons. When a nucleus captures a neutron, its mass increases by one atomic unit and its charge remains the same. Such a nucleus is often too heavy for its charge and might emit an electron (beta particle) to attain a more stable state. It then becomes a nucleus of the next higher element in the periodic table of the elements. In the first such process, called the slow, or s, process, the flux of neutrons is low. A nucleus captures a neutron and leisurely emits a beta particle; its nuclear charge then increases by one.

Beta decay is often very slow, and, if the flux of neutrons is high, the nucleus might capture another neutron before there is time for it to undergo decay. In this rapid, or *r*, process, the evolution of a nucleus can be very different from that in a slow process. In supernova explosions, vast quantities of neutrons can be produced, and these could result in the rapid buildup of massive elements. One interesting feature of the synthesis of heavy elements by neutron capture at a high rate in a supernova explosion is that nuclei much heavier than lead or even uranium can be fashioned. These in turn can decay by fission, releasing additional amounts of energy.

The superabundant elements in the S-type stars come from the slow neutron process. Moreover, the observation of technetium-99 is ample evidence that these processes are at work in stars today. Even so, some low-abundance atomic nuclei are proton-rich (i.e., neutron-deficient) and cannot be produced by either the *s* or the *r* process. Presumably, they have been created in relatively rare events—e.g., one in which a quantum of hard radiation, a gamma-ray photon, causes a neutron to be ejected.

In addition, no known nuclear process is capable of producing lithium, beryllium, and boron in stellar interiors. These lightweight nuclei are probably produced by the breakdown, or spallation, of heavier elements, such as iron and magnesium, by high-energy particles in stellar atmospheres or in the early stages of star formation. Apparently, these high-energy particles, called cosmic rays, originate by means of electromagnetic disturbances in the neighbourhood of starspots and stellar flares, and they also arise from supernova explosions themselves. Some of these light-element nuclei also might be produced by cosmic rays shattering atoms of carbon, nitrogen, oxygen, and other elements in the interstellar medium.

Finally, the peculiar A-type stars comprise a class of cosmic objects with strange elemental abundance anomalies. These might arise from mechanical effects—for example, selective radiation pressure or photospheric diffusion and element separation—rather than from nuclear effects. Some stars show enhanced silicon, others enhanced lanthanides. The so-called manganese stars show great overabundances of manganese and gallium, usually accompanied by an excess of mercury. The latter stars exhibit weak helium lines, low rotational velocities, and excess amounts of gallium, strontium, yttrium, mercury, and platinum, as well as absences of such elements as aluminum and nickel. When these types of stars are found in binaries, the two members often display differing chemical compositions. It is most difficult to envision plausible nuclear events that can account for the peculiarities of these abundances, particularly the strange isotope ratios of mercury.

END STATES OF STARS

The final stages in the evolution of a star depend on its mass and angular momentum and whether it is a member of a close binary.

WHITE DWARFS

The faint white dwarf stars represent the endpoint of the evolution of intermediate- and low-mass stars. White dwarf stars, so called because of the white colour of the first few that were discovered, are characterized by a low luminosity, a mass on the order of that of the Sun, and a radius comparable to that of Earth. Because of their large mass and small dimensions, such stars are dense and compact objects with average densities approaching 1,000,000 times that of water.

Unlike most other stars that are supported against their own gravitation by normal gas pressure, white dwarf stars are supported by the degeneracy pressure of the electron gas in their interior. Degeneracy pressure is the increased resistance exerted by electrons composing the gas, as a result of stellar contraction. The application of the so-called Fermi-Dirac statistics and of special relativity to the study of the equilibrium structure of white dwarf stars leads to the existence of a mass-radius relationship through which a unique radius is assigned to a white dwarf of a given mass; the larger the mass, the smaller the radius. Furthermore, the existence of a limiting mass is predicted, above which no stable white dwarf star can exist. This limiting mass, known as the Chandrasekhar limit, is on the order of 1.4 solar masses. Both predictions are in excellent agreement with observations of white dwarf stars.

The central region of a typical white dwarf star is composed of a mixture of carbon and oxygen. Surrounding this core is a thin envelope of helium and, in most cases, an even thinner layer of hydrogen. A very few white dwarf stars are surrounded by a thin carbon envelope. Only the outermost stellar layers are accessible to astronomical observations.

White dwarfs evolve from stars with an initial mass of up to three or four solar masses or even possibly higher. After quiescent phases of hydrogen and helium burning in its core—separated by a first red-giant phase—the star becomes a red giant for a second time. Near the end of this second red-giant phase, the star loses its extended envelope in a catastrophic event, leaving behind a dense, hot, and luminous core surrounded by a glowing spherical shell. This is the planetary-nebula phase. During the entire course of its evolution, which typically takes several billion years, the star will lose a major fraction of its original mass through stellar winds in the giant phases and through its ejected envelope. The hot planetary-nebula nucleus left behind has a mass of 0.5–1.0 solar mass and will eventually cool down to become a white dwarf.

White dwarfs have exhausted all their nuclear fuel and so have no residual nuclear energy sources. Their compact structure also prevents further gravitational contraction. The energy radiated away into the interstellar medium is thus provided by the residual thermal energy of the nondegenerate ions composing its core. That energy slowly diffuses outward through the insulating stellar envelope, and the white dwarf slowly cools down. Following the complete exhaustion of this reservoir of thermal energy, a process that takes several additional billion years, the white dwarf stops radiating and has by then reached the final stage of its evolution and becomes a cold and inert stellar remnant. Such an object is sometimes called a black dwarf.

White dwarf stars are occasionally found in binary systems, as is the case for the white dwarf companion to the brightest star in the night sky, Sirius. Aside from playing an essential role in Type Ia supernovae, they are also behind the outbursts of novae and of other cataclysmic variable stars.

Novae are a class of exploding stars whose luminosity temporarily increases from several thousand to as much as 100,000 times its normal level. A nova reaches maximum luminosity within hours after its outburst and may shine intensely for several days or occasionally for a few weeks, after which it slowly returns to its former level of luminosity. Stars that become novae are nearly always too faint before eruption to be seen with the unaided eye. Their sudden increase in luminosity, however, is sometimes great enough to make them readily visible in the nighttime sky. To observers, such objects may appear to be new stars; hence the name nova from the Latin word for "new."

Most novae are thought to occur in double-star systems in which members revolve closely around each other. Both members of such a system, commonly called a close binary star, are aged: one is a red giant and the other a white dwarf. In certain cases, the red giant expands into the gravitational domain of its companion. The gravitational field of the white dwarf is so strong that hydrogen-rich matter from the outer atmosphere of the red giant is pulled onto the smaller star. When a sizable quantity of this material accumulates on the surface of the white dwarf, a nuclear explosion occurs there, causing the ejection of hot surface gases on the order of $\frac{1}{10,000}$ the amount of material in the Sun. According to the prevailing theory, the white dwarf settles down after the explosion; however, the flow of hydrogen-rich material resumes immediately, and the whole process that produced the outburst repeats itself, resulting in another explosion about 1,000 to 10,000 years later. Recent research, however, suggests that such outbursts may recur at much longer intervals—every 100,000 years or so. It is explained that a nova eruption separates the members of the binary system, interrupting the transfer of matter until the two stars move close together again after a considerable length of time.

NEUTRON STARS

When the mass of a star's remnant core lies between 1.4 and about 2 solar masses, it apparently becomes a neutron star with a density more than a million times greater than even that of a white dwarf. These extremely dense, compact stars are thought to be composed primarily of

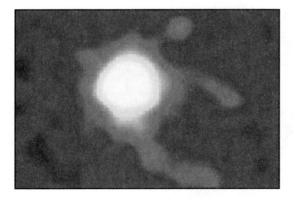

Geminga pulsar, imaged in X-ray wavelengths by the Earth-orbiting XMM-Newton X-ray Observatory. The pair of bright X-ray "tails" outline the edges of a cone-shaped shock wave produced by the pulsar as it moves through space nearly perpendicular to the line of sight (from lower right to upper left in the image). European Space Agency

neutrons. Neutron stars are typically about 20 km (12 miles) in diameter. Their masses range between 1.18 and 1.44 times that of the Sun, but most are 1.35 times that of the Sun. Thus, their mean densities are extremely high—about 10^{14} times that of water. This approximates the density inside the atomic nucleus, and in some ways a neutron star can be conceived of as a gigantic nucleus.

It is not known definitively what is at the centre of the star, where the pressure is greatest; theories include hyperons, kaons, pions, and strange quark matter. The intermediate layers are mostly neutrons and are probably in a "superfluid" state. The outer 1 km (0.6 mile) is solid, in spite of the high temperatures, which can be as high as 1,000,000 K. The surface of

this solid layer, where the pressure is lowest, is composed of an extremely dense form of iron.

Another important characteristic of neutron stars is the presence of very strong magnetic fields, upwards of 10^{12} Gauss (Earth's magnetic field is 0.5 Gauss), which causes the surface iron to be polymerized in the form of long chains of iron atoms. The individual atoms become compressed and elongated in the direction of the magnetic field and can bind together end-to-end. Below the surface, the pressure becomes much too high for individual atoms to exist.

The discovery of pulsars provided the first evidence of the existence of neutron stars. Pulsars are neutron stars that emit pulses of radiation once per rotation. The radiation emitted is usually radio waves. However, some objects are known to give off short rhythmic bursts of visible light, X-rays, and gamma radiation as well, and others are "radio-quiet" and emit only at X- or gamma-ray wavelengths. The very short periods of, for example, the Crab (NP 0532) and Vela pulsars (33 and 83 milliseconds, respectively) rule out the possibility that they might be white dwarfs. The pulses result from electrodynamic phenomena generated by their rotation and their strong magnetic fields, as in a dynamo. In the case of radio pulsars, neutrons at the surface of the star decay into protons and electrons. As these charged particles are released from the surface, they enter the intense magnetic field (10^{12} Gauss; Earth's magnetic field is 0.5 Gauss) that surrounds the star and rotates along with it. Accelerated to speeds approaching that of light, the particles give off electromagnetic radiation by synchrotron emission. This radiation is released as intense radio beams from the pulsar's magnetic poles.

These magnetic poles do not coincide with the rotational poles, and so the rotation of the pulsar swings the radiation beams around. As the beams sweep regularly past Earth with each complete rotation, an evenly spaced series of pulses is detected by ground-based telescopes.

Antony Hewish and Jocelyn Bell, astronomers working at the University of Cambridge, first discovered pulsars in 1967 with the aid of a radio telescope specially designed to record very rapid fluctuations in radio sources. Subsequent searches have resulted in the detection of about 2,000 pulsars. A significant percentage of these objects are concentrated toward the plane of the Milky Way Galaxy, the enormous galactic system in which Earth is located.

Although all known pulsars exhibit similar behaviour, they show considerable variation in the length of their periods—i.e., the intervals between successive pulses. The period of the slowest pulsar so far observed is about 11.8 seconds in duration. The pulsar designated PSR J1939+2134 was the fastest-known for more than two decades. Discovered in 1982, it has a period of 0.00155 second, or 1.55 milliseconds, which means it is spinning 642 times per second. In 2006 an even faster one was reported; known as

J1748-2446ad, it has a period of 1.396 milliseconds, which corresponds to a spin rate of 716 times per second. These spin rates are close to the theoretical limit for a pulsar because a neutron star rotating only about four times faster would fly apart as a result of "centrifugal force" at its equator, notwithstanding a gravitational pull so strong that the star's escape velocity is about half the speed of light.

These fast pulsars are known as millisecond pulsars. They form in supernovae like slower rotating pulsars; however, millisecond pulsars often occur in binary star systems. After the supernova, the neutron star accretes matter from its companion, causing the pulsar to spin faster.

Careful timing of radio pulsars shows that they are slowing down very gradually at a rate of typically a millionth of a second per year. The ratio of a pulsar's present period to the average slow-down rate gives some indication of its age. This so-called characteristic, or timing, age can be in close agreement with the actual age. For example, the Crab Pulsar, which was formed during a supernova explosion observed in 1054 CE, has a characteristic age of 1,240 years; however, pulsar J0205+6449, which was formed during a supernova in 1181 CE, has a characteristic age of 5,390 years.

Because pulsars slow down so gradually, they are very accurate clocks. Since pulsars also have strong gravitational fields, this accuracy can be used to test theories of gravity. American physicists Joseph Taylor and Russell Hulse won the Nobel Prize for Physics in 1993 for their study of timing variations in the pulsar PSR 1913+16. PSR 1913+16 has a companion neutron star with which it is locked in a tight orbit. The two stars' enormous interacting gravitational fields affect the regularity of the radio pulses, and by timing these and analyzing their variations, Taylor and Hulse found that the stars were rotating ever faster around each other in an increasingly tight orbit. This orbital decay is presumed to occur because the system is losing energy in the form of gravity waves. This was the first experimental evidence for the existence of the gravitational waves predicted by Albert Einstein in his general theory of relativity.

Some pulsars, such as the Crab and Vela pulsars, are losing rotational energy so precipitously that they also emit radiation of shorter wavelength. The Crab Pulsar appears in optical photographs as a moderately bright (magnitude 16) star in the centre of the Crab Nebula. Soon after the detection of its radio pulses in 1968, astronomers at the Steward Observatory in Arizona found that visible light from the Crab Pulsar flashes at exactly the same rate. The star also produces regular pulses of X-rays and gamma rays. The Vela Pulsar is much fainter at optical wavelengths (average magnitude 24) and was observed in 1977 during a particularly sensitive search with the large Anglo-Australian Telescope situated at Parkes, Australia. It also pulses at X-ray wavelengths. The Vela Pulsar does, however, give off gamma rays in regular pulses and is the most intense source of such radiation in the sky.

Pulsars also experience much more drastic period changes, which are called glitches, in which the period suddenly increases and then gradually decreases to its pre-glitch value. Some glitches are caused by "starquakes," or sudden cracks in the rigid iron crust of the star. Others are caused by an interaction between the crust and the more fluid interior. Usually the interior is loosely coupled to the crust, so the crust can slow down relative to the interior. However, sometimes the coupling between the crust and interior becomes stronger, spinning up the pulsar and causing a glitch.

Some X-ray pulsars are "accreting" pulsars. These pulsars are in binaries; the neutron star accretes material from its companion. This material flows to the magnetic polar caps, where it releases X-rays. Another class of X-ray pulsars is called "anomalous." These pulsars have periods of more than five seconds, sometimes give off bursts of X-rays, and are often associated with supernova remnants. These pulsars arise from highly magnetized neutron stars, or magnetars, which have a magnetic field of between 10^{14} and 10^{15} Gauss. (The magnetars also have been identified with another class of objects, the soft gamma-ray repeaters, which give off bursts of gamma rays.)

Some pulsars emit only in gamma rays. In 2008 the Fermi Gamma-ray Space Telescope discovered the first such pulsar within the supernova remnant CTA 1; since then, it has found 11 others. Unlike radio pulsars, the gamma-ray emission does not come from the particle beams at the poles but arises far from the neutron star surface. The precise physical process that generates the gamma-ray pulses is unknown.

Many binary X-ray sources, such as Hercules X-1, contain neutron stars. Cosmic objects of this kind emit X-rays by compression of material from companion stars accreted onto their surfaces.

Neutron stars are also seen as objects called rotating radio transients (RRATs) and as magnetars. The RRATs are sources that emit single radio bursts but at irregular intervals ranging from four minutes to three hours. The cause of the RRAT phenomenon is unknown. Magnetars are highly magnetized neutron stars that have a magnetic field of between 10^{14} and 10^{15} Gauss.

Most investigators believe that neutron stars are formed by supernova explosions in which the collapse of the central core of the supernova is halted by rising neutron pressure as the core density increases to about 10^{15} grams per cubic cm. If the collapsing core is more massive than about three solar masses, however, a neutron star cannot be formed, and the core would presumably become a black hole.

Black Holes

A black hole can be formed by the death of a massive star that exceeds about two solar masses. When such a star has exhausted its internal thermonuclear fuels at the end of its life, it becomes unstable and gravitationally collapses inward upon itself. The crushing weight of constituent matter falling in from all sides compresses the dying star to a point of zero volume and infinite density called the singularity. Details of the structure of a black hole are calculated from Albert Einstein's general theory of relativity. The singularity constitutes the centre of a black hole and is hidden by the object's "surface," the event horizon. Inside the event horizon the escape velocity (i.e., the velocity required for matter to escape from the gravitational field of a cosmic object) exceeds the speed of light, so that not even rays of light can escape into space.

The radius of the event horizon is called the Schwarzschild radius, after the German astronomer Karl Schwarzschild, who in 1916 predicted the existence of collapsed stellar bodies that emit no radiation. The Schwarzschild radius (R_g) of an object of mass M is given by the following formula, in which G is the universal gravitational constant and c is the speed of light:

$$R_g = 2GM/c^2.$$

The size of the Schwarzschild radius is proportional to the mass of the collapsing star. For a black hole with a mass 10 times as great as that of the Sun, the radius would be 30 km (18.6 miles).

Black holes cannot be observed directly on account of both their small size and the fact that they emit no light. They can be "observed," however, by the effects of their enormous gravitational fields on nearby matter. For example, if a black hole is a member of a binary star system, matter flowing into it from its companion becomes intensely heated and then radiates X-rays copiously before entering the event horizon of the black hole and disappearing forever. One of the component stars of the binary X-ray system Cygnus X-1 is a black hole. Discovered in 1971 in the constellation Cygnus, this binary consists of a blue supergiant and an invisible companion 8.7 times the mass of the Sun that revolve about one another in a period of 5.6 days.

Some black holes apparently have nonstellar origins. Various astronomers have speculated that large volumes of interstellar gas collect and collapse into supermassive black holes at the centres of quasars and galaxies. A mass of gas falling rapidly into a black hole is estimated to give off more than 100 times as much energy as is released by the identical amount of mass through nuclear fusion. Accordingly, the collapse of millions or billions of solar masses of interstellar gas under gravitational force into a large black hole would account for the enormous energy output of quasars and certain galactic systems. One such supermassive black hole, Sagittarius A*, exists at the centre of the Milky Way Galaxy. In 2005, infrared observations of stars orbiting around the position of Sagittarius A* demonstrated the presence of a black hole with a mass equivalent to 4,310,000 Suns.

Supermassive black holes have been seen in other galaxies as well. In 1994 the Hubble Space Telescope provided conclusive evidence for the existence of a supermassive black hole at the centre of the M87 galaxy. It has a mass equal to two to three billion Suns but is no larger than the solar system. The black hole's existence can be inferred from its energetic effects on an envelope of gas swirling around it at extremely high velocities.

The existence of another kind of nonstellar black hole has been proposed by the British astrophysicist Stephen Hawking. According to Hawking's theory, numerous tiny primordial black holes, possibly with a mass equal to that of an asteroid or less, might have been created during the big bang, a state of extremely high temperatures and density in which the universe is thought to have originated 13.7 billion years ago. These so-called mini black holes, like the more massive variety, lose mass over time through Hawking radiation and disappear. If certain theories of the universe that require extra dimensions are correct, the Large Hadron Collider (the world's most powerful particle accelerator) could produce significant numbers of mini black holes.

CHAPTER 4

STAR CLUSTERS

Our Sun is not part of a multiple star system. It floats alone in space, serene and solitary. However, many stars can be found in groups called star clusters. There are two general types of these stellar assemblages. They are held together by the mutual gravitational attraction of their members, which are physically related through common origin. The two types are open (formerly called galactic) clusters and globular clusters.

OPEN CLUSTERS

Open clusters contain from a dozen to many hundreds of stars, usually in an unsymmetrical arrangement. By contrast, globular clusters are old systems containing thousands to hundreds of thousands of stars closely packed in a symmetrical, roughly spherical form. In addition, groups called associations, made up of a few dozen to hundreds of stars of similar type and common origin whose density in space is less than that of the surrounding field, are also recognized.

Four open clusters have been known from earliest times: the Pleiades and Hyades in the constellation Taurus, Praesepe (the Beehive) in the constellation Cancer, and Coma Berenices. The Pleiades was so important to some early peoples that its rising at sunset determined the start of their year. The appearance of the Coma Berenices cluster to the

NGC 6705, a rich cluster (left), *and NGC 1508, a poor cluster* (right). Courtesy of Lick Observatory, University of California

naked eye led to the naming of its constellation for the hair of Berenice, wife of Ptolemy Euergetes of Egypt (3rd century BCE); it is the only constellation named after a historical figure.

Open clusters are strongly concentrated toward the Milky Way. They form a flattened disklike system 2,000 light-years thick, with a diameter of about 30,000 light-years. The younger clusters serve to trace the spiral arms of the Galaxy, since they are found invariably to lie in them. Very distant clusters are hard to detect against the rich Milky Way background. A classification based on central concentration and richness is used and has been extended to nearly 1,000 open clusters. Probably about half the known open clusters contain fewer than 100 stars, but the richest have 1,000 or more. The largest have apparent diameters of several degrees, the diameter of the Taurus cluster being 400 arc minutes (nearly seven arc degrees) and that of the Perseus cluster being 240 arc minutes.

The linear diameters range from the largest, 75 light-years, down to 5 light-years. Increasingly, it has been found that a large halo of actual cluster members surrounds the more-noticeable core and extends the diameter severalfold. Cluster membership is established through common motion, common distances, and so on. Tidal forces and stellar encounters lead to the disintegration of open clusters over long periods of time as stars "evaporate" from the cluster.

Stars of all spectral classes from O to M (high to low temperatures) are found in open clusters, but the frequency of types varies from one cluster to another, as does concentration near the centre. In some (O or OB clusters), the brightest stars are blue, very hot spectral types O or B. In others, they are whitish yellow, cooler spectral type F. High-luminosity stars are more common than in the solar neighbourhood, and dwarfs are much more scarce. The brightest stars in some open clusters are 150,000 times as bright as the Sun. The luminosity of the brightest stars at the upper end of the main sequence varies in clusters from about -8 to -2 visual magnitude. (Visual magnitude is a magnitude measured through a yellow filter, the term arising because the eye is most sensitive to yellow light.)

Because of the high luminosity of their brightest stars, some open clusters have a total luminosity as bright as that of some globular clusters (absolute magnitude of -8), which contain thousands of times as many stars. In the centre of rich clusters, the stars may be only one light-year apart. The density can be 100 times that of the solar neighbourhood. In some, such as the Pleiades and the Orion clusters, nebulosity is a prominent feature, while others have none. In clusters younger than 25 million years, masses of neutral hydrogen extending over three times the optical diameter of the cluster have been detected with radio telescopes. Many of the OB clusters mentioned above contain globules—relatively small, apparently spherical regions of absorbing matter.

The most-numerous variables connected with young open clusters are the T Tauri type and related stars that occur by the hundreds in some nebulous regions of the sky. Conspicuously absent from open clusters is the type most common in globular clusters, the RR Lyrae stars. Other variables include eclipsing binary stars (both Algol type and contact binaries), flare stars, and spectrum variables, such as Pleione. The last-named star, one of the Pleiades, is known to cast off shells of matter from time to time, perhaps as a result of its high rotational speed (up to 322 km/sec [20 miles/sec]). About two dozen open clusters are known to contain Population I Cepheids, and since the distances of these clusters can be determined accurately, the absolute magnitudes of those Cepheids are well-determined. This has been of paramount importance in calibrating the period-luminosity relation for Cepheids, and thus in determining the distance scale of the universe.

The colour- or spectrum-magnitude diagram derived from the individual stars holds vital information. Colour-magnitude diagrams are available for about 200 clusters on the UBV photometric system, in which colour is measured from the amount of light radiated by the stars in the ultraviolet, blue, and visual (yellow) wavelength regions.

In young clusters, stars are found along the luminous bright blue branch, whereas in old clusters, beyond a turnoff only a magnitude or two brighter than the Sun, they are red giants and supergiants.

Distances can be determined by many methods—geometric, photometric, and spectroscopic—with corrections for interstellar absorption. For the very nearest clusters, direct (trigonometric) parallaxes may be obtained, and these are inversely proportional to the distance. Distances can be derived from proper motions, apparent magnitudes of the brightest stars, and spectroscopically from individual bright stars. Colour-magnitude diagrams, fitted to a standard plot of the main sequence, provide a common and reliable tool for determining distance. The nearest open cluster is the nucleus of the Ursa Major group at a distance of 65 light-years; the farthest clusters are thousands of light-years away.

Motions, including radial velocities and proper motion, have been measured for thousands of cluster stars. The radial velocities of open cluster stars are much smaller than those of globular clusters, averaging tens of kilometres per second, but their proper motions are larger. Open clusters share in the galactic rotation. Used with galactic rotation formulas, the radial velocities provide another means of distance determination.

A few clusters are known as moving clusters because the convergence of the proper motions of their individual stars toward a "convergent point" is pronounced. The apparent convergence is caused by perspective: the cluster members are really moving as a swarm in almost parallel directions and with about the same speeds. The Hyades is the most-prominent example of a moving cluster. (The Hyades stars are converging with a velocity of 45 km/sec (28 miles/sec) toward the point in the sky with position coordinates right ascension 94 arc degrees, declination +7.6 arc degrees.) The Ursa Major group, another moving cluster, occupies a volume of space containing the Sun, but the Sun is not a member. The cluster consists of a compact nucleus of 14 stars and an extended stream.

Stellar groups are composed of stars presumed to have been formed together in a batch, but the members are now too widely separated to be recognized as a cluster.

Of all the open clusters, the Pleiades is the best known and perhaps the most thoroughly studied. This cluster, with a diameter of 35 light-years at a distance of 380 light-years, is composed of about 500 stars and is 100 million years old. Near the Pleiades in the sky but not so conspicuous, the Hyades is the second nearest cluster at 150 light-years. Its stars are similar to those in the solar neighbourhood, and it is an older cluster (about 615 million years in age). Measurements of the Hyades long formed a basis for astronomical determinations of distance and age because its thoroughly studied main sequence was used as a standard. The higher-than-usual metal abundance in its stars, however, complicated matters, and it is no longer favoured in this way. Coma Berenices, located 290 light-years away, is an example of a "poor" cluster, containing only about 40 stars. There are some extremely young open clusters. Of these, the one associated with the Orion Nebula, which is some 4 million years old, is the closest at a distance of 1,400 light-years. A still younger cluster is NGC 6611, some of the stars in which formed only a few hundred thousand years ago. At the other end of the scale, some open clusters have ages approaching those of the globular clusters. M67 in the constellation Cancer is 4.5 billion years old, and NGC 188 in Cepheus is 6.5 billion years of age. The oldest known open cluster, Collinder 261 in the southern constellation of Musca, is 8.9 billion years old.

Globular Clusters

Though several globular clusters, such as Omega Centauri and Messier 13 in the constellation Hercules, are visible to the unaided eye as hazy patches of light, attention was paid to them only after the invention of the telescope. The first record of a globular cluster, in the constellation Sagittarius, dates to 1665 (it was later named Messier 22); the next, Omega Centauri, was recorded in 1677 by the English astronomer and mathematician Edmund Halley.

Investigations of globular and open clusters greatly aided the understanding of the Milky Way Galaxy. In 1917, from a study of the distances and distributions of globular clusters, the American astronomer Harlow Shapley, then of the Mount Wilson Observatory in California, determined that its galactic centre lies in the Sagittarius region. In 1930, from measurements of angular sizes and distribution of open clusters, Robert J. Trumpler of Lick Observatory in California showed that light is absorbed as it travels through many parts of space.

More than 150 globular clusters were known in the Milky Way Galaxy by the early years of the 21st century. Most are widely scattered in galactic latitude, but about a third of them are concentrated around the galactic centre, as satellite systems in the rich Sagittarius-Scorpius star fields. Individual cluster masses include up to one million suns, and their linear diameters can be several hundred light-years; their apparent diameters range from one degree for Omega Centauri down to knots of one minute of arc. In a cluster such as M3, 90 percent of the light is contained within a diameter of 100 light-years, but star counts and the study of RR Lyrae member stars (whose intrinsic brightness varies regularly within well-known limits) include a larger one of 325 light-years. The clusters differ markedly in the degree to which stars are concentrated at their centres. Most of them appear circular and are probably spherical, but a few (e.g., Omega Centauri) are noticeably elliptical. The most elliptical cluster is M19, its major axis being about double its minor axis.

Globular clusters are composed of Population II objects (i.e., old stars). The brightest stars are the red giants, bright red stars with an absolute magnitude of -2, about 600 times the Sun's brightness or luminosity. In relatively few globular clusters have stars as intrinsically faint as the Sun been measured, and in no such clusters have the faintest stars yet been recorded. The luminosity function for M3 shows that 90 percent of the visual light comes from stars at least twice as bright as the Sun, but more than 90 percent of the cluster mass is made up of fainter stars. The density near the centres of globular clusters is roughly two stars per cubic light-year, compared with one star per 300 cubic light-years in the solar neighbourhood. Studies of globular clusters have shown a difference in spectral properties from stars in the solar neighbourhood—a difference that proved to be due to a deficiency of metals in the clusters, which have been classified on the basis of increasing metal abundance. Globular cluster stars are between 2 and 300 times poorer in metals than stars like the Sun, with the metal abundance being higher for clusters near the galactic centre than for those in the halo (the outermost reaches of the Galaxy extending far above and below its plane). The amounts of other elements, such as helium, may also differ from cluster to cluster. The hydrogen in cluster stars is thought to amount to 70–75 percent by mass, helium 25–30 percent, and the heavier elements 0.01–0.1 percent. Radio astronomical studies have set a low upper limit on the amount of neutral hydrogen in globular clusters. Dark lanes of nebulous matter are puzzling features in some of these clusters. Though it is difficult to explain the presence of distinct, separate masses of unformed matter in old systems, the nebulosity cannot be foreground material between the cluster and the observer.

About 2,000 variable stars are known in the 100 or more globular clusters that have been examined. Of these, perhaps 90 percent are members of the class called RR Lyrae variables. Other variables that occur in globular clusters are Population II Cepheids, RV Tauri, and U Geminorum stars, as well as Mira stars, eclipsing binaries, and novae.

The colour of a star, as previously noted, has been found generally to correspond to its surface temperature, and in a somewhat similar way the type of spectrum shown by a star depends on the degree of excitation of the light-radiating atoms in it and therefore also on the temperature. All stars in a given globular cluster are, within a very small percentage of the total distance, at equal distances from the Earth so that the effect of distance on brightness is common to all. Colour-magnitude and spectrum-magnitude diagrams can thus be plotted for the stars of a cluster, and the position of the stars in the array, except for a factor that is the same for all stars, will be independent of distance.

In globular clusters all such arrays show a major grouping of stars along the lower main sequence, with a giant branch containing more-luminous stars curving from there upward to the red and with a horizontal branch starting about halfway up the giant branch and extending toward the blue.

This basic picture was explained as owing to differences in the courses of evolutionary change that stars with similar compositions but different masses would follow after long intervals of time. The absolute magnitude at which the brighter main-sequence stars leave the main sequence (the turnoff point, or "knee") is a measure of the age of the cluster, assuming that most of the stars formed at the same time. Globular clusters in the Milky Way Galaxy prove to be nearly as old as the universe, averaging perhaps 14 billion years in age and ranging between approximately 12 billion and 16 billion years, although these figures continue to be revised. RR Lyrae variables, when present, lie in a special region of the colour-magnitude diagram called the RR Lyrae gap, near the blue end of the horizontal branch in the diagram.

Two features of globular cluster colour-magnitude diagrams remain enigmatic. The first is the so-called "blue straggler" problem. Blue stragglers are stars located near the lower main sequence, although their temperature and mass indicate that they already should have evolved off the main sequence, like the great majority of other such stars in the cluster. A possible explanation is that a blue straggler is the coalescence of two lower mass stars in a "born-again" scenario that turned them into a single, more-massive, and seemingly younger star farther up the main sequence, although this does not fit all cases.

The other enigma is referred to as the "second parameter" problem. Apart from the obvious effect of age, the shape and extent of the various sequences in a globular cluster's colour-magnitude diagram are governed by the abundance of metals in the chemical makeup of the cluster's members. This is the "first parameter." Nevertheless, there are cases in which two clusters, seemingly almost identical in age and metal abundance, show horizontal branches that are quite different—one may be short and stubby, and the other may extend far toward the blue. There is thus evidently another, as-yet-unidentified parameter involved. Stellar rotation has been mooted as a possible second parameter, but that now seems unlikely.

Integrated magnitudes (measurements of the total brightness of the cluster), cluster diameters, and the mean magnitude of the 25 brightest stars made possible the first distance determinations on the basis of the assumption that the apparent differences were due entirely to distance. The colour-magnitude diagram, or the apparent magnitudes of the RR Lyrae variables, however, leads to the best distance estimates. The correction factor for interstellar reddening, which is caused by the presence of intervening matter that absorbs and reddens stellar light, is substantial for many globular clusters but small for those in high galactic latitudes, away from the plane of the Milky Way. Distances range from about 8,000 light-years for NGC 6397 to an intergalactic distance of 390,000 light-years for the cluster called AM-1.

The radial velocities (the speed at which objects approach or recede from an observer, taken as positive when the distance is increasing) measured by the Doppler effect have been determined from integrated spectra for some 138 globular clusters. The largest negative velocity is 384 km/sec (239 miles/sec) for NGC 7006, while the largest positive velocity is 494 km/sec (307 miles/sec) for NGC 3201. These velocities suggest that the globular clusters are moving around the galactic centre in highly elliptical orbits. The globular cluster system as a whole has a rotational velocity of about 180 km/s relative to the Sun, or 30 km/s on an absolute basis. For one cluster, Omega Centauri, motions of the individual stars around the massive centre have actually been observed and measured. Though proper motions of the clusters are very small, those for individual stars provide a useful criterion for cluster membership.

The two globular clusters of highest absolute luminosity are in the Southern Hemisphere in the constellations Centaurus and Tucana. Omega Centauri, with an (integrated) absolute visual magnitude of –10.2, is the richest cluster in variables, with nearly 300 known in the early 21st century. From this large group, three types of RR Lyrae stars were first distinguished in 1902. Omega Centauri is relatively nearby, at a distance of 16,000 light-years, and it lacks a sharp nucleus. The cluster designated 47 Tucanae (NGC 104), with an absolute visual magnitude of –9.3 at a similar distance of 13,500 light-years, has a different appearance with strong central concentration. It is located near the Small Magellanic Cloud but is not connected with it. For an observer situated at the centre of this great cluster, the sky would have the brightness of twilight on the Earth because of the light of the thousands of stars nearby. In the Northern Hemisphere, M13 in the constellation Hercules is the easiest to see and is the best known. At a distance of 22,000 light-years, it has been thoroughly investigated and is relatively poor in variables. M3 in Canes Venatici, 32,000 light-years away, is the cluster second richest in variables, with well more than 200 known. Investigation of these variables resulted in the placement of the RR Lyrae stars in a special region of the colour-magnitude diagram.

OB and T Associations

The discovery of stellar associations depended on knowledge of the characteristics and motions of individual stars scattered over a substantial area. In the 1920s it was noticed that young, hot blue stars (spectral types O and B) apparently congregated together. In 1949 Victor A. Ambartsumian, a Soviet astronomer, suggested that these stars are members of physical groupings of stars with a common origin and named them O associations (or OB associations, as they are often designated today). He also applied the term T associations to groups of dwarf, irregular T Tauri variable stars, which were first noted at Mount Wilson Observatory by Alfred Joy.

The chief distinguishing feature of the members of a stellar association is that the large majority of constituent stars have similar physical characteristics. An OB association consists of many hot, blue giant stars, spectral classes O and B, and a relatively small number of other objects. A T association consists of cooler dwarf stars, many of which exhibit irregular variations in brightness. The stars clearly must be relatively close to each other in space, though in some cases they might be widely dispersed in the sky and are less closely placed than in the open clusters.

The existence of an OB association is usually established through a study of the space distribution of early O- and B-type stars. It appears as a concentration of points in a three-dimensional plot of galactic longitude and latitude and distance. More than 70 have been cataloged and are designated by constellation abbreviation and number (e.g., Per OB 1 in the constellation Perseus). In terms of dimensions, they are larger than open clusters, ranging from 100 to 700 light-years in diameter, and usually contain one or more open clusters as nuclei. They frequently contain a special type of multiple star, the Trapezium (named for its prototype in Orion), as well as supergiants, binaries, gaseous nebulae, and globules. Associations are relatively homogeneous in age. The best distance determinations are from spectroscopic parallaxes of individual stars—i.e., estimates of their absolute magnitudes made from studies of their spectra. Most of those known are closer than 10,000 light-years, with the nearest association, straddling the boundary between Centaurus and Crux, at 385 light-years.

Associations appear to be almost spherical, though rapid elongation would be expected from the shearing effect of differential galactic rotation. Expansion, which is on the order of 10 km/sec (6 miles/sec), may well mask the tendency to elongate, and this is confirmed in some. Tidal forces break up an association in less than 10 million years through differences in the attraction by an outside body on members in different parts of the association.

A good example of an OB association is Per OB 1 at a distance of some 7,500 light-years, which spreads out from the double cluster h and χ Persei. A large group of 20 supergiant stars of spectral type M belongs to Per OB 1. Associations with red supergiants may be in a relatively advanced evolutionary stage, almost ready to disintegrate.

The T associations (short for T Tauri associations) are formed by groups of T Tauri stars associated with the clouds of interstellar matter (nebulae) in which they occur. About three dozen are recognized. A T Tauri star is characterized by irregular variations of light, low luminosity, and hydrogen line (H-alpha) emission. It is a newly formed star of intermediate mass that is still in the process of contraction from diffuse matter. The small motions of T Tauri stars relative to a given nebula indicate that they are not field stars passing through the nebula. They are found in greatest numbers in regions with bright O- and B-type stars.

T associations occur only in or near regions of galactic nebulosity, either bright or dark, and only in obscured regions showing the presence of dust. Besides T Tauri stars, they include related variables, nonvariable stars, and Herbig-Haro objects—small nebulosities 10,000 astronomical units in diameter, each containing several starlike condensations in configurations similar to the Trapezium, Theta Orionis, in the sword of Orion. These objects are considered to be star groups at the very beginning of life.

The constellation of Cygnus has five T associations, and Orion and Taurus have four each. The richest is Ori T2, with more than 400 members; it has a diameter of 50 by 90 light-years and lies at a distance of 1,300 light-years around the variable star T Ori.

DYNAMICS OF STAR CLUSTERS

Seen from intergalactic space, the Milky Way Galaxy would appear as a giant luminous pinwheel, with more than 150 globular clusters dotted around it. The richest parts of the spiral arms of the pinwheel would be marked by dozens of open clusters. If this panorama could be seen as a time-lapse movie, the great globular clusters would wheel around the galactic centre in elliptical orbits with periods of hundreds of millions of years. The open clusters and stellar associations would be seen to form out of knots of diffuse matter in the spiral arms, gradually disperse, run through their life cycle, and fade away, while the Sun pursued its course around the galactic centre for billions of years.

Young open clusters and associations, occupying the same region of space as clouds of ionized hydrogen (gaseous nebulae), help to define the spiral arms. A concentration of clusters in the bright inner portion of the Milky Way between galactic longitudes 283° and 28° indicates an inner arm in Sagittarius. Similarly, the two spiral arms of Orion and Perseus are defined between 103° and 213°, with a bifurcation of the Orion arm. Associations show the existence of spiral structure in the Sun's vicinity. Older clusters, whose main sequence does not reach to the blue stars, show no correlation with spiral arms because in the intervening years their motions have carried them far from their place of birth.

All the O- and B-type stars in the Galaxy might have originated in OB associations. The great majority, if not all, of the O-type stars were formed and still exist in clusters and associations. Though only 10 percent of the total number of B-type stars are now in OB associations or clusters, it is likely that all formed in them. At the other (fainter) end of the range of stellar luminosities, the number of dwarf variable stars in the nearby T associations is estimated at 12,000. These associations are apparently the main source of low-luminosity stars in the neighbourhood of the Sun.

While large numbers of associations have formed and dispersed and provided a population of stars for the spiral arms, the globular clusters have survived relatively unchanged except for the evolutionary differences that time brings. They are too massive to be disrupted by the tidal forces of the Galaxy, though their limiting dimensions are set by these forces when they most closely approach the galactic centre. Impressive as they are individually, their total mass of 10 million suns is small compared with the mass of the Galaxy as a whole—only about 1/10,000. Their substance is that of the Galaxy in a very early stage. The Galaxy probably collapsed from a gaseous cloud composed almost entirely of hydrogen and helium. About 14 billion years ago, before the last stages of the collapse, matter forming the globular clusters may have separated from the rest. The fact that metal-rich clusters are near the galactic nucleus while metal-poor clusters are in the halo or outer fringes may indicate a nonuniform distribution of elements throughout the primordial mass. However, there is evidence that galaxies are given to cannibalism, in which smaller galaxies merge with larger ones that do not necessarily have the same properties. This has complicated the picture of chemical evolution. The case of the globular cluster Omega Centauri suggests this merging also may happen on smaller scales. Its stars are unusual, perhaps unique, in having a variety of chemical compositions, as though they came from more than one earlier cluster.

In a study of star clusters, a time panorama unfolds—from the oldest objects existing in the Galaxy, the globular clusters, through clusters in existence only half as long, to extremely young open clusters and associations that have come into being since humans first trod the Earth.

CLUSTERS IN EXTERNAL GALAXIES

The study of clusters in external galaxies began in 1847, when Sir John Herschel at the Cape Observatory (in what is now South Africa) published lists of such objects in the nearest galaxies, the Magellanic Clouds. During the 20th century the identification of clusters was extended to more remote galaxies by the use of large reflectors and other more specialized instruments, including Schmidt telescopes.

Clusters have been discovered and studied in many external galaxies, particularly members of the Local Group (a group of about 40 stellar systems to which the Galaxy belongs). At their great distances classification is difficult, but it has been accomplished from studies of the colours of the light from an entire cluster (integrated colours) or, for relatively few, from colour-magnitude diagrams.

Clusters have been found by the hundreds in some of the nearest galaxies. At the distance of the Magellanic Clouds, a cluster like the Pleiades would appear as a faint 15th magnitude object, subtending 15 seconds of arc instead of several degrees. Nevertheless, it is estimated that the Small Magellanic Cloud, at a distance of 200,000 light-years, contains about 2,000 open clusters. In the Large Magellanic Cloud, at a distance of 163,000 light-years, over 1,200 of an estimated 4,200 have been cataloged. Most of them are young blue-giant open clusters such as NGC 330 and NGC 1866. The open clusters contain some Cepheid variables and in chemical composition are similar to, but not exactly the same as, those of the Galaxy. The globular clusters fall into two distinct groups. Those of the first group, the red, have a large metal deficiency similar to the globular clusters in the Galaxy, and some are known to contain RR Lyrae variables. The globular clusters of the second group are large and circular in outline, with colours much bluer than normal galactic globular clusters and with ages of about one million to one billion years. They are similar to the open clusters of the Magellanic Clouds but are very populous. The observed differences between clusters in the Galaxy and the Magellanic Clouds result from small differences in helium or heavy-element abundances. There are at least

122 associations with a mean diameter of 250 light-years, somewhat richer and larger than in the Galaxy. Sixteen of the associations contain coexistent clusters. Also, 15 star clouds (aggregations of many thousands of stars dispersed over hundreds or even thousands of light-years) are recognized.

In the great Andromeda spiral galaxy (M31) some 2.2 million light-years away, about 500 globular clusters are known. Colour studies of some of these clusters reveal that they have a higher metal content than globular clusters of the Galaxy. Nearly 200 OB associations are known, with distances up to 80,000 light-years from the nucleus. The diameters of their dense cores are comparable to those of galactic associations. NGC 206 (OB 78) is the richest star cloud in M31, having a total mass of 200,000 suns and bearing a strong resemblance to the double cluster in Perseus. Some globular clusters have been found around the dwarf elliptical companions to M31, NGC 185, and NGC 205.

M33 in the constellation Triangulum—a spiral galaxy with thick, loose arms (an Sc system in the Hubble classification scheme)—has about 300 known clusters, not many of which have globular characteristics. Of the six dwarf spheroidal galaxies in the Local Group, only the one in the constellation Fornax has clusters. Its five globular clusters are similar to the bluest globular clusters of the Galaxy. No clusters have been discovered in the irregular galaxies NGC 6822 and IC 1613.

Beyond the Local Group, at a distance of 45 million light-years, the giant elliptical galaxy M87 in the Virgo cluster of galaxies is surrounded by an estimated 13,000 globular star clusters. Inspection of other elliptical galaxies in Virgo shows that they too have globular clusters whose apparent magnitudes are similar to those in M87, though their stellar population is substantially smaller. It appears that the mean absolute magnitudes of globular clusters are constant and independent of the absolute luminosity of the parent galaxy.

The total number of clusters now known in external galaxies far exceeds the number known in the Milky Way system.

NOTABLE STARS AND STAR CLUSTERS

Of the billions of stars and star clusters in the universe, some have stood out among the rest for a variety of reasons.In the section that follows, greater detail is presented on many of those that have distinguished themselves as distinctive objects in the sky or in the history of astronomy itself.

51 Pegasi

The fifth-magnitude star 51 Pegasi is located 48 light-years away from Earth in the constellation Pegasus and was the first sunlike star confirmed to possess a planet. 51 Pegasi, which has physical properties (luminosity and temperature, for example) very similar to those of the Sun, became the focus of attention in 1995 when astronomers announced the detection of a planet orbiting it. The extrasolar planet is not visible from Earth, but its presence was deduced from the wobble that its gravity induces in the parent star's motion in a 4.23-day cycle. It has a mass 47 percent that of Jupiter and orbits surprisingly close (7.8 million km [4.8 million miles]) to the star—much closer than Mercury, which orbits the Sun at a distance of 57.9 million km (35.9 million miles).

Alpha Centauri

Alpha Centauri is a triple star, the faintest component of which, Proxima Centauri, is the closest star to the Sun, at about 4.2 light-years' distance. The two brighter components, about ⅕ light-year farther from the Sun, revolve around each other with a period of about 80 years, while Proxima may be circling them with a period probably of 500,000 years. The brightest component star resembles the Sun in spectral type, diameter, and absolute magnitude. Its apparent visual magnitude is 0.0. The second brightest component, of visual magnitude 1.4, is a redder star. The third component, of 11th magnitude, is a red dwarf star.

As seen from Earth, the system is the fourth brightest star (after Sirius, Canopus, and Arcturus); the red dwarf Proxima is invisible to the unaided eye. Alpha Centauri lies in the southern constellation Centaurus and can be seen only from south of about 40° north latitude.

Arcturus

Arcturus (also called Alpha Boötis,) is one of the five brightest stars in the night sky and the brightest star in the northern constellation Boötes, with an apparent visual magnitude of -0.05. It is an orange-coloured giant star 36.7 light-years from Earth. It lies in an almost direct line with the tail of Ursa Major (the Great Bear); hence its name, derived from the Greek words for "bear guard."

Betelgeuse

Betelgeuse, or Alpha Orionis, is the brightest star in the constellation Orion, marking the eastern shoulder of the hunter. Its name is derived from the Arabic word *bat al-dshauzâ*, which means "the giant's shoulder." Betelgeuse has a variable apparent magnitude of about 0.6 and is one of the most luminous stars in the night sky. It is easily discernible to even the casual observer, not only because of its brightness and position in the brilliant Orion but also because of its deep-reddish colour. The star is approximately 640 light-years from Earth.

Betelgeuse is a red supergiant star roughly 950 times as large as the Sun, making it one of the largest stars known. For comparison, the diameter of Mars's orbit around the Sun is 328 times the Sun's diameter. Infrared studies from spacecraft have revealed that Betelgeuse is surrounded by immense shells of material evidently shed by the star during episodes of mass loss over the past 100,000 years. The largest of these shells has a radius of nearly 7.5 light-years.

Deneb

Deneb, which is also called Alpha Cygni, is one of the brightest stars, with an apparent magnitude of 1.25. Its name is Arabic for "tail" (of the Swan, Cygnus). This star, at about 1,500 light-years' distance, is the most remote (and brightest intrinsically) of the 20 apparently brightest stars. It lies in the northern constellation Cygnus and, with Vega and Altair, forms the prominent "Summer Triangle."

Fomalhaut

Fomalhaut, or Alpha Piscis Austrini, is the 17th star (in order of apparent brightness). It is used in navigation because of its conspicuous place in a sky region otherwise lacking in bright stars. It lies in the southern constellation Piscis Austrinus, 25 light-years from Earth. A white star, it has an apparent magnitude of 1.16. A sixth-magnitude companion star, HR 8721, is yellow and orbits at a distance of about 0.9 light-year. A belt of dust orbits between 19.9 and 23.6 billion km (12.4 and 14.7 billion miles) from the star. Images taken with the Hubble Space Telescope in 2004 and 2006 showed a planet, Fomalhaut b, orbiting inside the dust belt at a distance of 17.8 billion km (11.1 billion miles) from the star. These

Bright nebulosity in the Pleiades (M45, NGC 1432), distance 430 light-years. Cluster stars provide the light, and surrounding clouds of dust reflect and scatter the rays from the stars. Hale Observatories © 1961

were the first confirmed images of an extrasolar planet. The planet has a mass three times that of Jupiter and an orbital period of 872 years.

Fomalhaut was associated with the Roman goddess Ceres (associated with the analogous Sicilian and Greek goddess Demeter) and was worshipped; in astrology it is one of four royal stars.

PLEIADES

The Pleiades (catalog number M45) is an open cluster of young stars in the zodiacal constellation Taurus, about 430 light-years from the solar system. It contains a large amount of bright nebulous material and more than 1,000 stars, of which six or seven can be seen by the unaided eye and have figured prominently in the myths and literature of many cultures. In Greek mythology the Seven Sisters (Alcyone, Maia, Electra, Merope, Taygete, Celaeno, and Sterope, names now assigned to individual stars), daughters of Atlas and Pleione, were changed into the stars. The heliacal (near dawn) rising of the Pleiades in spring of the Northern Hemisphere has marked from ancient times the opening of seafaring and farming seasons, as the morning setting of the group in autumn signified the seasons' ends. Some South American Indians use the same word for "Pleiades" and "year."

The cluster was first examined telescopically by Galileo, who found more than 40 members; it was first photographed by Paul and Prosper Henry in 1885.

POLARIS

Polaris, which is also called Alpha Ursae Minoris, is Earth's present northern polestar, or North Star. It can be found at the end of the "handle" of the so-called Little Dipper in the constellation Ursa Minor. Polaris is actually a triple star, the brighter of two visual components being a spectroscopic binary with a period of about 30 years and a Cepheid variable with a period of about 4 days. Its changes in brightness are too slight to be detected with the unaided eye. Apparent visual magnitude of the Polaris system is 2.00.

SIRIUS

Sirius—which is also called Alpha Canis Majoris, or the Dog Star—is the brightest star in the night sky, with apparent visual magnitude of -1.44. It is a binary star in the constellation Canis Major. The bright component of the binary is a blue-white star 23 times as luminous as the Sun and somewhat larger and considerably hotter than the Sun. Its distance from the solar system is about 8.6 light-years, only twice the distance of the nearest known star beyond the Sun. Its name probably comes from a Greek word meaning "sparkling," or "scorching."

Sirius was known as Sothis to the ancient Egyptians, who were aware that it made its first heliacal rising (i.e., rose just before sunrise) of the year at about the

Sirius A and B (lower left) *photographed by the Hubble Space Telescope.* NASA, ESA, H. Bond (STScI), and M. Barstow (University of Leicester)

time the annual floods were beginning in the Nile River delta. They long believed that Sothis caused the Nile floods; and they discovered that the heliacal rising of the star occurred at intervals of 365.25 days rather than the 365 days of their calendar year, a correction in the length of the year that was later incorporated in the Julian calendar. Among the ancient Romans, the hottest part of the year was associated with the heliacal rising of the Dog Star, a connection that survives in the expression "dog days."

That Sirius is a binary star was first reported by the German astronomer Friedrich Wilhelm Bessel in 1844. He had observed that the bright star was pursuing a slightly wavy course among its neighbours in the sky and concluded that it had a companion star, with which it revolved in a period of about 50 years. The companion was first seen in 1862 by Alvan Clark, an American astronomer and telescope maker.

Sirius and its companion revolve together in orbits of considerable eccentricity and with average separation of the stars of about 20 times the Earth's distance from the Sun. Despite the glare of the bright star, the seventh-magnitude companion is readily seen with a large telescope. This companion star, known as Sirius B, is about as massive as the Sun, though much more condensed, and was the first white dwarf star to be discovered.

VEGA

Vega, or Alpha Lyrae, is the brightest star in the northern constellation Lyra and the fifth brightest in the night sky, with a visual magnitude of 0.03. It is also one of the Sun's closer neighbours, at a distance of about 25 light-years. Vega's spectral type is A (white) and its luminosity class V (main sequence). It will become the northern polestar by about 14,000 CE because of the precession of the equinoxes. Vega is surrounded by a disk of circumstellar dust that may be similar to the solar system's Kuiper Belt.

CHAPTER 5

NEBULAE

Scattered between the stars in interstellar space are various tenuous clouds of gas and dust. These clouds are called nebulae (Latin: "mist" or "cloud"). The term was formerly applied to any object outside the solar system that had a diffuse appearance rather than a pointlike image, as in the case of a star. This definition, adopted at a time when very distant objects could not be resolved into great detail, unfortunately includes two unrelated classes of objects: the extragalactic nebulae, the enormous collections of stars and gas now called galaxies, and the galactic nebulae, which are composed of the interstellar medium (the gas between the stars, with its accompanying small solid particles) within a single galaxy. Today, the term *nebula* generally refers exclusively to the interstellar medium.

In a spiral galaxy the interstellar medium makes up 3 percent to 5 percent of the galaxy's mass, but within a spiral arm its mass fraction increases to about 20 percent. About 1 percent of the mass of the interstellar medium is in the form of "dust"—small solid particles that are efficient in absorbing and scattering radiation. Much of the rest of the mass within a galaxy is concentrated in visible stars, but there is also some form of dark matter that accounts for a substantial fraction of the mass in the outer regions.

The most conspicuous property of interstellar gas is its clumpy distribution on all size scales observed, from the

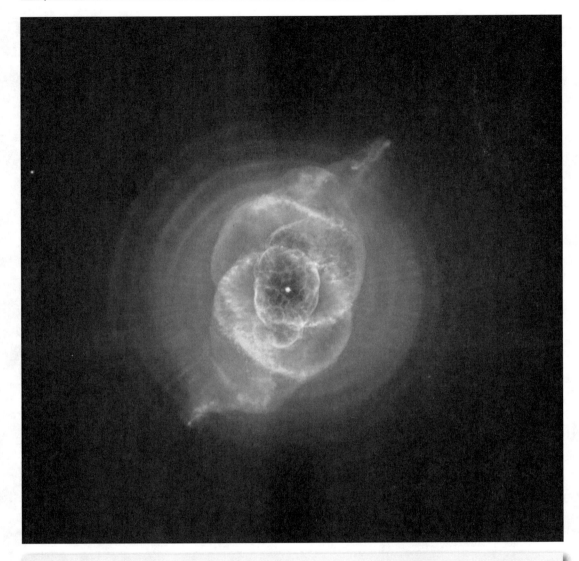

The Cat's Eye nebula. NASA, ESA, HEIC, and The Hubble Heritage Team (STScI/AURA)

size of the entire Milky Way Galaxy (about 10^{20} metres, or hundreds of thousands of light-years) down to the distance from Earth to the Sun (about 10^{11} metres, or a few light-minutes). The large-scale variations are seen by direct observation; the small-scale variations are observed by fluctuations in the intensity of radio waves, similar to the "twinkling" of starlight caused by unsteadiness in the Earth's atmosphere. Various regions exhibit an enormous range of densities and temperatures. Within the Galaxy's spiral arms about half the mass of the interstellar medium is concentrated in molecular clouds, in which hydrogen occurs in molecular form (H_2) and temperatures are as low as 10 kelvins (K). These clouds are inconspicuous optically and are detected principally by their carbon monoxide (CO) emissions in the millimetre wavelength range. Their densities in the regions studied by CO emissions are typically 1,000 H_2 molecules per cubic cm (1 cubic cm = .06 cubic in). At the other extreme is the gas between the clouds, with a temperature of 10 million K and a density of only 0.001 H^+ ion per cubic cm. Such gas is produced by supernovae, the violent explosions of unstable stars.

CLASSES OF NEBULAE

All nebulae observed in the Milky Way Galaxy are forms of interstellar matter. Their appearance differs widely, depending not only on the temperature and density of the material observed but also on how the material is spatially situated with respect to the observer. Their chemical composition, however, is fairly uniform. It corresponds to the composition of the universe in general in that approximately 90 percent of the constituent atoms are hydrogen and nearly all the rest are helium, with oxygen, carbon, neon, nitrogen, and the other elements together making up about two atoms per thousand.

On the basis of appearance, nebulae can be divided into two broad classes: dark nebulae and bright nebulae. Dark nebulae appear as irregularly shaped black patches in the sky and blot out the light of the stars that lie beyond them. They are very dense and cold molecular clouds; they contain about half of all interstellar material. Typical densities range from hundreds to millions (or more) of hydrogen molecules per cubic centimetre. These clouds are the sites where new stars are formed through the gravitational collapse of some of their parts. Most of the remaining gas is in the diffuse interstellar medium, relatively inconspicuous because of its very low density (about 0.1 hydrogen atom per cubic cm) but detectable by its radio emission of the 21-cm line of neutral hydrogen.

Bright nebulae appear as faintly luminous glowing surfaces; they either emit their own light or reflect the light of nearby stars. They are comparatively dense clouds of gas within the diffuse interstellar medium. They have several subclasses: (1) reflection nebulae, (2) H II regions, (3) diffuse ionized gas, (4) planetary nebulae, and (5) supernova remnants.

Reflection nebulae reflect the light of a nearby star from their constituent dust grains. The gas of reflection nebulae is cold, and such objects would be seen as dark nebulae if it were not for the nearby light source.

H II regions are clouds of hydrogen ionized (separated into positive H⁺ ions and free electrons) by a neighbouring hot star. The star must be of stellar type O or B, the most massive and hottest of normal stars in the Galaxy, in order to produce enough of the radiation required to ionize the hydrogen.

Diffuse ionized gas, so pervasive among the nebular clouds, is a major component of the Galaxy. It is observed by faint emissions of positive hydrogen, nitrogen, and sulfur ions (H^+, N^+, and S^+) detectable in all directions. These emissions collectively require far more power

than the much more spectacular H II regions, planetary nebulae, or supernova remnants that occupy a tiny fraction of the volume.

Planetary nebulae are ejected from stars that are dying but are not massive enough to become supernovae—namely, red giant stars. That is to say, a red giant has shed its outer envelope in a less-violent event than a supernova explosion and has become an intensely hot star surrounded by a shell of material that is expanding at a speed of tens of

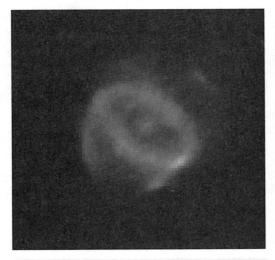

Planetary Nebula Hen 1357, as photographed by the Hubble Space Telescope. Located about 18,000 light-years from Earth in the constellation Ara the Altar, this expanding cloud of gas was expelled from an aging star in the nebula's centre. National Aeronautics and Space Administration

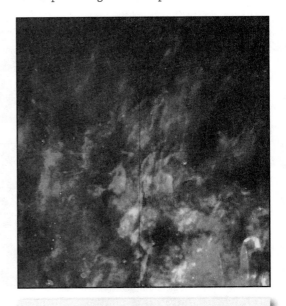

A star-forming region in the Orion Nebula (M42, NGC 1976). This composite image shows an area one light-year square near the edge of a cavity of ionized hydrogen heated by ultraviolet radiation from a star cluster at the nebula's centre. National Aeronautics and Space Administration

kilometres per second. Planetary nebulae typically appear as rather round objects of relatively high surface brightness. Their name is derived from their superficial resemblance to planets—i.e., their regular appearance when viewed telescopically as compared with the chaotic forms of other types of nebula.

Supernova remnants are the clouds of gas expanding at speeds of hundreds or even thousands of kilometres per second from comparatively recent explosions of massive stars. If a supernova remnant is younger than a few thousand years, it may be assumed that the gas in the nebula was mostly ejected by the exploded star. Otherwise, the nebula would consist chiefly of interstellar gas that has been swept up by the expanding remnant of older objects.

EARLY OBSERVATIONS OF NEBULAE

In 1610, two years after the invention of the telescope, the Orion Nebula, which looks like a star to the naked eye, was discovered by the French scholar and naturalist Nicolas-Claude Fabri de Peiresc. In 1656 Christiaan Huygens, the Dutch scholar and scientist, using his own greatly superior instruments, was the first to describe the bright inner region of the nebula and to determine that its inner star is not single but a compact quadruple system.

Early 18th-century observational astronomers gave high priority to comet seeking. A by-product of their search was the discovery of many bright nebulae. Several catalogs of special objects were compiled by comet researchers; by far the best known is that of the Frenchman Charles Messier, who in 1781 compiled a catalog of 103 nebulous, or extended, objects in order to prevent their confusion with comets. Most are clusters of stars, 35 are galaxies, and 11 are nebulae. Even today many of these objects are commonly referred to by their Messier catalog number; M20, for instance, is the great Trifid Nebula, in the constellation Sagittarius.

THE WORK OF THE HERSCHELS

By far the greatest observers of the early and middle 19th century were the English astronomers William Herschel and his son John. Between 1786 and 1802 William Herschel, aided by his sister Caroline, compiled three catalogs totaling about 2,500 clusters, nebulae, and galaxies. John Herschel later added to the catalogs 1,700 other nebulous objects in the southern sky visible from the Cape Observatory in South Africa but not from London and 500 more objects in the northern sky visible from England.

The catalogs of the Herschels formed the basis for the great *New General Catalogue* (*NGC*) of J.L. Dreyer, published in 1888. It contains the location and a brief description of 7,840 nebulae, galaxies, and clusters. In 1895 and 1908 it was supplemented by two *Index*

Catalogues (*IC*) of 5,386 additional objects. The list still included galaxies as well as true nebulae, for they were often at this time still indistinguishable. Most of the brighter galaxies are still identified by their NGC or IC numbers according to their listing in the *New General Catalogue* or *Index Catalogues*.

Advances Brought by Photography and Spectroscopy

The advent of photography, which allows the recording of faint details invisible to the naked eye and provides a permanent record of the observation for study of fine details at leisure, caused a revolution in the understanding of nebulae. In 1880 the first photograph of the Orion Nebula was made, but really good ones were not obtained until 1883. These early photographs showed a wealth of detail extending out to distances unsuspected by visual observers.

Much can be learned about the physical nature of an astronomical object by studying its spectrum—i.e., the resolution of its light into different wavelengths (or colours). Study of the spectrum of an object provides a decisive test as to whether it is composed of unresolved stars (as are galaxies) or glowing gas. Stars radiate at all wavelengths, almost always with dark absorption lines superimposed, while hot, transparent gas clouds radiate only emission lines at certain wavelengths characteristic of their constituent gases. In 1864 observation of the spectrum of the Orion Nebula showed bright emission lines of glowing gases, with conspicuous hydrogen lines and some green lines even brighter. By contrast, the spectrum of galaxies was found to be stellar, so a distinction between galaxies and nebulae—that nebulae are gaseous and galaxies are stellar—was appreciated at this time, although the true sizes and distances of galaxies were not demonstrated until the 20th century.

20TH-CENTURY DISCOVERIES

The 20th century witnessed enormous advances in observational techniques as well as in the scientific understanding of the physical processes that operate in interstellar matter. In 1930 a German optical worker, Bernhard Schmidt, invented an extremely fast wide-angled camera ideal for photographing faint extended nebulae. Photographic plates became progressively more sensitive to an ever-widening range of colours, but photography has been completely replaced by photoelectric devices. Most images are now recorded with so-called charge-coupled devices (CCDs) that act as arrays of tiny photoelectric cells, each recording the light from a small patch of sky. Modern CCDs consist of square arrays of up to 4,000 cells on each side, or 16 million independent photocells, capable of observing the sky simultaneously. Electronic detectors are up to 100 times more sensitive than photography, can record a much wider range of light levels, and are sensitive to a much wider range of wavelengths, from

0.1 micrometre (3.93700787 x 10^{-6} inch) in the ultraviolet (accessible only from satellites orbiting above Earth's atmosphere) to more than 1.2 micrometres (4.72440945 x 10^{-5} inch) in the infrared.

Spacecraft allow the observation of radiation normally absorbed by Earth's atmosphere: gamma and X-rays (which have very short wavelengths), far-ultraviolet radiation (with wavelengths shorter than about 0.3 micrometre [1.18110236 x 10^{-5} inch], below which atmospheric ozone is strongly absorbing), and infrared (from about 3 micrometres to 1 mm [.00012 inches to .039 inch]), strongly absorbed by atmospheric water vapour and carbon dioxide. Gamma rays, X-rays, and ultraviolet radiation reveal the physical conditions in the hottest regions in space (extending to some 100 million kelvins in shocked supernova gas). Infrared radiation reveals the conditions within dark cold molecular clouds, into which starlight cannot penetrate because of absorbing dust layers.

The primary means of studying nebulae is not by images but by spectra, which show the relative distribution of the radiation among various wavelengths (or colours for optical radiation). Spectra can be obtained by means of prisms (as in the earlier part of the 20th century), diffraction gratings, or crystals, in the case of X-rays. A particularly useful instrument is the echelle spectrograph, in which one coarsely ruled grating spreads the electromagnetic radiation in one direction, while another finely ruled grating disperses it in the perpendicular direction. This device, often used both in spacecraft and on the ground, allows astronomers to record simultaneously a wide range of wavelengths with very high spectral resolution (i.e., to distinguish slightly differing wavelengths). For even higher spectral resolution astronomers employ Fabry-Pérot interferometers. Spectra provide powerful diagnostics of the physical conditions within nebulae. Images and spectra provided by Earth-orbiting satellites, especially the Hubble Space Telescope, have yielded data of unprecedented quality.

Ground-based observations also have played a major role in recent advances in scientific understanding of nebulae. The emission of gas in the radio and submillimetre wavelength ranges provides crucial information regarding physical conditions and molecular composition. Large radio telescope arrays, in which several individual telescopes function collectively as a single enormous instrument, give spatial resolutions in the radio regime far superior to any yet achieved by optical means.

CHEMICAL COMPOSITION AND PHYSICAL PROCESSES

Many characteristics of nebulae are determined by the physical state of their constituent hydrogen, by far the most abundant element. For historical reasons, nebulae in which hydrogen is mainly ionized (H^+) are called H II regions, or diffuse nebulae. Those in which hydrogen is mainly neutral are designated H I regions, and those in which the gas is in molecular form (H_2) are referred to as molecular clouds. The distinction is important because of major differences in the radiation that is present in the various regions and consequently in the physical conditions and processes that are important.

Radiation is a wave but is carried by packets called photons. Each photon has a specified wavelength and precise energy that it carries, with gamma rays (short wavelengths) carrying the most and X-rays, ultraviolet, optical, infrared, microwave, and radio waves following in order of decreasing energies (or increasing wavelengths). Neutral hydrogen atoms are extremely efficient at absorbing ionizing radiation—that is, an energy per photon of at least 13.6 electron volts (or, equivalently, a wavelength of less than 0.0912 micrometre [$3.59055118 \times 10^{-6}$ in]). If the hydrogen is mainly neutral, no radiation with energy above this threshold can penetrate except for photons with energies in the X-ray range and above (thousands of electron volts or more), in which case the hydrogen becomes somewhat transparent. The absorption by neutral hydrogen abruptly reduces the radiation field to almost zero for energies above 13.6 electron volts. This dearth of hydrogen-ionizing radiation implies that no ions requiring more ionizing energy than hydrogen can be produced, and the ionic species of all elements are limited to the lower stages of ionization. Within H II regions, with almost all the hydrogen ionized and thereby rendered nonabsorbing, photons of all energies propagate, and ions requiring energetic radiation for their production (e.g., O^{++}) occur.

Ultraviolet photons with energies of more than 11.2 electron volts can dissociate molecular hydrogen (H_2) into two H atoms. In H I regions there are enough of these photons to prevent the amount of H_2 from becoming large, but the destruction of H_2 as fast as it forms takes its toll on the number of photons of suitable energies. Furthermore, interstellar dust is a fairly efficient absorber of photons throughout the optical and ultraviolet range. In some regions of space the number of photons with energies higher than 11.2 volts is reduced to the level where H2 cannot be destroyed as fast as it is produced on grain surfaces. In this case, H_2 becomes the dominant form of hydrogen present. The gas is then part of a molecular cloud. The role of interstellar dust in this process is crucial because H_2 cannot be formed efficiently in the gas phase.

Interstellar Dust

Only about 0.7 percent of the mass of the interstellar medium is in the form of solid grains, but these grains have a profound effect on the physical conditions within the gas. Their main effect is to absorb stellar radiation; for photons unable to ionize hydrogen and for wavelengths outside absorption lines or bands, the dust grains are much more opaque than the gas. The dust absorption increases with photon energy, so long-wavelength radiation (radio and far-infrared) can penetrate dust freely, near-infrared rather well, and ultraviolet relatively poorly.

Dark, cold molecular clouds, within which all star formation takes place, owe their existence to dust. Besides absorbing starlight, the dust acts to heat the gas under some conditions (by ejecting electrons produced by the photoelectric effect, following the absorption of a stellar photon) and to cool the gas under other conditions (because the dust can radiate energy more efficiently than the gas and so in general is colder). The largest chemical effect of dust is to provide the only site of molecular hydrogen formation on grain surfaces. It also removes some heavy elements (especially iron and silicon) that would act as coolants to the gas. The optical appearance of most nebulae is significantly modified by the obscuring effects of the dust.

The chemical composition of the gas phase of the interstellar medium alone, without regard to the solid dust, can be determined from the strength of narrow absorption lines that are produced by the gas in the spectra of background stars. Comparison of the composition of the gas with cosmic (solar) abundances shows that almost all the iron, magnesium, and silicon, much of the carbon, and only some of the oxygen and nitrogen are contained in the dust. The absorption and scattering properties of the dust reveal that the solid grains are composed partially of silicaceous material similar to terrestrial rocks, though of an amorphous rather than crystalline variety. The grains also have a carbonaceous component. The carbon dust probably occurs in at least two forms:

(1) grains, either free-flying or as components of composite grains that also contain silicates, and (2) individual, freely floating aromatic hydrocarbon molecules, with a range varying from 70 to several hundred carbon atoms and some hydrogen atoms that dangle from the outer edges of the molecule or are trapped in the middle of it.

It is merely convention that these molecules are referred to as dust, since the smallest may be only somewhat larger than the largest molecules observed with a radio telescope. Both of the dust components are needed to explain spectroscopic features arising from the dust. In addition, there are probably mantles of hydrocarbon on the surfaces of the grains. The size of the grains ranges from perhaps as small as 0.0003 micrometre ($1.18110236 \times 10^{-8}$ in) for the tiniest hydrocarbon molecules to a substantial fraction of a micrometre; there are many more small grains than large ones.

The dust cannot be formed directly from purely gaseous material at the low densities found even in comparatively dense interstellar clouds, which would be considered an excellent laboratory vacuum. For a solid to condense, the gas density must be high enough to allow a few atoms to collide and stick together long enough to radiate away their energy to cool and form a solid. Grains are known to form in the outer atmospheres of cool supergiant stars, where the gas density is comparatively high (perhaps 10^9 times what it is in typical nebulae). The grains are then blown out of the stellar atmosphere by radiation pressure (the mechanical force of the light they absorb and scatter). Calculations indicate that refracting materials, such as the constituents of the grains proposed above, should condense in this way.

There is clear indication that the dust is heavily modified within the interstellar medium by interactions with itself and with the interstellar gas. The absorption and scattering properties of dust show that there are many more smaller grains in the diffuse interstellar medium than in dense clouds. Apparently in the dense medium the small grains have coagulated into larger ones, thereby lowering the ability of the dust to absorb radiation with short wavelengths (namely, ultraviolet, near 0.1 micrometre). The gas-phase abundances of some elements, such as iron, magnesium, and nickel, also are much lower in the dense regions than in the diffuse gas, although even in the diffuse gas most of these elements are missing from the gas and are therefore condensed into dust. These systematic interactions of gas and dust show that dust grains collide with gas atoms much more rapidly than one would expect if the dust and gas simply drifted together. There must be disturbances, probably magnetic in nature, that keep the dust and gas moving with respect to each other.

The motions of gas within nebulae of all types are clearly chaotic and complicated. There are sometimes large-scale flows, such as when a hot star forms on the outer edge of a cold, quiescent dark molecular cloud and ionizes an H II region in its vicinity. The pressure strongly increases in the newly ionized zone, so the ionized gas flows out through the surrounding material. There are also expanding structures resembling bubbles surrounding stars that are ejecting their outer atmospheres into stellar winds.

TURBULENCE

Besides these organized flows, nebulae of all types always show chaotic motions called turbulence. This is a well-known phenomenon in gas dynamics that results when there is low viscosity in flowing fluids, so the motions become chaotic eddies that transfer kinetic and magnetic energy and momentum from large scales down to small sizes. On small-enough scales viscosity always becomes important, and the energy is converted into heat, which is kinetic energy on a molecular scale. Turbulence in nebulae has profound, but poorly understood, effects on their energy balance and pressure support.

Turbulence is observed by means of the widths of the emission or absorption lines in a nebular spectrum. No line can be precisely sharp in wavelength, because the energy levels of the atom or ion from which it arises are not precisely sharp. Actual lines are usually much broader than this intrinsic width because of the Doppler effect arising from motions of the atoms along the line of sight. The emission line of an atom is shifted to longer wavelengths if it is receding from the observer and to shorter wavelengths if it is approaching. Part of the observed broadening is easily explained by thermal motions, since v^2, the averaged squared speed, is proportional to T/m, where T is the temperature and m is the mass of the atom. Thus, hydrogen atoms move the fastest at any given temperature.

Observations show that, in fact, hydrogen lines are broader than those of other elements but not as much as expected from thermal motions alone. Turbulence represents bulk motions, independent of the mass of the atoms. This chaotic motion of gas atoms of all masses would explain the observations. The physical question, though, is what maintains the turbulence. Why do the turbulent cascades not carry kinetic energy from large-size scales into ever-shorter-size scales and finally into heat?

The answer is that energy is continuously injected into the gases by a variety of processes. One involves strong stellar winds from hot stars, which are blown off at speeds of thousands of kilometres per second. Another arises from the violently expanding remnants of supernova explosions, which sometimes start at 20,000 km (12,000 miles) per second and gradually slow to typical cloud speeds (10 km [6 miles] per second). A third process is the occasional collision of clouds moving in the overall galactic gravitational potential. All these processes inject energy on large scales that can undergo turbulent cascading to heat.

GALACTIC MAGNETIC FIELD

There is a pervasive magnetic field that threads the spiral arms of the Milky Way Galaxy and extends to thousands of light-years above the galactic plane. The evidence for the existence of this field comes from radio synchrotron emission produced by very energetic electrons moving through it and from the polarization of starlight that is produced by elongated dust grains that tend to be aligned with the magnetic field. The magnetic field is very strongly coupled to the gas because it acts upon the embedded electrons, even the few in H I regions, and the electrons impart some motion of the other constituents by means of collisions. The gas and field are effectively confined to moving together, even though the gas can slip along the field freely. The field has an important influence upon the turbulence because it exerts a pressure similar to gas pressure, thereby influencing the motions of the gas. The resulting complex interactions and wave motions have been studied in extensive numerical calculations.

MOLECULAR CLOUDS

A molecular cloud, or a dark nebula, is an interstellar clump or cloud that is opaque because of its internal dust grains. The form of such dark clouds is very irregular:

they have no clearly defined outer boundaries and sometimes take on convoluted serpentine shapes because of turbulence. The largest molecular clouds are visible to the naked eye, appearing as dark patches against the brighter background of the Milky Way Galaxy. An example is the Coalsack in the southern sky. Stars are born within molecular clouds.

COMPOSITION

The hydrogen of these opaque dark clouds exists in the form of H_2 molecules. The largest nebulae of this type, the so-called giant molecular clouds, are a million times more massive than the Sun. They contain much of the mass of the interstellar medium, are some 150 light-years across, and have an average density of 100 to 300 molecules per cubic centimetre (1 cubic cm = .06 cubic in) and an internal temperature of only 7 to 15 K. Molecular clouds consist mainly of gas and dust but contain many stars as well. The central regions of these clouds are completely hidden from view by dust and would be undetectable except for the far-infrared thermal emission from dust grains and the microwave emissions from the constituent molecules. This radiation is not absorbed by dust and readily escapes the cloud. The material within the clouds is clumped together on all size scales, with some clouds ranging down to the masses of individual stars. The density within the clumps may reach up to 10^5 H_2 molecules per cubic centimetre or more. Small clumps may extend about one light-year across. Turbulence

and the internal magnetic field provide support against the clouds' own gravity.

The chemistry and physical conditions of the interior of a molecular cloud are quite different from those of the surrounding low-density interstellar medium. In the outer parts of the dark cloud, hydrogen is neutral. Deeper within it, as dust blocks out an increasing amount of stellar ultraviolet radiation, the cloud becomes darker and colder. Approaching the centre, the predominant form of gaseous carbon changes successively from C^+ on the outside to neutral C (C^0) and finally to the molecule carbon monoxide (CO), which is so stable that it remains the major form of carbon in the gas phase in the darkest regions. At great depths within the cloud, other molecules can be seen from their microwave transitions, and more than 150 chemical species have been identified within the constituent gas.

Because of the comparatively low densities and temperatures, the chemistry is very exotic, as judged by terrestrial experiments; some rather unstable species can exist in space because there is not enough energy to convert them to more-stable forms. An example is the near equality of the abundances of the interstellar molecule HNC (hydroisocyanic acid) and its isomer HCN (hydrocyanic acid); in ordinary terrestrial conditions there is plenty of energy to allow the nitrogen and carbon atoms in HNC to exchange positions and produce HCN, by far the preferred species for equilibrium chemistry. In the cold clouds, however, not enough energy exists for the exchange to occur. There is less than one-thousandth as much starlight within a cloud as in the interstellar space outside the cloud, and the heating of the material in the cloud is provided primarily by cosmic rays. Cooling within the cloud occurs chiefly by transitions between low-lying levels of the carbon monoxide molecule.

The emission lines from C^+, C^0, and CO show that the edges of the molecular clouds are very convoluted spatially, with stellar ultraviolet radiation able to penetrate surprisingly far throughout the cloud despite the absorption of dust. Stellar radiation can apparently enter the cloud through channels where the dust (and gas) density is lower than average. The clumpiness of the interstellar material has profound effects on its properties.

FORMATION OF STARS

In the inner regions of molecular clouds an important event takes place: the formation of stars from the gravitational collapse of dense clumps within the nebula. Initially the cloud consists of a chaotic jumble of smaller clouds, each of which is destined to be an individual stellar system. Each system has a rotary motion arising from the original motions of the material that is falling into it. Because of this spin, the collapsing cloud flattens as it shrinks. Eventually most of its mass is in a rotating condensation near its centre, a "protostar" destined to become one or more closely spaced stars. Surrounding the protostar is a rotating disk larger than the solar system that collapses into "protoplanets" and comets.

These ideas are given encouraging confirmation by observations of molecular clouds in very long wavelength infrared radiation. Some of the brightest infrared sources are associated with such dark dust clouds; a good example is the class of T Tauri variables, named for their prototype star in the constellation Taurus. The T Tauri stars are known for a variety of reasons to be extremely young. The variables are always found in or near molecular clouds; they often are also powerful sources of infrared radiation, corresponding to warm clouds of dust heated by the T Tauri star to a few hundred kelvins. There are some strong infrared sources (especially in the constellation of Orion) that have no visible stars with them; these are presumably "cocoon stars" completely hidden by their veils of dust.

One of the remarkable features of molecular clouds is their concentration in the spiral arms in the plane of the Milky Way Galaxy. While there is no definite boundary to the arms, which have irregularities and bifurcations, the nebulae in other spiral galaxies are strung out along these narrow lanes and form a beautifully symmetric system when viewed from another galaxy. The nebulae are remarkably close to the galactic plane; most are within 300 light-years, only 1 percent of the Sun's distance from the centre. The details of the explanation of why the gas is largely confined to the spiral arms is beyond the scope of this book. Briefly, the higher density of the stars in the arms produces sufficient gravity to hold the gas to them.

Why doesn't the gas simply condense into stars and disappear? The present rate of star formation is about one solar mass per year in the entire Galaxy, which contains something like 2×10^9 solar masses of gas. Clearly, if the gas received no return of material from stars, it would be depleted in roughly 2×10^9 years, about one-sixth the present age of the Galaxy. There are several processes by which gas is returned to the interstellar medium. Possibly the most important is the ejection of planetary nebula shells; other processes are ejection of material from massive O- and B-type normal stars or from cool M giants and supergiants. The rate of gas ejection is roughly equal to the rate of star formation, so that the mass of free gas is declining very slowly. (Some gas is also falling into the Galaxy that has never been associated with any galaxy.)

This cycling of gas through stars has had one major effect: the chemical composition of the gas has been changed by the nuclear reactions inside the stars. There is excellent evidence that the Galaxy originally consisted of 77 percent hydrogen by mass and that almost all of the rest of the constituent matter was helium. All heavy elements have been produced inside stars by being subjected to the exceedingly high temperatures and densities in the central regions. Thus, most of the atoms and molecules on Earth, as well as in human bodies, owe their very existence to processes that occur within stars.

HYDROGEN CLOUDS

A different type of nebula is the hydrogen cloud, or the H I region; this region is interstellar matter in which hydrogen is mostly neutral, rather than ionized or molecular. Most of the matter between the stars in the Milky Way Galaxy, as well as in other spiral galaxies, occurs in the form of relatively cold neutral hydrogen gas. Neutral hydrogen clouds are easily detectable at radio wavelengths because they emit a characteristic energy at a wavelength of 21 cm (8 in).

Neutral hydrogen is dominant in clouds that have enough starlight to dissociate molecular hydrogen into atoms but lack hydrogen-ionizing photons from hot stars. These clouds can be seen as separate structures within the lower-density interstellar medium or else on the outer edges of the molecular clouds. Because a neutral cloud moves through space as a single entity, it often can be distinguished by the absorption line that its atoms or ions produce at their common radial velocity in the spectrum of a background star.

If neutral clouds at a typical pressure were left alone until they could reach an equilibrium state, they could exist at either of two temperatures: "cold" (about 80 K) or "warm" (about 8,000 K), both determined by the balance of heating and cooling rates. There should be little material in between. Observations show that these cold and warm clouds do exist, but roughly half the material is in clouds at intermediate temperatures, which implies that turbulence and collisions between clouds can prevent the equilibrium states from being reached. Cold H I regions are heated by electrons ejected from the dust grains by interstellar ultraviolet radiation incident upon such a cloud from outside. Cooling is mainly by C^+ because passing electrons or hydrogen atoms can excite it from its normal energy state, the lowest, to one slightly higher, which is then followed by emission of radiation at 158 micrometres. This line is observed to be very strong in the spectrum of the Milky Way Galaxy as a whole, which indicates that a great deal of energy is removed from interstellar gas by this process. Cold H I regions have densities of 10 to 100 hydrogen atoms per cubic cm. Warm H I regions are cooled by excitation of the $n = 2$ level of hydrogen, which is at a much higher energy than the lowest level of C^+ and therefore requires a higher temperature for its excitation. The density of 0.5 atom per cubic cm (1 cubic cm = .06 in) is much lower than in the colder regions. At any particular density there is far more neutral hydrogen available for cooling than C^+.

REFLECTION NEBULAE

The reflection nebulae are interstellar clouds that would normally be dark nebulae but whose dust reflects the light from a nearby bright star that is not hot enough to ionize the cloud's hydrogen. The famous nebulosity in the Pleiades star cluster is of this type. It was discovered in 1912 that the spectrum of this nebula mimics the absorption lines of the nearby stars, whereas bright nebulae that emit their own light show their own characteristic emission lines. The brightest reflection nebulae are illuminated by B-type stars that are very luminous but have temperatures lower than about 25,000 K, cooler than the O-type stars that would ionize the hydrogen in the gas and produce an H II region.

The extent and brightness of reflection nebulae show conclusively that dust grains are excellent reflectors in the broad range of wavelengths extending from the ultraviolet (as determined from observations from space) through the visible. Optical observations suggest that about 60–70 percent of the light is reflected rather than absorbed, while the corresponding fraction for Earth is only 35 percent and for the Moon a mere 5 percent. Grains reflect light almost as well as fresh snow, more because of their favourable size (which promotes scattering rather than absorption) than their chemical composition. Calculations show that even graphite, which is black in bulk, reflects visible light well when dispersed into small particles.

H II REGION

Nebulae that are full of ionized hydrogen atoms are H II regions. (These regions are also called diffuse nebulae or emission nebulae.) The energy that is responsible for ionizing and heating the hydrogen in an emission nebula comes from a central star that has a surface temperature in excess of 20,000 K. The density of these clouds normally ranges from 10 to 100,000 particles per cubic cm (1 cubic cm = .06 in); their temperature is about 8,000 K.

Like molecular clouds, H II regions typically have little regular structure or sharp boundaries. Their sizes and masses vary widely. There is even a faint region of ionized gas around the Sun and other comparatively cool stars, but it cannot be observed from nearby stars with existing instruments.

The largest H II regions (none of which occur in the Milky Way Galaxy) are 500 light-years across and contain at least 100,000 solar masses of ionized gas. These enormous H II regions are

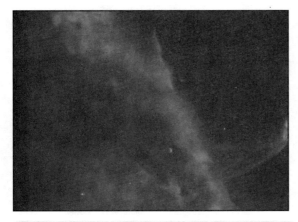

A plume of gas (lower right) in the Orion Nebula. A highly supersonic shock wave—moving at a speed of more than 238,000 km (148,000 miles) per hour—was produced by a beam of material emanating from a newly formed star. National Aeronautics and Space Administration

powered by clusters of massive hot stars rather than by any single stellar body. A typical H II region within the Galaxy measures about 30 light-years in diameter and has an average density of about 10 atoms per cubic cm. The mass of such a cloud amounts to several hundred solar masses. The only H II region visible to the naked eye is the beautiful Orion Nebula. It is located in the constellation named for the Greek mythological hunter and is seen as the central "star" in Orion's sword. The entire constellation is enveloped in faint emission nebulosity, powered by several stars in Orion's belt rather than by the star exciting the much smaller Orion Nebula. The largest H II region in terms of angular size is the Gum Nebula, discovered by Australian astronomer Colin S. Gum. It measures 40° in angular diameter and is mainly ionized by two very hot stars (Zeta Puppis and Gamma Velorum).

High-resolution studies of H II regions reveal one of the surprises that make the study of astrophysics delightful. Instead of the smooth structure that might be expected of a gas, a delicate tracery of luminous filaments can be detected down to the smallest scale that can be resolved. In the Orion Nebula this is about 6 billion km (4 billion miles), or about the radius of the orbit of Pluto around the Sun. Even finer details almost surely exist, and there is evidence from spectra that much of the matter may be gathered into dense condensations, or knots, the rest of the space being comparatively empty. Unrestrained gas would fill a vacuum between the visible filaments in about 200 years, an astronomical instant. The nebular gas must be restrained from expansion by the pressure of million-degree tenuous material between the filaments. Its pressure, however, is comparable to that in the visible "warm" (8,000 K) gas of the H II region. Hence, the density of the hot material is several hundred times lower, which effectively prevents it from being observable except in X-rays. The space throughout the plane of the Milky Way Galaxy is largely filled with this hot component, which is mainly produced and heated by supernovae.

In H II regions, hot gas also arises from the stellar winds of the exciting stars. These winds create a large cavity or bubble in the denser, cooler gas originally surrounding such a star. In the interior of the bubble, the radially flowing stellar wind passes through a transition in which its radial motion is converted into heat. The hot gas then fills most of the cavity (perhaps 90 percent or more) and serves to separate the filaments of the warm, comparatively dense H II region. Within the condensations of visible plasma, there are neutral globules in which the gas is quite cold (about 100 K) but is dense enough (typically, 10,000 atoms per cubic cm) to have about the same pressure as the hot and warm materials. In short, an H II region is much more complicated than its visual radiation would suggest.

H II regions are almost always accompanied by molecular clouds on their borders. The Orion Nebula, for example, is merely a conspicuous ionized region on the nearby face of a much larger dark cloud; the H II region is almost entirely produced by the ionization provided by a single hot star, one of the four bright central stars (the Trapezium) identified by Dutch astronomer Christiaan Huygens in 1656. The shape of the Orion Nebula appears at visible wavelengths as irregular. However, much of this seeming chaos is spurious, caused by obscuration of dust in dark foreground neutral material rather than by the actual distribution of ionized material. Radio waves can penetrate the dust unhindered, and the radio emission from the ionized gas reveals it to be quite circular in shape and surprisingly symmetrical as seen in projection on the sky. The foreground dark material obscures about half the ionized nebula.

An H II region on the outer edge of a large molecular cloud can induce star formation. For instance, behind the bright Orion Nebula, deeper within the dark cold Orion molecular cloud, new stars are being formed today. At present, none of the new stars is massive and hot enough to produce its own H II region, but presumably some of them eventually will be. When an H II region is produced from cold molecular gas by the formation of a hot star, the temperature is raised from roughly 25 to 8,000 K, and the number of particles per cubic centimetre is almost quadrupled because each H_2 molecule is split into two ions and two electrons. Gas pressure is proportional to the product of the temperature and number of particles per cubic centimetre (regardless of their mass, so electrons are as important as the much heavier ions). Thus, the pressure in an H II region is some 800 times the pressure of the cold gas from which it formed. The excess pressure causes a violent expansion of the gas into the dense cloud. Rapid star formation may occur in the compressed region, producing an expanding group of young stars. Such groups, the so-called O Associations (with O stars) or T Associations (with T Tauri stars), have been observed. The component stars simultaneously generate extremely fast outflows from their atmospheres. These winds create regions of hot, tenuous gas surrounding the association. Eventually the massive stars in the association explode as supernovae, which further disturb the surrounding gas.

Ultracompact H II Regions

This picture of the evolution of H II regions and molecular clouds is one of constant turmoil, a few transient O stars serving to keep the material stirred, in constant motion, continually producing new stars and churning clouds of gas and dust. In this way some of the stellar thermonuclear energy is converted into the kinetic energy of interstellar gas. This process begins just after the formation of the massive star that will power the mature H II region. The star begins producing copious amounts of ultraviolet radiation, converting the surrounding H_2 to atomic hydrogen, and then ionizing it to very dense high-pressure H^+.

The very dense, very young H II regions within molecular clouds are called "ultracompact" because of their small sizes and high densities. These nebulae are observed only at the wavelengths of radio and far-infrared radiation, both of which are able to penetrate the thick dust in the clouds. They are extremely bright at wavelengths of 50 micrometres (.002 in). There are about 2,500 in the Milky Way Galaxy, representing 10 to 20 percent of the total O-type star population. Usually only a light-month in size, 100 times smaller than a typical H II region, they show densities in the ionized region of 10^5 hydrogen atoms per cubic cm. They cannot be at rest with respect to the surrounding gas; if they were, the immense pressure exerted by their dense hot gas would cause a violent expansion. (Their lifetimes would be only about 3,000 years—exceedingly short on an astronomical timescale—and not nearly as many could be seen as the number observed by astronomers.) Rather, their gas is kept confined because they are moving through the surrounding cloud at speeds of about 10 km (6 miles) per second, and what is observed is the cloud of freshly ionized gas ahead of them that has not yet had time to expand. The ultracompact H II regions leave behind a trail of ionized material that is not as bright as the confined gas ahead of them. This trail gradually fades as it recombines after the ionizing star has passed. The radio radiation is produced by the ionized gas, but the far-infrared radiation is emitted by the 5,000 solar masses of surrounding dust warmed by the luminosity of the embedded star.

SUPERGIANT NEBULAE

The most energetic H II regions within nearby galaxies have over 1,000 times more ionizations per second than does the Orion Nebula, too many to be provided by a single star. Indeed, there are clumps of ionized gas ionized by tight groupings of single stars that are embedded in rather diffuse material. These objects are more than 10 times as luminous as any in the Milky Way Galaxy and are about 200 light-years in diameter. If they were located at the Orion Nebula, they would cover the entire constellation of Orion with brightly glowing gas. These

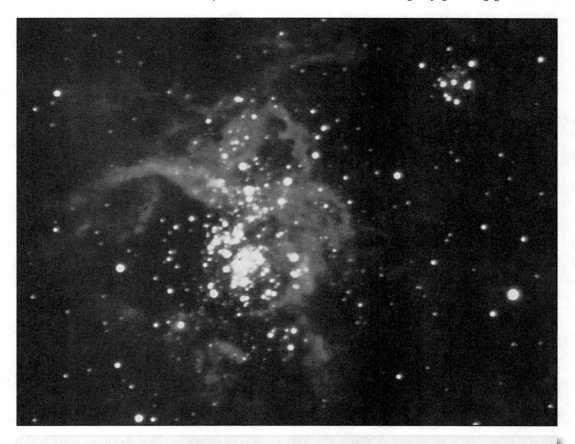

The inner part of the 30 Doradus Nebula, the most luminous nebula in the entire Local Group of galaxies, located in the Large Magellanic Cloud. National Optical Astronomy Observatories

supergiant nebulae are more than 10 times as luminous as any in the Galaxy.

The entire Local Group—the cluster of galaxies consisting of the Milky Way Galaxy, the great spiral galaxy in Andromeda, the smaller spiral in Triangulum, and more than 50 other stellar assemblages—contains but one supergiant nebula, the object called 30 Doradus, in the Large Magellanic Cloud. It contains a stellar cluster called R136, the source of most of the energy radiated by the nebula. This grouping consists of dozens of the most massive known stars of the Milky Way Galaxy, all packed into a volume only a thousandth of a typical stellar spacing in size. How such a cluster could form is a fascinating puzzle. There are other supergiant nebulae outside the Local Group, some of which radiate 10 times the energy of 30 Doradus.

CHEMICAL COMPOSITION OF H II REGIONS

The chemical composition of H II regions (the numbers of atoms of each chemical element, relative to hydrogen) can be estimated from nebular spectra. Each element is found in more than one stage of ionization, so the first step is to use the emission-line strengths of each stage of ionization, relative to those of the hydrogen lines, to obtain the abundance of that particular stage of ionization. All abundant elements have some stages of ionization that produce observable emission lines. On the other hand, some elements, such as argon, sulfur, and carbon, have important ions that do not show easily observable lines. Elaborate computer calculations predict the ionization structure of gas ionized by a hot star whose temperature is determined by its spectrum. The calculations then provide predictions of the abundances of the invisible ions, relative to the observable, and the total elemental abundance follows.

The main difficulty with this straightforward procedure is that there are two methods for determining the observed ionic abundances; each should be reliable, but they give quite different answers. By far the easier method of determining ionic abundances is to observe the bright lines produced by collisions between the ion and energetic electrons. The brightest lines from this process in the entire spectrum of H II regions arise from either O^+ or O^{+2}. These bright lines (and others such as N^+) are the basis of the abundance determinations in other galaxies.

Alternatively, the ionic abundances can be determined from the very faint emission lines that follow recombination, the process by which the higher stage of ionization captures an electron (usually at low energies) into a high level of the ion. Following recombination, there is a cascade from the high energy levels to the ground state, with photons in the observed emission line being emitted at each downward transition. These emission lines are fainter than the hydrogen emissions by roughly the ratio of abundances, which is more than 1,000, so only in bright nebulae can this method be used. However, modern spectrographs on large telescopes have provided strengths of these faint recombination lines for many objects, with good agreement among observers. Checks are provided by comparison of several lines of the same stage of ionization. The relative strengths of the observed lines agree well with the expectations of the cascading process in the excited ions.

The results are interesting and controversial. For H II regions that are bright enough for the faint heavy-element recombination lines to be measured, the carbon, nitrogen, neon, and oxygen abundances from recombination lines are uniformly about 1.8 times those from the collisionally excited lines. A common interpretation is that there are strong temperature fluctuations within the nebulae. In the warmer regions the collisionally excited lines are strongly overproduced per heavy ion, so fewer heavy ions are needed to account for the observed line strengths. The hydrogen lines are hardly affected by the postulated temperature fluctuations. The temperature fluctuations, which must be large (about 20 percent of the average), are unexplained. Turbulence and magnetic fields are prime suspects.

The nebular temperature can be estimated directly from collisional lines alone by comparing emission lines from high-energy levels, populated by collisions, with lines from lower levels. This process can be carried out at various places on the sky within each nebula, and large-scale temperature fluctuations would appear as variations from place to place.

However, no such variations have been convincingly detected. Some astronomers have proposed that there are chemical inhomogeneities within nebulae that give rise to the differences between the abundances derived from recombination and collisionally excited lines, but how such variations could be maintained is unexplained.

Nevertheless, abundances are estimated on the basis of a simple interpretation of the mysterious postulated temperature excursions, but no better procedure has been suggested to deal with the startling discrepancies in the derived abundances. The other class of ionized nebulae, the planetary nebulae, show the same effect. The local estimated abundances (say, for the Orion Nebula) are roughly solar. The abundances of heavy elements per million hydrogen atoms are 500 for carbon, 80 for nitrogen, 600 for oxygen, and 100 for neon. There is a gradient of these abundances within the Milky Way Galaxy. At a distance halfway to the centre, 12,000 light-years inward, they are 50 percent larger than locally. Beyond Earth the gradient seems to persist, but there are very few observations. Helium is about 0.1 times as abundant as hydrogen, by number of atoms, throughout the Milky Way Galaxy.

Except for a few cases, compositions of nebulae in galaxies outside the Milky Way Galaxy are measured by collisionally excited lines. The Large Magellanic Cloud has compositions that are uniformly about one-half those of the local Milky Way for oxygen, neon, argon, and sulfur and are one-quarter for carbon and nitrogen. It appears that the first group of elements must be manufactured together, presumably in massive stars, and ejected together into the interstellar gas. Stars of a different (probably lower) mass must produce carbon and nitrogen. Planetary nebulae suggest the same scenario.

The abundance of helium in nebulae has received considerable attention because the helium content of the oldest objects provides clues to the origin of the universe. The value cited above for the Orion Nebula is in agreement with the predictions of the big-bang model.

PLANETARY NEBULAE

Some nebulae, called planetary nebulae, are expanding shells of luminous gas expelled by dying stars. Observed telescopically, they have a relatively round compact appearance rather than the chaotic patchy shapes of other nebulae— hence their name, which was given because of their resemblance to planetary disks when viewed with the instruments of the late 1700s, when the first planetary nebulae were discovered.

There are believed to be about 20,000 objects called planetary nebulae in the Milky Way Galaxy, each representing gas expelled relatively recently from a central star very late in its evolution. Because of the obscuration of dust in the Galaxy, only about 1,800 planetary nebulae have been cataloged. Planetary nebulae are important sources of the gas in the interstellar medium.

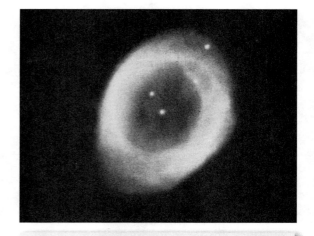

Ring Nebula (M57, NGC 6720) in the constellation Lyra, a planetary nebula consisting mainly of gases thrown off by the star in the centre. Hale Observatories © 1959

FORMS AND STRUCTURE

Compared with diffuse nebulae, planetary nebulae are small objects, having a radius typically of 1 light-year and containing a mass of gas of about 0.3 solar mass. One of the largest-known planetary nebulae, the Helix Nebula (NGC 7293) in the constellation Aquarius, subtends an angle of about 20 minutes of arc—two-thirds the angular size of the Moon. Planetary nebulae are considerably denser than most H II regions, typically containing 1,000–10,000 atoms per cubic cm (1 cubic cm = .06 in) within their dense regions, and have a surface brightness 1,000 times larger. Many are so far away that they appear stellar when photographed directly, but the conspicuous examples have an angular size up to 20 minutes of arc across, with 10–30 seconds of arc being usual. Those that show a bright disk have much more-regular forms than the chaotic H II regions, but there are still usually some brightness fluctuations over the disk. The planetaries generally have regular, sharp outer boundaries; often they have a relatively regular inner boundary as well, giving them the appearance of a ring. Many have two lobes of bright material, resembling arcs of a circle, connected by a bridge, somewhat resembling the letter Z.

Most planetaries show a central star, called the nucleus, which provides the ultraviolet radiation required for ionizing the gas in the ring or shell surrounding it. Those stars are among the hottest known and are in a state of comparatively rapid evolution.

As with H II regions, the overall structural regularity conceals large-scale fluctuations in density, temperature, and chemical composition. High-resolution images of a planetary nebula usually reveal tiny knots and filaments down to the resolution limit. The spectrum of the planetary nebula is basically the same as that of the H II region; it contains bright lines from hydrogen and helium recombinations and the bright, collisionally excited forbidden lines and faint recombination lines of other ions. (Recombination is the process by which the higher stage of ionization captures an electron [usually at low energies] into a high level of the ion.) The central stars show a much greater range of temperatures than those in H II regions, ranging from relatively cool (25,000 K) to some of the hottest known (200,000 K).

In the nebulae with hot stars, most of the helium is doubly ionized, and appreciable amounts of five-times-ionized oxygen and argon and four-times-ionized neon exist. In H II regions helium is mainly once ionized and neon and argon only once or twice. This difference in the states of the atoms results from the temperature of the planetary nucleus (up to about 150,000 K), which is much higher than that of the exciting star of the H II regions (less than 60,000 K for an O star, the hottest). High stages of ionization are found close to the central star. The rare heavy ions, rather than hydrogen, absorb the photons of several hundred electron volt energies. Beyond a certain distance from the central star, all the photons of energy sufficient to ionize a given species of ion have been absorbed, and that species therefore cannot exist farther out. Detailed theoretical calculations have rather successfully predicted the spectra of the best-observed nebulae.

The spectra of planetary nebulae reveal another interesting fact: they are expanding from the central star at 24–56 km (15–35 miles) per second. The gravitational pull of the star is quite small at the distance of the shell from the star, so the shell will continue its expansion until it finally merges with the interstellar gas around it. The expansion is proportional to the distance from the central star, consistent with the entire mass of gas having been ejected at one brief period from the star in some sort of instability.

The Distances of Planetary Nebulae

Estimating the distance to any particular planetary nebula is challenging because of the variety of shapes and masses of the ionized gas. There is uncertainty about the amount of ionizing radiation from the central star that escapes from the nebula and the amount of hot low-density material that fills part of the volume but does not emit appreciable radiation. Thus, planetary nebulae are not a homogeneous class of objects.

Distances are estimated by obtaining measurements for about 40 objects that happen to have especially favourable properties. The favourable properties involve association with other objects whose distance can be estimated independently, such as membership in a stellar cluster or association with a star of known properties. Statistical methods, calibrated by these objects, provide rough estimates (about 30 percent errors) of distances for all others. The statistical method involves assuming that all shells have similar masses when all of the shell is ionized and correcting for the fraction that is neutral for the rest.

From the best available distance determination, the true size of any nebula can be found from its angular size. Typically, planetary nebulae are a few tenths of a light-year in radius. If this distance is divided by the expansion speed, the age of the nebula since ejection is obtained. Values range up to roughly 30,000 years, after which the nebula is so tenuous that it cannot be distinguished from the surrounding interstellar gas. This lifetime is much shorter than the lifetimes of the parent stars, so the nebular phase is relatively brief.

Chemical Composition

Planetary nebulae are chemically enriched in elements produced by nuclear processing within the central star. Some are carbon-rich, with twice as much carbon as oxygen, while there is more oxygen than carbon in the Sun. Others are over-abundant in nitrogen; the most luminous ones, observed in external galaxies, are conspicuous examples. Helium is modestly enhanced in many. There are objects that contain almost no hydrogen; it is as if the gas had been ejected from these object at the very end of the nuclear-burning process. Planetary nebulae also show a clear indication of the general heavy-element abundance gradient in the Galaxy, presumably a reflection of the original composition of the stars that gave rise to the present nebulae.

As in the case of H II regions, planetary nebulae show discrepancies between the determinations of abundances of heavy elements from faint recombination lines as opposed to those determined from collisionally excited lines, but in a much more severe form. There are some nebulae for which the two methods give the same abundances. However, the most extreme discrepancies are factors of 30 or more in the oxygen abundances. Perhaps this wild variation in planetary nebulae is not surprising, since they surely have regions of material that are strongly enriched in heavy elements and deficient in hydrogen. These regions originate in the complicated nuclear processing of the expelled material ejected from the evolved central star. They would have strong cooling from the heavy-element emissions and thus much lower temperatures than the regions of normal composition. These regions would contribute very little to the hydrogen emission lines because they are hydrogen-poor.

Some, but not all, planetary nebulae contain internal dust. In general, this dust cannot be seen directly but can be detected from the infrared radiation it emits after being heated by nebular and stellar radiation. The presence of dust implies that planetary nebulae are even richer in heavy elements than gas-phase abundance studies suggest.

Among nebulae so far discovered, two are particularly deviant in chemical composition: one is in the globular cluster M15 and the other in the halo (tenuous outer regions) of the Galaxy. Both have very low heavy-element content (down from normal by factors of about 50) but normal helium. Both objects are very old, suggesting that the primeval gas in the Galaxy had a low heavy-element content but an almost normal amount of helium. The origin of most helium in the Galaxy was the big bang, the initial explosion of the universe itself.

POSITIONS IN THE GALAXY

One of the best indicators of the average age of astronomical objects is their position and motion in the Galaxy. The youngest are in the spiral arms, near the gas from which they have formed; the oldest are not concentrated in the plane of the Galaxy, nor are they found within the spiral arms. By these criteria, the planetaries reveal themselves to be rather middle-aged; they are moderately but not strongly concentrated in the plane; rather, they are concentrated toward the galactic centre, as the older objects are. Their motions in the Galaxy follow elliptical paths, whereas circular orbits are characteristic of younger stars. They belong to the type of distribution often called a "disk population," to distinguish them from the Population II (very old) and Population I (young) objects proposed by the German American astronomer Walter Baade. There is a wide variation in the ages of planetaries, and some are very young objects.

EVOLUTION OF PLANETARY NEBULAE

A description of the evolution of a planetary nebula begins before the ejection of the nebula itself. As will be discussed below, the central star is a red giant before the ejection. In such a phase it experiences a rapid loss of mass, up to 0.01 Earth mass per day, in the form of a comparatively slowly expanding stellar wind.

At this stage the red giant might be heavily obscured by dust that forms from the heavy elements in the wind. Eventually the nature of both the star and its wind changes. The star becomes hotter because its hot core is exposed by the loss of the overlying atmosphere. The inner gas is ionized by radiation from the hot star. The ionization zone moves steadily outward through the slowly moving material of what was formerly the stellar wind. The expansion speed of the gas is typically 30 km (19 miles) per second. Nebulae in this stage are bright but have starlike images as seen from Earth, because they are too small to show a disk. The gas is at a relatively high density—about one million atoms per cubic centimetre (1 cubic cm = .06 cubic in)—but becomes more dilute as the gas expands. During this stage the nebula is surrounded by neutral hydrogen. It appears to expand faster than the individual atoms of gas in it are moving; the ionized shell is "eating into" the neutral material as the density falls.

The middle stage of evolution occurs when the density has dropped to the point at which the entire mass of gas is ionized. After this stage is reached, some of the ultraviolet radiation escapes into space, and the expansion of the nebula is caused entirely by the motion of the gas. Most planetaries are now in this middle stage. Finally the central star becomes less luminous and can no longer provide enough ultraviolet radiation to keep even the dilute nebula ionized. Once again the outer regions of the nebula become neutral and therefore invisible. Eventually the gas is mingled with the general interstellar gas. A curious feature of several planetaries is that faint rings surrounding the bright inner nebula can be observed; they are the remnants of a previous shell ejected earlier by the star.

CENTRAL STARS

Many central stars are known from their spectra to be very hot. A common type of spectrum has very broad emission lines of carbon or nitrogen, as well as of ionized helium, superimposed upon a bluish continuum. These spectra are indistinguishable from those from the very bright rare stars known as Wolf-Rayet stars, but the planetary nuclei are about 100 times fainter than true Wolf-Rayet objects. The stars appear to be losing some mass at the present time, though evidently not enough to contribute appreciably to the shell.

The presence of the nebula allows a fairly precise determination of the central star's evolution. The temperature of the star can be estimated from the nebula from the amounts of emission of ionized helium and hydrogen by a method devised by the Dutch astronomer H. Zanstra. The amount of ionized-helium radiation is determined by the number of photons with energy of more than 54 electron volts, while hydrogen is ionized by photons in excess of 13.6 electron volts. The relative numbers of photons in the two groups depend strongly on temperature, since the spectrum shifts dramatically to higher energies as the temperature of the star increases. Hence, the temperature can be found from the observed strengths of the hydrogen and helium lines. The rate of evolution of the stars can be determined from the sizes of their nebulae, as the time since ejection of the shell is the radius of the nebula divided by the expansion rate. The energy output, or luminosity, of the central star can be estimated from the brightness of the nebula, because the nebula is converting the star's invisible ultraviolet radiation (which contains the greater part of the star's luminous energy) into visible radiation.

The resulting theoretical description of the star's evolution is quite interesting. While there seem to be real differences in stars at a given stage, the trends are quite clear. The central stars in young planetary nebulae are about as hot as the massive O and B stars—35,000–40,000 K—but roughly 10 times fainter. They have half the diameter of the Sun but are 1,000 times as luminous. As the nebula expands, the star increases its brightness and temperature, but its radius decreases steadily. It reaches a maximum energy output when it is roughly 10,000 times as luminous as the Sun, about 5,000 years after the initial expansion. This is a very small fraction of the star's age of several billion years; it represents a period equivalent to about half an hour in a human life. From this point on, the star becomes fainter, but for some time the temperature continues to increase while the shrinkage of the star continues. At its hottest the star is perhaps 200,000 K, almost five times hotter than the hottest of most of the stars. It then cools and after about 10,000 years becomes a very dense white dwarf star, scarcely larger than Earth but with a density of thousands of kilograms per cubic centimetre (1 cubic cm = .06 cubic in). From this point it cools very slowly, becoming redder and fainter indefinitely.

While there is not yet a very detailed theoretical picture of this contraction, a few results have emerged rather clearly: (1) white dwarf stars must obtain nearly all their energy from the contraction noted above, not from nuclear sources; therefore, (2) they must contain practically no hydrogen or helium, except perhaps in a very thin shell on their surfaces. These conditions would have to be met for the evolution to take place so quickly.

The absence of hydrogen in the star's interior is quite surprising; the planetary nebulae are all found to have a normal hydrogen abundance of about 1,000 times as many hydrogen atoms as heavy elements, such as oxygen. Thus, it can be concluded that the mechanism of expulsion of the envelope must be very efficient at ejecting the hydrogen-rich outer layers of a star while leaving heavy-element-rich material behind.

THE NATURE OF THE PROGENITOR STARS

The progenitor must have mass not much in excess of a solar mass because of the distribution of the planetaries in the Galaxy. Very massive stars are young and more closely confined than are nebulae to the galactic plane. Also, the mass of the nebula is roughly 0.3 solar mass, and the mass of a typical white dwarf (the final state of the central star) is roughly 0.7 solar mass. Next, the expansion velocity of the nebula is probably comparable to the velocity of escape from its progenitor, which implies that the progenitor was a red giant star, large and cool, completely unlike the small, hot, blue, nuclear star remaining after the ejection. Likely candidates are members of the class of long-period variable stars, which have about the right size and mass and are known to be unstable. Symbiotic stars (i.e., stars with characteristics of both cool giants and very hot stars) also are candidates. Novae, stars that brighten temporarily while ejecting a shell explosively, are definitely not candidates; the nova shell is expanding at hundreds of kilometres per second.

The cause of the ejection is the outward force of radiation on the outer layers of red giant stars. The ejection is triggered by a rapid variation in the nuclear luminosity in the interior of the giant, caused by instability in the helium-burning shell. The ejection takes place during more than one phase of the giant's evolution. Nitrogen-rich nebulae develop during an early episode when convection inside the star carries nitrogen, produced from carbon in a series of nuclear reactions (i.e., the carbon-nitrogen cycle of hydrogen burning), to the surface. A later ejection takes place with an enrichment of both nitrogen and helium, which also is produced by hydrogen burning. A still later phase occurs when convection carries carbon, the product of helium burning, to the surface.

SUPERNOVA REMNANTS

Like the planetary nebulae, supernova remnants are clouds left behind by a dying star. In this case, a star goes supernova, a spectacular explosion in which a star ejects most of its mass in a violently expanding cloud of debris. At the brightest phase of the explosion, the expanding cloud radiates as much energy in a single day as the Sun has done in the past three million years. Such explosions occur roughly every 50 years within a large galaxy. They have been observed less frequently in the Milky Way Galaxy because most of them have been hidden by the obscuring clouds of dust. Galactic supernovae were observed in 1006 in Lupus, in 1054 in Taurus, in 1572 in Cassiopeia (Tycho's nova, named after Tycho Brahe, its observer), and finally in 1604 in Serpens, called Kepler's nova. The stars became bright enough to be visible in the daytime.

The only naked-eye supernova to occur since 1604 was Supernova 1987A in the Large Magellanic Cloud (the galaxy nearest to the Milky Way system), visible only from the Southern Hemisphere. On Feb. 23, 1987, a blue supergiant star brightened to gradually become third magnitude, easily visible at night, and it has subsequently been followed in every wavelength band available to scientists. The spectrum

A small part of the Cygnus Loop supernova remnant, which marks the edge of an expanding blast wave from an enormous stellar explosion that occurred about 10,000 years ago. The remnant is located in the constellation Cygnus, the Swan. National Aeronautics and Space Administration

within the molecular cloud in which it formed, the expanding remnant might compress the surrounding interstellar gas and trigger subsequent star formation. The remnants contain strong shock waves that create filaments of material emitting gamma-ray photons with energies up to 10^{14} electron volts and accelerating electrons and atomic nuclei up to cosmic-ray energies, from 10^9 up to 10^{15} electron volts per particle. In the solar neighbourhood, these cosmic rays carry about as much energy per cubic metre as starlight in the plane of the galaxy, and they carry it to thousands of light-years above the plane.

Much of the radiation from supernova remnants is synchrotron radiation, which is produced by electrons spiraling in a magnetic field at almost the speed of light. This radiation is dramatically different from the emission from electrons moving at low speeds: it is (1) strongly concentrated in the forward direction, (2) spread out over a broad range of frequencies, with the average frequency increasing with the electron's energy, and (3) highly polarized. Electrons of many different energies produce radiation at essentially all wavelengths, from radio through infrared, optical, and ultraviolet up to X- and gamma rays.

showed hydrogen lines expanding at 12,000 km per second (7,456 miles per second), followed by a long period of slow decline. There are 270 known supernova remnants, almost all observed by their strong radio emission, which can penetrate the obscuring dust in the galaxy.

Supernova remnants are very important to the structure of galaxies. They are a major source of heating of interstellar gas by means of the magnetic turbulence and violent shocks that they produce. They are the main source of most heavy elements, from oxygen on up. If the exploding massive star is still

About 50 supernova remnants contain pulsars, the spinning neutron star remnants of the former massive star. The name comes from the exceedingly regularly pulsed radiation that propagates into space in a narrow beam that sweeps past the observer similarly to the beam from a lighthouse. There are several reasons why most supernova remnants do not contain visible pulsars. Perhaps the original pulsar was ejected because there was a recoil from an asymmetrical explosion, or the supernova formed a black hole instead of a pulsar, or the beam of the rotating pulsar does not sweep past the solar system.

Supernova remnants evolve through four stages as they expand. At first, they expand so violently that they simply sweep all older interstellar material before them, acting as if they were expanding into a vacuum. The shocked gas, heated to millions of kelvins by the explosion, does not radiate its energy very well and is readily visible only in X-rays. This stage typically lasts several hundred years, after which time the shell has a radius of about 10 light-years. As the expansion occurs, little energy is lost, but the temperature falls because the same energy is spread into an ever-larger volume. The lower temperature favours more emission, and during the second phase the supernova remnant radiates its energy at the outermost, coolest layers. This phase can last thousands of years. The third stage occurs after the shell has swept up a mass of interstellar material

that is comparable to or greater than its own; the expansion has by then slowed substantially. The dense material, mostly interstellar at its outer edge, radiates away its remaining energy for hundreds of thousands of years. The final phase is reached when the pressure within the supernova remnant becomes comparable to the pressure of the interstellar medium outside the remnant, so the remnant loses its distinct identity. In the later stages of expansion, the magnetic field of the galaxy is important in determining the motions of the weakly expanding gas. Even after the bulk of the material has merged with the local interstellar medium, there might be remaining regions of very hot gas that produce soft X-rays (i.e., those of a few hundred electron volts) observable locally.

The recent galactic supernovae observed are in the first phases of the evolution suggested above. At the sites of Kepler's and Tycho's novae, there exist heavy obscuring clouds, and the optical objects remaining are now inconspicuous knots of glowing gas. Near Tycho's nova, in Cassiopeia, there are similar optically insignificant wisps that appear to be remnants of yet another supernova explosion. To a radio telescope, however, the situation is spectacularly different: the Cassiopeia remnant is the strongest radio source in the entire sky. Study of this remnant, called Cassiopeia A, reveals that a supernova explosion occurred there in approximately 1680, missed by observers because of the obscuring dust.

THE CRAB NEBULA

At the site of the 1054 supernova is one of the most remarkable objects in the sky, the Crab Nebula, now about 10 light-years across. Photographed in colour, it is revealed as a beautiful red lacy network of long and sinuous glowing hydrogen filaments surrounding a bluish structure-less region whose light is strongly polarized. The filaments emit the spectrum characteristic of a diffuse nebula. The gas is expanding at 1,100 km (700 miles) per second—slower than the 10,000–20,000 km per second in the shells of new supernovae in other galaxies. The bluish amorphous inner region of the Crab Nebula is radiating synchrotron radiation, and the spectrum extends up to gamma-ray energies. The Crab is the second brightest X-ray source in the sky, after Scorpius X-1 (an X-ray binary star). After almost 1,000 years, the nebula is still losing 100,000 times as much energy per second as the Sun.

On the basis of this huge outpouring of energy, it is easy to calculate how long the nebula can shine without a new supply of energy. The electrons emitting the X-rays should decay, or drop to lower energies, in about 30 years—far less than the age of the nebula. The source of energy of the electrons that emit the X-rays was discovered in 1969 to be a pulsar, which has been found to flash optically, as well as at radio wavelengths, blinking on and off with a period of 0.033 second. This period is slowly increasing (at the rate of 0.0012 second per century), which implies that the pulsar is slowing down and thereby losing its energy to the nebula. The corresponding rate of energy loss is about equal to the nebula's rate of energy loss, convincing evidence that a tiny, extremely dense pulsar can supply the energy to the nebula. The Crab Nebula is unique in being a young supernova remnant and relatively

The Crab Nebula (M1, NGC 1952) in the constellation Taurus is a gaseous remnant of the galactic supernova of 1054 CE. The nebula, 6,500 light-years away, is expanding at 1,100 km (700 miles) per second. Hale Observatories © 1959

free from obscuration, while Tycho's and Kepler's supernovae are conspicuous radio sources, radiating by synchrotron emission; in neither case has a detectable pulsar been found.

THE CYGNUS LOOP

The best-observed old supernova remnant is the Cygnus Loop (or the Veil Nebula), a beautiful filamentary object roughly in the form of a circular arc in Cygnus. Its patchiness is striking: the loop consists of a series of wisps rather than a continuous cloud of gas. The most likely interpretation of this patchiness is that the interstellar medium into which the shock wave is propagating contains

Veil Nebula (NGC 6992) in the constellation Cygnus, which glows as it collides with dust and gas in interstellar space. Palomar Observatory; photograph © California Institute of Technology 1959

small clouds of denser material; many lines of reasoning from other evidence lead to the same result. The present speed of the filaments is about 100 km per second (62 miles per second); the approximate age of the Cygnus Loop is 10,000 years.

DIFFUSE IONIZED GAS

A major component of the interstellar medium, or the warm ionized medium (WIM), is the diffuse ionized gas, dilute interstellar material that makes up about 90 percent of the ionized gas in the Milky Way Galaxy. It produces a faint emission-line spectrum that is seen in every direction. It was first detected from a thin haze of electrons that affect radio radiation passing through the Milky Way Galaxy. Similar layers are now seen in many other galaxies. The American astronomer Ronald Reynolds and his collaborators have mapped ionized hydrogen and a few other ions (N^+, S^+, and O^{++}). The total power required for the ionization is amazingly large: about 15 percent of the luminosity of all O and B stars. This energy output is about equal to the total power provided by supernovae, but the latter radiate most of their energy either in nonionizing radiation or in providing kinetic energies to their expanding shells. Other potential energy sources fall far short.

Unlike H II regions, the diffuse ionized gas is found far from the galactic plane as well as close to it. Pulsars (spinning neutron stars emitting pulsed radio waves) occasionally reside at large distances from the plane and emit radio waves. The electrons in the diffuse ionized gas slow these waves slightly in a manner that depends on the frequency, allowing observers to determine the number of electrons per square metre (1 square metre = 10.8 square feet) on the path to the pulsar. These observations show that the diffuse ionized gas extends more than 3,000 light-years above and below the galactic plane, which is much farther than the 300-light-year thickness of distributions of molecular clouds, H II regions, and O and B stars.

On average, the densities of the electrons are only about 0.05 per cubic cm (a fifth of the average density in the galactic plane), and only 10 to 20 percent of the volume is occupied by gas even at this low density. The rest of the volume can be filled by very hot, even lower density gas or by magnetic pressure. In the diffuse ionized gas, the comparatively low stages of ionization of the common elements ($O^{\pm}$, N^+, and S^+) are much more abundant relative to higher stages (O^{++}, N^{++}, and S^{++}) than in typical diffuse nebulae. Such an effect is caused by the extremely low density of the diffuse ionized gas; in this case, even hot stars fail to produce high stages of ionization. Thus, it seems possible to explain the peculiar ionization of the diffuse ionized gas with ionization powered by O and B stars, which are mostly found in the plane of the Milky Way Galaxy. Apparently the stars are able to ionize passages through the clouds enveloping them so that a substantial part of the ionizing radiation can escape into the regions far from the galactic plane.

NOTABLE NEBULAE

Nearly all nebulae are beautiful objects when seen up close, through a telescope. Some of the most notable nebulae also are fascinating subjects when considered in depth, with attention to detail.

CASSIOPEIA A

Cassiopeia A is the strongest source of radio emission in the sky beyond the solar system, located in the direction of the constellation Cassiopeia about 9,000 light-years from Earth. Cassiopeia A, abbreviated Cas A, is the remnant of a supernova explosion caused by the collapse of a massive star. The light from the

Cassiopeia A supernova remnant, in a composite image synthesized from observations gathered in different spectral regions by three space-based observatories. NASA/JPL/California Institute of Technology

event is estimated to have reached Earth about 1667, which makes Cas A the youngest known supernova remnant in the Milky Way Galaxy. Although the explosion must have been very powerful, no contemporary record exists of its having been observed, so the explosion may have happened behind an interstellar dust cloud. Today the remnant is also weakly observable at visible, infrared, and X-ray wavelengths, and it appears as an expanding ring of material approximately five arc minutes in diameter. The expansion rate of the remnant has been used to estimate how long ago the explosion occurred.

Coalsack

The Coalsack is a dark nebula in the Crux constellation (Southern Cross). Easily visible against a starry background, it is perhaps the most conspicuous dark nebula. Starlight coming to Earth through it is reduced by 1 to 1.5 magnitudes. The Coalsack is about 500 light-years from Earth and 50 light-years in diameter. It figures in legends of peoples of the Southern Hemisphere and has been known to Europeans since about 1500. The Northern Coalsack, in the constellation Cygnus, is similar in nature and appearance but somewhat less prominent.

Great Rift

The Great Rift is a complex of dark nebulae that seems to divide the bright clouds of the Milky Way Galaxy lengthwise through about one-third of their extent. From the constellation Cygnus, the rift reaches through Aquila and Sagittarius, where the centre of the Galaxy lies hidden behind it, to Centaurus. The clouds of dark material making up the Great Rift are several thousand light-years from the Earth.

Gum Nebula

The largest known emission nebula in terms of angular diameter as seen from Earth is the Gum Nebula, which extends about 35° in the southern constellations Puppis and Vela. A complex of diffuse, glowing gas too faint to be seen with the unaided eye, it was discovered by the Australian-born astrophysicist Colin S. Gum, who published his findings in 1955. The Gum Nebula lies roughly 1,000 light-years from Earth and is about 1,000 light-years in diameter. It may be the remnant of an ancient supernova—i.e., violently exploding star.

Horsehead Nebula

The Horsehead Nebula (catalog number IC 434) is an H II region in the constellation Orion. The nebula consists of a cloud of ionized gas lit from within by young, hot stars; a dark cloud containing interstellar dust lies immediately in front. The dust absorbs the light from part of the ionized cloud. A portion of this dark cloud has a shape somewhat resembling a horse's head. The nebula is located 400 parsecs (1,300 light-years) from the Sun. It has a diameter of approximately 4 parsecs (13 light-years) and a total mass of about 250 solar masses.

Lagoon Nebula

The Lagoon Nebula (catalog numbers NGC 6523 and M8) is an H II region located in the constellation Sagittarius at 1,250 parsecs (4,080 light-years) from the solar system. The nebula is a cloud of interstellar gas and dust approximately 10 parsecs (33 light-years) in diameter. A group of young, hot stars in the cloud ionize the nearby gas. As the atoms in the gas recombine, they produce the light emitted by the nebula. Interstellar dust within the nebula absorbs some of this light and appears almost to divide the nebula, thus producing a lagoonlike shape.

Lagoon Nebula (M8, NGC 6523) in the constellation Sagittarius. This bright diffuse nebula is so large that light from the stars involved does not penetrate its boundaries, and the bright nebula appears to be seen against a larger, darker one. Palomar Observatory; photograph © California Institute of Technology 1961

North American Nebula

The North American Nebula (NGC 7000) is an ionized-hydrogen region in the constellation Cygnus. The nebula is a cloud of interstellar gas ionized from within by young, hot stars. Interstellar dust particles in part of this cloud absorb the light emitted by recombining atoms. The shape of the nebula roughly resembles that of North America, with the dusty region being shaped like the Gulf of Mexico. The North American Nebula is approximately 520 parsecs (1,700 light-years) from the Sun. It has a diameter of about 30 parsecs (100 light-years) and a total mass equal to about 4,000 solar masses.

Orion Nebula

The bright diffuse Orion Nebula is faintly visible to the unaided eye in the sword of the hunter's figure in the constellation Orion. The nebula lies about 1,350 light-years from Earth and contains hundreds of very hot (O-type) young stars clustered about a nexus of four massive stars known as the Trapezium. Radiation from these stars excites the nebula to glow. It was discovered in 1610 by the French scholar Nicolas-Claude Fabri de Peiresc and independently in 1618 by the Swiss astronomer Johann Cysat. It was the first nebula to be photographed (1880), by Henry Draper in the United States.

Images of the nebula continued to improve, and technological advances in the late 1980s enabled scientists to photograph infrared-emitting objects in the Orion Nebula that had never before been observed optically. The Hubble Space Telescope in 1991 revealed the sharpest details yet available of known features of the nebula, including what appeared to be a jet (an energetic outflow) related to the birth of a young star.

R Monocerotis

R Monocerotis (NGC 2261) is a stellar infrared source and nebula in the constellation Monoceros (Greek: Unicorn). The star, one of the class of dwarf stars called T Tauri variables, is immersed in a cloud of matter that changes in brightness erratically, reflecting or re-radiating energy from the star.

Ring Nebula

The Ring Nebula (catalog numbers NGC 6720 and M57) is a bright planetary nebula in the constellation Lyra, about 2,300 light-years from the Earth. It was discovered in 1779 by the French astronomer Augustin Darquier. Like other nebulae of its type, it is a sphere of glowing gas thrown off by a central star. Seen from a great distance, such a sphere appears brighter at the edge than at the centre and thus takes on the appearance of a luminous ring. It is a popular object for amateur astronomers.

Trifid Nebula

The Trifid Nebula (catalog numbers NGC 6514 and M 20) is a bright, diffuse nebula in the constellation Sagittarius, lying several thousand light-years from the Earth. It was discovered by the French astronomer Legentil de La Galaisière before 1750 and named by the English astronomer Sir John Herschel for the three dark rifts that seem to divide the nebula and join at its centre. Of about the ninth magnitude optically, the Trifid is also a radio source.

CHAPTER 6

GALAXIES

The Milky Way Galaxy is just one of many galaxies, the systems of stars and interstellar matter that make up the universe. Many galaxies are so enormous that they contain hundreds of billions of stars.

Nature has provided an immensely varied array of galaxies, ranging from faint, diffuse dwarf objects to brilliant spiral-shaped giants. Virtually all galaxies appear to have been formed soon after the universe began, and they pervade space, even into the depths of the farthest reaches penetrated by powerful modern telescopes. Galaxies usually exist in clusters, some of which in turn are grouped into larger clusters that measure hundreds of millions of light-years across. These so-called superclusters are separated by nearly empty voids, and this causes the gross structure of the universe to look somewhat like a network of sheets and chains of galaxies.

Galaxies differ from one another in shape, with variations resulting from the way in which the systems were formed and subsequently evolved. Galaxies are extremely varied not only in structure but also in the amount of activity observed. Some are the sites of vigorous star formation, with its attendant glowing gas and clouds of dust and molecular complexes. Others, by contrast, are quiescent, having long ago ceased to form new stars. Perhaps the most conspicuous activity in galaxies occurs in their nuclei, where evidence suggests that

The Whirlpool Galaxy (left), also known as M51, an Sc galaxy accompanied by a small, irregular companion galaxy, NGC 5195 (right). NASA, ESA, S. Beckwith (STScI), and The Hubble Heritage Team (STScI/AURA)

in many cases supermassive objects—probably black holes—lurk. These central black holes apparently formed several billion years ago; they are now observed forming in galaxies at large distances (and, therefore, because of the time it takes light to travel to Earth, at times in the far distant past) as brilliant objects called quasars.

The existence of galaxies was not recognized until the early 20th century. Since then, however, galaxies have become one of the focal points of astronomical investigation. The notable developments and achievements in the study of galaxies are surveyed here. Included in the discussion are the external galaxies (i.e., those lying outside the Milky Way Galaxy, the local galaxy to which the Sun and Earth belong), their distribution in clusters and superclusters, and the evolution of galaxies and quasars.

THE EVOLUTION OF GALAXIES

The study of the origin and evolution of galaxies and the quasar phenomenon has only just begun. Many models of galaxy formation and evolution have been constructed on the basis of what we know about conditions in the early universe, which is in turn based on models of the expansion of the universe after the big bang (the primordial explosion from which the universe is thought to have originated) and on the characteristics of the cosmic microwave background (the observed photons that show us the light-filled universe as it was when it was a few hundred thousand years old).

According to the big-bang model, the universe expanded rapidly from a highly compressed primordial state, which resulted in a significant decrease in density and temperature. Soon afterward, the dominance of matter over antimatter (as observed today) may have been established by processes that also predict proton decay. During this stage many types of elementary particles may have been present. After a few seconds, the universe cooled enough to allow the formation of certain nuclei. The theory predicts that definite amounts of hydrogen, helium, and lithium were produced. Their abundances agree with what is observed today. About one million years later the universe was sufficiently cool for atoms to form.

When the universe had expanded to be cool enough for matter to remain in neutral atoms without being instantly ionized by radiation, structure apparently had already been established in the form of density fluctuations. At a crucial point in time, there condensed from the expanding matter small clouds (protogalaxies) that could collapse under their own gravitational field eventually to form galaxies.

For the latter half of the 20th century, there were two competing models of galaxy formation: "top-down" and "bottom-up." In the top-down model, galaxies formed out of the collapse of much larger gas clouds. In the bottom-up model, galaxies formed from the merger of smaller entities that were the size of globular clusters. In both models the angular momentum of the original clouds determined the form of the galaxy that eventually evolved. It is thought that a protogalaxy with a large amount of angular momentum tended to form a flat, rapidly rotating system (a spiral galaxy), whereas one with very little angular momentum developed into a more nearly spherical system (an elliptical galaxy).

The transition from the 20th to the 21st century coincided with a dramatic transition in our understanding of the evolution of galaxies. It is no longer believed that galaxies have evolved smoothly and alone. Indeed, it has become clear that collisions between galaxies have occurred all during their evolution—and these collisions, far from being rare events, were the mechanism by which galaxies developed in the distant past and are the means by which they are changing their structure and appearance even now. Evidence for this new understanding of galactic evolution comes primarily from two sources: more detailed studies of nearby galaxies with new, more sensitive instruments and deep surveys of extremely distant galaxies, seen when the universe was young.

Recent surveys of nearby galaxies, including the Milky Way Galaxy, have shown evidence of past collisions and capture of galaxies. For the Milky Way the most conspicuous example is the Sagittarius Galaxy, which has been absorbed by our Galaxy. Now its stars lie spread out across the sky, its seven globular clusters intermingling with the globular clusters of the Milky Way Galaxy. Long tails of stars around the Milky Way were formed by the encounter and act as clues to the geometry of the event. A second remnant galaxy, known as the Canis Major Dwarf Galaxy, can also be traced by the detection of star streams in the outer parts of our Galaxy. These galaxies support the idea that the Milky Way Galaxy is a mix of pieces, formed by the amalgamation of many smaller galaxies.

The Andromeda Galaxy (M31) also has a past involving collisions and accretion. Its peculiar close companion, M32, shows a structure that indicates that it was formerly a normal, more massive galaxy that lost much of its outer parts and possibly all of its globular clusters to M31 in a past encounter. Deep surveys of the outer parts of the Andromeda Galaxy have revealed huge coherent structures of star streams and clouds, with properties indicating that these include the outer remnants of smaller galaxies

"eaten" by the giant central galaxy, as well as clouds of M31 stars ejected by the strong tidal forces of the collision.

More spectacular are galaxies presently in the process of collision and accretion in the more distant, but still nearby, universe. The symptoms of the collision are the distortion of the galaxies' shape (especially that of the spiral arms), the formation of giant arcs of stars by tidal action, and the enhanced rate of star and star cluster formation. Some of the most massive and luminous young star clusters observed anywhere lie in the regions where two galaxies have come together, with their gas and dust clouds colliding and merging in a spectacular cosmic fireworks display.

A second type of evidence for the fact that galaxies grow by merging comes from very deep surveys of the very distant universe, especially those carried out with the Hubble Space Telescope (HST). These surveys, especially the Hubble Deep Field and the Hubble Ultra Deep Field, found galaxies so far away that the light observed by the HST left them when they were very young, only a few hundred million years old. This enables the direct detection and measurement of young galaxies as they were when the universe was young. The result is a view of a very different universe of galaxies. Instead of giant elliptical galaxies and grand spirals, the universe in its early years was populated with small, irregular objects that looked like mere fragments. These were the building blocks that eventually formed bigger galaxies such as the Milky

Way. Many show active formation of stars that are deficient in heavy elements because many of the heavy elements had not yet been created when these stars were formed.

The rate of star formation in these early times was significant, but it did not reach a peak until about one billion years later. Galaxies from this time show a maximum in the amount of excited hydrogen, which indicates a high rate of star formation, as young, very hot stars are necessary for exciting interstellar hydrogen so that it can be detected. Since that time, so much matter has been locked up in stars (especially white dwarfs) that not enough interstellar dust and gas are available to achieve such high rates of star formation.

An important development that has helped our understanding of the way galaxies form is the great success of computer simulations. High-speed calculations of the gravitational history of assemblages of stars, interstellar matter, and dark matter suggest that after the big bang the universe developed as a networklike arrangement of material, with gradual condensation of masses where the strands of the network intersected. In simulations of this process, massive galaxies form, but each is surrounded by a hundred or so smaller objects. The small objects may correspond to the dwarf galaxies, such as those that surround the Milky Way Galaxy but of which only a dozen or so remain, the rest having presumably been accreted by the main galaxy. Such computer models, called "n-body simulations," are especially successful in mimicking galaxy collisions and in helping to explain the presence of various tidal arms and jets observed by astronomers.

In summary, the current view of galactic history is that present-day galaxies are a mix of giant objects that accreted lesser galaxies in their vicinities, especially early in the formation of the universe, together with some remnant lesser, or dwarf, galaxies that have not yet come close enough to a more massive galaxy to be captured. The expansion of the universe gradually decreases the likelihood of such captures, so some of the dwarfs may survive to old age—eventually dying, like their giant cousins, when all of their stars become dim white dwarfs or black holes and slowly disappear.

HISTORICAL SURVEY OF THE STUDY OF GALAXIES

Most nebulae look as amorphous and ephemeral as clouds in the sky. However, in 1845, the Irish astronomer William Parsons discovered that some nebulae had a spiral shape. Why did these objects have such a well-ordered appearance?

The dispute over the nature of what were once termed spiral nebulae stands as one of the most significant in the development of astronomy. On this dispute hinged the question of the magnitude of the universe: were we confined to a single, limited stellar system that lay embedded alone in empty space, or was our Milky Way Galaxy just one of millions of galaxies that pervaded space, stretching beyond the vast distances probed by our most powerful telescopes? How this question arose, and how it was resolved, is an important element in the development of our prevailing view of the universe.

Up until 1925, spiral nebulae and their related forms had uncertain status. Some scientists, notably Heber D. Curtis of the United States and Knut Lundmark of Sweden, argued that they might be remote aggregates of stars similar in size to the Milky Way Galaxy. Centuries earlier the German philosopher Immanuel Kant, among others, had suggested much the same idea, but that was long before the tools were available to actually measure distances and thus prove it. During the early 1920s astronomers were divided. Although some deduced that spiral nebulae were actually extragalactic star systems, there was evidence that convinced many that such nebulae were local clouds of material, possibly new solar systems in the process of forming.

The Problem of the Magellanic Clouds

It is now known that the nearest external galaxies are the Magellanic Clouds, two patchy irregular objects visible in the skies of the Southern Hemisphere. For years, most experts who regarded the Magellanic Clouds as portions of the Milky Way Galaxy system separated from the main stream could not study them because of their position. (Both Magellanic Clouds are too far south to be seen from northern latitudes.) Moreover, the irregular shapes of the objects and their numerous hot blue stars, star clusters, and gas clouds did indeed make them resemble the southern Milky Way Galaxy.

The American astronomer Harlow Shapley, noted for his far-reaching work on the size and structure of the Milky Way Galaxy, was one of the first to appreciate the importance of the Magellanic Clouds in terms of the nature of spiral nebulae. To gauge the distance of the Clouds, he made use of the period-luminosity (P-L) relation discovered by Henrietta Leavitt of the Harvard College Observatory. In 1912 Leavitt had found that there was a close correlation between the periods of pulsation (variations in light) and the luminosities (intrinsic, or absolute, brightnesses) of a class of stars called Cepheid variables in the Small Magellanic Cloud. Leavitt's discovery, however, was of little practical value until Shapley worked out a calibration of the absolute brightnesses of pulsating stars closely analogous to the Cepheids, the so-called RR Lyrae variables. With this quantified form of the P-L relation, he was able to calculate the distances to the Magellanic Clouds, determining that they were about 75,000 light-years from Earth. The significance of the Clouds, however, continued to elude scientists of the time. For them, these objects still seemed to be anomalous, irregular patches of the Milky Way Galaxy, farther away than initially thought but not sufficient to settle the question of the nature of the universe.

NOVAE IN THE ANDROMEDA NEBULA

An unfortunate misidentification hampered the early recognition of the northern sky's brightest nearby galaxy, the Andromeda Nebula, also known as M31. In 1885 a bright star, previously invisible, appeared near the centre of M31, becoming almost bright enough to be seen without a telescope. As it slowly faded again, astronomers decided that it must be a nova, a "new star," similar to the class of temporary stars found relatively frequently in populous parts of the Milky Way Galaxy. If this was the case, it was argued, then its extraordinary brightness must indicate that M31 cannot be very far away, certainly not outside the local system of stars. Designated S Andromeda in conformity with the pattern of terminology applied to stars of variable brightness, this supposed nova was a strong argument in favour of the hypothesis that nebulae are nearby objects in the Milky Way Galaxy.

By 1910, however, there was evidence that S Andromeda might have been wrongly identified. Deep photographs were being taken of M31 with the Mount Wilson Observatory's newly completed 152-cm (60-inch) telescope, and the astronomers at the observatory, especially J.C. Duncan and George W. Ritchey, were finding faint objects, just resolved by the longest exposures, that also seemed to behave like novae. These objects, however, were about 10,000 times fainter than S Andromeda. If they were ordinary novae, then M31 must be millions of light-years away, but then the nature of S Andromeda became a difficult question. At this vast distance its total luminosity would have to be immense—an incomprehensible output of energy for a single star.

Completion of the 254-cm (100-inch) telescope on Mount Wilson in 1917 resulted in a new series of photographs that captured even fainter objects. More novae were found in M31, mainly by Milton L. Humason, who was an assistant at the time to Edwin P. Hubble, one of the truly outstanding astronomers of the day. Hubble eventually studied 63 of these stars, and his findings proved to be one of the final solutions to the controversy.

THE SCALE OF THE MILKY WAY GALAXY

At the same time that spiral nebulae were being studied and debated, the Milky Way Galaxy became the subject of contentious discussion. During the early years of the 20th century, most astronomers believed that the Milky Way Galaxy was a disk-shaped system of stars with the Sun near the centre and with the edge along a thick axis only about 15,000 light-years away. This view was based on statistical evidence involving star counts and the spatial distribution of a variety of cosmic objects—open star clusters, variable stars, binary systems, and clouds of interstellar gas. All these objects seemed to thin out at distances of several thousand light-years.

This conception of the Milky Way Galaxy was challenged by Shapley in 1917, when he released the findings of his study of globular clusters. He had found that these spherically symmetrical groups of densely packed stars, as compared with the much closer open clusters, were unusual in their distribution. While the known open clusters are concentrated heavily in the bright belt of the Milky Way Galaxy, the globular clusters are for the most part absent from those areas except in the general direction of the constellation Sagittarius, where there is a concentration of faint globular clusters. Shapley's plot of the spatial distribution of these stellar groupings clarified this peculiar fact: the centre of the globular cluster system—a huge almost spherical cloud of clusters—lies in that direction, some 30,000 light-years from the Sun. Shapley assumed that this centre must also be the centre of the Milky Way Galaxy. The globular clusters, he argued, form a giant skeleton around the disk of the Milky Way Galaxy, and the system is thus immensely larger than was previously thought, its total extent measuring nearly 100,000 light-years.

Shapley succeeded in making the first reliable determination of the size of the Milky Way Galaxy largely by using Cepheids and RR Lyrae stars as distance indicators. His approach was based on the P-L relation discovered by Leavitt and on the assumption that all these variables have the same P-L relation. As he saw it, this assumption was most likely true in the case of the RR Lyrae stars, because all

variables of this type in any given globular cluster have the same apparent brightness. If all RR Lyrae variables have the same intrinsic brightness, then it follows that differences in apparent brightness must be due to different distances from Earth. The final step in developing a procedure for determining the distances of variables was to calculate the distances of a handful of such stars by an independent method so as to enable calibration. Shapley could not make use of the trigonometric parallax method, since there are no variables close enough for direct distance measurement. However, he had recourse to a technique devised by the Danish astronomer Ejnar Hertzsprung that could determine distances to certain nearby field variables (i.e., those not associated with any particular cluster) by using measurements of their proper motions and the radial velocity of the Sun. Accurate measurements of the proper motions of the variables based on long-term observations were available, and the Sun's radial velocity could be readily determined spectroscopically. Thus, by availing himself of this body of data and adopting Hertzsprung's method, Shapley was able to obtain a distance scale for Cepheids in the solar neighbourhood.

Shapley applied the zero point of the Cepheid distance scale to the globular clusters he had studied with the 152-cm (60-inch) telescope at Mount Wilson. Some of these clusters contained RR Lyrae variables, and for these Shapley could calculate distances in a straightforward manner from the P-L relation. For other globular clusters he made distance determinations, using a relationship that he discovered between the brightnesses of the RR Lyrae stars and the brightness of the brightest red stars. For still others he made use of apparent diameters, which he found to be relatively uniform for clusters of known distance. The final result was a catalog of distances for 69 globular clusters, from which Shapley deduced his revolutionary model of the Milky Way Galaxy—one that not only significantly extended the limits of the galactic system but that also displaced the Sun from its centre to a location nearer its edge.

Shapley's work caused astronomers to ask themselves certain questions: How could the existing stellar data be so wrong? Why couldn't they see something in Sagittarius, the proposed galactic centre, 30,000 light-years away? The reason for the incorrectness of the star count methods was not learned until 1930, when Lick Observatory astronomer Robert J. Trumpler, while studying open clusters, discovered that interstellar dust pervades the plane of the Milky Way Galaxy and obscures objects beyond only a few thousand light-years. This dust thus renders the centre of the system invisible optically and makes it appear that globular clusters and spiral nebulae avoid the band of the Milky Way.

Shapley's belief in the tremendous size of the local galactic system helped to put him on the wrong side of the argument about other galaxies. He thought that, if the Milky Way Galaxy was so immense, then the spiral nebulae must lie within it. His conviction was reinforced by two lines of evidence. One of these has already been mentioned—the nova S Andromeda was so bright as to suggest that the Andromeda Nebula most certainly was only a few hundred light-years away. The second came about because of a very curious error made by one of Shapley's colleagues at Mount Wilson Observatory, Adrian van Maanen.

THE VAN MAANEN ROTATION

During the early 20th century, one of the most important branches of astronomy was astrometry, the precise measurements of stellar positions and motions. Van Maanen was one of the leading experts in this field. Most of his determinations of stellar positions were accurate and have stood the test of time, but he made one serious and still poorly understood error when he pursued a problem tangential to his main interests. In a series of papers published in the early 1920s, van Maanen reported on his discovery and measurement of the rotation of spiral nebulae. Using early plates taken by others at the 152-cm (60-inch) Mount Wilson telescope as well as more recent ones taken about 10 years later, van Maanen measured the positions of several knotlike, nearly stellar images in the spiral arms of some of the largest-known spiral nebulae (e.g., M33, M101, and M51). Comparing the positions, he found distinct changes indicative of a rotation of the spiral pattern against the background of surrounding field stars. In each case, the rotation occurs in the sense that the spiral arms trail. The periods of rotation were all approximately 100,000 years. Angular motions were about 0.02 second of arc per year.

Shapley seized the van Maanen results as evidence that the spirals had to be nearby; otherwise, their true space velocities of rotation would have to be impossibly large. For example, if M51 is rotating at an apparent rate of 0.02 second of arc per year, its true velocity would be immense if it is a distant galaxy. Assuming that a distance of 10,000,000 light-years would lead to an implausibly large rotation velocity of 12,000 km/sec (7,456 miles/sec), Shapley argued that, if a more reasonable velocity was adopted—say, 100 km/sec (62 miles/sec)—then the distances would all be less than 100,000 light-years, which would put all the spirals well within the Milky Way Galaxy.

It is unclear just why such a crucial measurement went wrong. Van Maanen repeated the measures and obtained the same answer even after Hubble demonstrated the truth about the distances to the spirals. However, subsequent workers, using the same plates, failed to find any rotation. Among the various hypotheses that science historians have proposed as an explanation for the error are two particularly reasonable ideas: (1) possibly the fact that spiral nebulae look like they are rotating (i.e., they resemble familiar rotational patterns that are perceivable in nature) may have influenced the observer subconsciously, and this subtle effect manifested itself in prejudicing the delicate measurements, or (2) possibly the first set of plates was the problem. Many of these plates had been taken in an unconventional manner by Ritchey, who swung the plate holder out of the field whenever the quality of the images was temporarily poor because of atmospheric turbulence. The resulting plates appeared excellent, having been exposed only during times of very fine seeing; however, according to some interpretations, the images had a slight asymmetry that led to a very small displacement of star images compared with nonstellar images. Such an error could look like rotation if not recognized for what it really was. In any case, the van Maanen rotation was accepted by many astronomers, including Shapley, and temporarily sidetracked progress toward recognizing the truth about galaxies.

THE SHAPLEY-CURTIS DEBATE

The nature of galaxies and scale of the universe were the subject of the Great Debate, a public program arranged in 1920 by the National Academy of Sciences at the Smithsonian Institution in Washington, D.C. Featured were talks by Shapley and the aforementioned Heber Curtis, who were recognized as spokesmen for opposite views on the nature of spiral nebulae and the Milky Way Galaxy. This so-called debate has often been cited as an illustration of how revolutionary new concepts are assimilated by science.

It is sometimes compared to the debate, centuries before, over the motions of the Earth (the Copernican revolution); however, though as a focal point the debate about Earth's motion can be used to define the modern controversy, the Shapley-Curtis debate actually was much more complicated.

A careful reading of the documents involved suggests that, on the broader topic of the scale of the universe, both men were making incorrect conclusions but for the same reasons—namely, for being unable to accept and comprehend the incredibly large scale of things. Shapley correctly argued for an enormous Milky Way Galaxy on the basis of the P-L relation and the globular clusters, while Curtis incorrectly rejected these lines of evidence, advocating instead a small galactic system. Given a Milky Way Galaxy system of limited scale, Curtis could argue for and consider plausible the extragalactic nature of the spiral nebulae. Shapley, on the other hand, incorrectly rejected the island universe theory of the spirals (i.e., the hypothesis that there existed comparable galaxies beyond the boundaries of the Milky Way Galaxy) because he felt that such objects would surely be engulfed by the local galactic system. Furthermore, he put aside the apparent faint novae in M31, preferring to interpret S Andromeda as an ordinary nova, for otherwise that object would have been unbelievably luminous. Unfortunately for him, such phenomena—called supernovae—do in fact exist, as was realized a few years later. Curtis was willing to concede that there might be two classes of novae, yet, because he considered the Milky Way Galaxy to be small, he underestimated their differences. The van Maanen rotation also entered into Shapley's arguments: if spiral nebulae were rotating so fast, they must be within the Milky Way Galaxy as he conceived it. For Curtis, however, the matter provided less of a problem: even if spiral nebulae did rotate as rapidly as claimed, the small scale of Curtis's universe allowed them to have physically reasonable speeds.

The Shapley-Curtis debate took place near the end of the era of the single-galaxy universe. In just a few years the scientific world became convinced that Shapley's grand scale of the Milky Way Galaxy was correct and at the same time that Curtis was right about the nature of spiral nebulae. Such objects indeed lie even outside Shapley's enormous Milky Way Galaxy, and they range far beyond the distances that in 1920 seemed too vast for many astronomers to comprehend.

HUBBLE'S DISCOVERY OF EXTRAGALACTIC OBJECTS

During the early 1920s Hubble detected 15 stars in the small, irregular cloudlike object NGC 6822 that varied in luminosity, and he suspected that they might include Cepheids. After considerable effort, he determined that 11 of them were in fact Cepheid variables, with properties indistinguishable from those of normal Cepheids in the Milky Way Galaxy and in the Magellanic Clouds. Their periods ranged from 12 to 64 days, and they were all very faint, much fainter than their Magellanic counterparts. Nevertheless, they fit a P-L relation of the same nature as had been discovered by Leavitt.

Hubble then boldly assumed that the P-L relation was universal and derived an estimate for the distance to NGC 6822, using Shapley's most recent (1925) version of the calibration of the relation. This calibration was wrong, as is now known, because of the confusion at that time over the nature of Cepheids. Shapley's calibration included certain Cepheids in globular clusters that subsequent investigators found to have their own fainter P-L relation. (Such Cepheids have been designated Type II Cepheids to distinguish them from the normal variety, which are referred to as Type I.) Thus, Hubble's distance for NGC 6822 was too small: he calculated a distance of only 700,000 light-years. Today it is recognized that the actual distance is closer to 2,000,000 light-years. In any case, this vast distance—even though underestimated—was large enough to convince Hubble that NGC 6822 must be a remote, separate galaxy, much too far away to be included even in Shapley's version of the Milky Way Galaxy system. Technically, then, this faint nebula can be considered the first recognized external galaxy. The Magellanic Clouds continued to be regarded simply as appendages to the Milky Way Galaxy, and the other bright nebulae, M31 and M33, were still being studied at the Mount Wilson Observatory. Although Hubble announced his discovery of Cepheids in

M31 at a meeting in 1924, he did not complete his research and publish the results for this conspicuous spiral galaxy until five years later.

While the Cepheids made it possible to determine the distance and nature of NGC 6822, some of its other features corroborated the conclusion that it was a separate, distant galaxy. Hubble discovered within it five diffuse nebulae, which are glowing gaseous clouds composed mostly of ionized hydrogen, designated H II regions. (H stands for hydrogen and II indicates that most of it is ionized; H I, by contrast, signifies neutral hydrogen.) He found that these five H II regions had spectra like those of gas clouds in the Milky Way Galaxy system—e.g., the Orion Nebula and Eta Carinae. Calculating their diameters, Hubble ascertained that the sizes of the diffuse nebulae were normal, similar to those of local examples of giant H II regions.

Five other diffuse objects discerned by Hubble were definitely not gaseous nebulae. He compared them with globular clusters (both in the Milky Way Galaxy and in the Magellanic Clouds) and concluded that they were too small and faint to be normal globular clusters. Convinced that they were most likely distant galaxies seen through NGC 6822, he dismissed them from further consideration. Modern studies suggest that Hubble was too hasty. Though probably not true giant globular clusters, these objects are in all likelihood star clusters in the system, fainter, smaller in population, and probably somewhat younger than normal globular clusters.

The Dutch astronomer Jacobus Cornelius Kapteyn showed in the early 20th century that statistical techniques could be used to determine the stellar luminosity function for the solar neighbourhood. (The luminosity function is a curve that shows how many stars there are in a given volume for each different stellar luminosity.) Eager to test the nature of NGC 6822, Hubble counted stars in the galaxy to various brightness limits and found a luminosity function for its brightest stars. When he compared it with Kapteyn's, the agreement was excellent—another indication that the Cepheids had given about the right distance and that the basic properties of galaxies were fairly uniform. Step by step, Hubble and his contemporaries piled up evidence for the fundamental assumption that has since guided the astronomy of the extragalactic universe, the uniformity of nature. By its bold application, astronomers have moved from a limiting one-galaxy universe to an immense vastness of space populated by billions of galaxies, all grander in size and design than the Milky Way Galaxy system was once thought to be.

THE DISTANCE TO THE ANDROMEDA NEBULA

In 1929 Hubble published his epochal paper on M31, the great Andromeda Nebula. Based on 350 photographic plates taken at Mount Wilson, his study provided evidence that M31 is a giant stellar system like the Milky Way Galaxy.

Because M31 is much larger than the field of view of the 152- and 254-cm (60- and 100-inch) telescopes at Mount Wilson, Hubble concentrated on four regions, centred on the nucleus and at various distances along the major axis. The total area studied amounted to less than half the galaxy's size, and the other unexplored regions remained largely unknown for 50 years. (Modern comprehensive optical studies of M31 have been conducted only since about 1980.)

Hubble pointed out an important and puzzling feature of the resolvability of M31. Its central regions, including the nucleus and diffuse nuclear bulge, were not well resolved into stars, one reason that the true nature of M31 had previously been elusive. However, the outer parts along the spiral arms in particular were resolved into swarms of faint stars, seen superimposed over a structured background of light. Current understanding of this fact is that spiral galaxies typically have central bulges made up exclusively of very old stars, the brightest of which are too faint to be visible on Hubble's plates. Not until 1944 did the German-born astronomer Walter Baade finally resolve the bulge of M31. Using red-sensitive plates and very long exposures, he managed to detect the brightest red giants of this old population. Out in the arms there exist many young, bright, hot blue stars, and these are easily resolved. The brightest are so luminous that they can be seen even with moderate-sized telescopes.

The most important of Hubble's discoveries was that of M31's population of

Cepheid variables. Forty of the 50 variables detected turned out to be ordinary Cepheids with periods ranging from 10 to 48 days. A clear relation was found between their periods and luminosities, and the slope of the relation agreed with those for the Magellanic Clouds and NGC 6822. Hubble's comparison indicated that M31 must be 8.5 times more distant than the Small Magellanic Cloud (SMC), which would imply a distance of two million light-years if the modern SMC distance was used (the 1929 value employed by Hubble was about two times too small). Clearly, M31 must be a distant, large galaxy.

Other features announced in Hubble's paper were M31's population of bright, irregular, slowly varying variables. One of the irregulars was exceedingly bright; it is among the most luminous stars in the galaxy and is a prototype of a class of high-luminosity stars now called Hubble-Sandage variables, which are found in many giant galaxies. Eighty-five novae, all behaving very much like those in the Milky Way Galaxy, were also analyzed. Hubble estimated that the true occurrence rate of novae in M31 must be about 30 per year, a figure that was later confirmed by the American astronomer Halton C. Arp in a systematic search.

Hubble found numerous star clusters in M31, especially globular clusters, 140 of which he eventually cataloged. He clinched the argument that M31 was a galaxy similar to the Milky Way Galaxy by calculating its mass and mass density. Using the velocities that had been measured for the inner parts of M31 by spectrographic work, he calculated (on the basis of the distance derived from the Cepheids) that M31's mass must be about 3.5 billion times that of the Sun. Today astronomers have much better data, which indicate that the galaxy's true total mass must be at least 100 times greater than Hubble's value, but even that value clearly showed that M31 is an immense system of stars. Furthermore, Hubble's estimates of star densities demonstrated that the stars in the outer arm areas of M31 are spread out with about the same density as in the Milky Way Galaxy system in the vicinity of the Sun.

THE GOLDEN AGE OF EXTRAGALACTIC ASTRONOMY

Until about 1950, scientific knowledge of galaxies advanced slowly. Only a very small number of astronomers took up galaxy studies, and only a very few telescopes were suitable for significant research. It was an exclusive field, rather jealously guarded by its practitioners, and so progress was orderly but limited.

During the decade of the 1950s, the field began to change. Ever-larger optical telescopes became available, and the space program resulted in a sizable increase in the number of astronomers emerging from universities. New instrumentation enabled investigators to explore galaxies in entirely new ways, making it possible to detect their radio, infrared, and ultraviolet emissions and eventually even radiation at X-ray and gamma-ray wavelengths. Whereas in the 1950s there was only one telescope larger than 254 cm (100 inches)—and only about 10 astronomers conducting research on galaxies worldwide—by the year 2000 the number of large telescopes had grown immensely, with 12 telescopes larger than 800 cm (300 inches), and the number of scientists devoted to galaxy study was in the thousands. By then, galaxies were being extensively studied with giant arrays of ground-based radio telescopes, Earth-orbiting optical, X-ray, ultraviolet, and infrared telescopes, and high-speed computers—studies that have given rise to remarkable advances in knowledge and understanding. The tremendous progress in both theoretical and observational work has led many to say that the turn of the 21st century happened during the "golden age" of extragalactic astronomy.

TYPES OF GALAXIES

All galaxies are not spirals like our own Milky Way. Some are elliptical systems. Others, the irregulars, have no definite shape at all. Astronomers have devised systems of classification that encompass all these types.

PRINCIPAL SCHEMES OF CLASSIFICATION

Almost all current systems of galaxy classification are outgrowths of the initial scheme proposed by the American astronomer Edwin Hubble in 1926. In Hubble's scheme, which is based on the optical appearance of galaxy images on photographic plates, galaxies are divided into three general classes: ellipticals, spirals, and irregulars. Hubble subdivided these three classes into finer groups.

In The Hubble Atlas of Galaxies (1961), the American astronomer Allan R. Sandage drew on Hubble's notes and his own research on galaxy morphology to revise the Hubble classification scheme. Some of the features of this revised scheme are subject to argument because of the findings of very recent research, but its general features, especially the coding of types, remain viable. A description of the classes as defined by Sandage is given here, along with observations concerning needed refinements of some of the details.

ELLIPTICAL GALAXIES

These systems exhibit certain characteristic properties. They have complete rotational symmetry; i.e., they are figures of revolution with two equal principal axes. They have a third smaller axis that is the presumed axis of rotation. The surface brightness of ellipticals at optical wavelengths decreases monotonically outward from a maximum value at the centre, following a common mathematical law of the form:

$$I = I_0 (r/a + 1)^{-2},$$

where I is the intensity of the light, I_0 is the central intensity, r is the radius, and a is a scale factor. The isophotal contours exhibited by an elliptical system are similar ellipses with a common orientation, each centred on its nucleus. No galaxy of this type is flatter than b/a = 0.3, with b and a the minor and major axes of the elliptical image, respectively. Ellipticals contain neither interstellar dust nor bright stars of spectral types O and B. Many, however, contain evidence of the presence of low-density gas in their nuclear regions. Ellipticals are red in colour, and their spectra indicate that their light comes mostly from old stars, especially evolved red giants.

Subclasses of elliptical galaxies are defined by their apparent shape, which is of course not necessarily their three-dimensional shape. The designation is En, where n is an integer defined by

$$n = 10(a- b)/a.$$

A perfectly circular image will be an E0 galaxy, while a flatter object might be an E7 galaxy. (As explained above, elliptical galaxies are never flatter than this, so there are no E8, E9, or E10 galaxies.)

Although the above-cited criteria are generally accepted, current high-quality measurements have shown that some significant deviations exist. Most elliptical galaxies do not, for instance, exactly fit the intensity law formulated by Hubble; deviations are evident in their innermost parts and in their faint outer parts. Furthermore, many elliptical galaxies have slowly varying ellipticity, with the images being more circular in the central regions than in the outer parts. The major axes sometimes do not line up either; their position angles vary in the outer parts. Finally, astronomers have found that a few ellipticals do in fact have small numbers of luminous O and B stars as well as dust lanes.

SPIRAL GALAXIES

Spirals are characterized by circular symmetry, a bright nucleus surrounded by a thin outer disk, and a superimposed spiral structure. They are divided into two parallel classes: normal spirals and barred spirals. The normal spirals have arms that emanate from the nucleus, while barred spirals have a bright linear feature called a bar that straddles the nucleus, with the arms unwinding from the ends of the bar. The nucleus of a spiral galaxy is a sharp-peaked area of smooth texture, which can be quite small or, in some cases, can make up the bulk of the galaxy. Both the arms and the disk of a spiral system are blue in colour, whereas its central areas are red like an elliptical galaxy. The normal spirals are designated S and the barred varieties SB. Each of these classes is subclassified into three types according to the size of the nucleus and the degree to which the spiral arms are coiled. The three types are denoted with the lowercase letters a, b, and c. There also exist galaxies that are intermediate between ellipticals and spirals. Such systems have the disk shape characteristic of the latter but no spiral arms. These intermediate forms bear the designation S0.

So Galaxies

These systems exhibit some of the properties of both the ellipticals and the spirals and seem to be a bridge between these two more common galaxy types. Hubble introduced the So class long after his original classification scheme had been universally adopted, largely because he noticed the dearth of highly flattened objects that otherwise had the properties of elliptical galaxies. Sandage's elaboration of the So class yielded the characteristics described here.

So galaxies have a bright nucleus that is surrounded by a smooth, featureless bulge and a faint outer envelope. They are thin; statistical studies of the ratio of the apparent axes (seen projected onto the sky) indicate that they have intrinsic ratios of minor to major axes in the range 0.1 to 0.3. Their structure does not generally follow the luminosity law of elliptical galaxies but has a form more like that for spiral galaxies. Some So systems have a hint of structure in the envelope, either faintly discernible arm-like discontinuities or narrow absorption lanes produced by interstellar dust. Several So galaxies are otherwise peculiar, and it is difficult to classify them with certainty. They can be thought of as peculiar irregular galaxies (i.e., Irr II galaxies) or simply as some of the 1 or 2 percent of galaxies that do not fit easily into the Hubble scheme. Among these are such galaxies as NGC 4753, which has irregular dust lanes across its image, and NGC 128, which has a double, almost rectangular bulge around a central nucleus. Another type of peculiar So is found in NGC 2685. This nebula in the constellation Ursa Major has an apparently edge-on disk galaxy at its centre, with surrounding hoops of gas, dust, and stars arranged in a plane that is at right angles to the apparent plane of the central object.

Sa Galaxies

These normal spirals have narrow, tightly wound arms, which usually are visible because of the presence of interstellar dust and, in many cases, bright stars. Most of them have a large amorphous bulge in the centre, but there are some that violate this criterion, having a small nucleus around which is arranged an amorphous disk with superimposed faint arms. NGC 1302 is an example of the normal type of Sa galaxy, while NGC 4866 is representative of one with a small nucleus and arms consisting of thin dust lanes on a smooth disk.

Sb Galaxies

This intermediate type of spiral typically has a medium-sized nucleus. Its arms are more widely spread than those of the Sa variety and appear less smooth. They contain stars, star clouds, and interstellar gas and dust. Sb galaxies show wide dispersions in details in terms of their shape. Hubble and Sandage observed, for example, that in certain Sb galaxies the arms emerge at the nucleus, which is often quite small. Other members of this subclass have arms that begin tangent to a bright, nearly circular ring, while still others reveal a small, bright spiral pattern inset into the nuclear bulge. In any of these cases, the spiral arms may be set at different pitch angles. (A pitch angle is defined as the angle between an arm and a circle centred on the nucleus and intersecting the arm.)

Hubble and Sandage noted further deviations from the standard shape established for Sb galaxies. A few systems exhibit a chaotic dust pattern superimposed upon the tightly wound spiral arms. Some have smooth, thick arms of low surface brightness, frequently bounded on their inner edges with dust lanes. Finally, there are those with a large, smooth nuclear bulge from which the arms emanate, flowing outward tangent to the bulge and forming short arm segments. This is the most familiar type of Sb galaxy and is best exemplified by the giant Andromeda Galaxy.

Many of these variations in shape remain unexplained. Theoretical models of spiral galaxies based on a number of different premises can reproduce the basic Sb galaxy shape, but many of the deviations noted above are somewhat mysterious in origin and must await more detailed and realistic modeling of galactic dynamics.

Sc Galaxies

These galaxies characteristically have a very small nucleus and multiple spiral arms that are open, with relatively large pitch angles. The arms, moreover, are lumpy, containing as they do numerous irregularly distributed star clouds, stellar associations, star clusters, and gas clouds known as emission nebulae.

As in the case of Sb galaxies, there are several recognizable subtypes among the Sc systems. Sandage has cited six subdivisions: (1) galaxies, such as the Whirlpool Galaxy (M51), that have thin branched arms that wind outward from a tiny nucleus, usually extending out about 180° before branching into multiple segments, (2) systems with multiple arms that start tangent to a bright ring centred on the nucleus, (3) those with arms that are poorly defined and that span the entire image of the galaxy, (4) those with a spiral pattern that cannot easily be traced and that are multiple and punctuated with chaotic dust lanes, (5) those with thick, loose arms that are not well defined—e.g., the nearby galaxy M33 (the Triangulum Nebula)—and (6) transition types, which are almost so lacking in order that they could be considered irregular galaxies.

Some classification schemes, such as that of the French-born American astronomer Gerard de Vaucouleurs, give the last of the above-cited subtypes a class of its own, type Sd. It also has been found that some of the variations noted here for Sc galaxies are related to total luminosity. Galaxies of the fifth subtype, in particular, tend to be intrinsically faint, while those of the first subtype are among the most luminous spirals known. This correlation is part of the justification for the luminosity classification discussed below.

SB Galaxies

The luminosities, dimensions, spectra, and distributions of the barred spirals tend to be indistinguishable from those of normal spirals. The subclasses of SB systems exist in parallel sequence to those of the latter.

There are SB0 galaxies that feature a large nuclear bulge surrounded by a disk-like envelope across which runs a luminous featureless bar. Some SB0 systems have short bars, while others have bars that extend across the entire visible image. Occasionally there is a ringlike feature external to the bar. SBa galaxies have bright, fairly large nuclear bulges and tightly wound, smooth spiral arms that emerge from the ends of the bar or from a circular ring external to the bar. SBb systems have a smooth bar as well as relatively smooth and continuous arms. In some galaxies of this type, the arms start at or near the ends of the bar, with conspicuous dust lanes along the inside of the bar that can be traced right up to the nucleus. Others have arms that start tangent to a ring external to the bar. In SBc galaxies, both the arms and the bar are highly resolved into star clouds and stellar associations. The arms are open in form and can start either at the ends of the bar or tangent to a ring.

Barred spiral galaxy NGC 1300. NASA, ESA, and The Hubble Heritage Team (STScI/AURA)

IRREGULAR GALAXIES

Most representatives of this class consist of grainy, highly irregular assemblages of luminous areas. They have neither noticeable symmetry nor an obvious central nucleus, and they are generally bluer in colour than are the arms and disks of spiral galaxies. An extremely small number of them, however, are red and have a smooth, though nonsymmetrical, shape.

Hubble recognized these two types of irregular galaxies, Irr I and Irr II. The Irr I type is the most common of the irregular systems, and it seems to fall naturally on an extension of the spiral classes, beyond Sc, into galaxies with no discernible spiral structure. They are blue, are highly resolved, and have little or no nucleus. The Irr II systems are red, rare objects. They include various kinds of chaotic galaxies for which there apparently are many different explanations, including most commonly the results of galaxy-galaxy interactions, both tidal distortions and cannibalism; therefore, this category is no longer seen as a useful way to classify galaxies.

Some irregular galaxies, like spirals, are barred. They have a nearly central bar structure dominating an otherwise chaotic arrangement of material. The Large Magellanic Cloud is a well-known example.

OTHER CLASSIFICATION SCHEMES AND GALAXY TYPES

Other classification schemes similar to Hubble's follow his pattern but subdivide the galaxies differently. A notable example of one such system is that of de Vaucouleurs. This scheme, which has evolved considerably since its inception in 1959, includes a large number of codes for indicating different kinds of morphological characteristics visible in the images of galaxies. The major Hubble galaxy classes form the framework of de Vaucouleurs's scheme, and its subdivision includes different families, varieties, and stages. The de Vaucouleurs system is so detailed that it is more of a descriptive code for galaxies than a commonly used classification scheme.

Galaxies with unusual properties often have shorthand names that refer to their characteristic properties. Common examples are:

D: Galaxies with abnormally large, distended shapes, always found in the central areas of galaxy clusters and hypothesized to consist of merged galaxies.

S: Seyfert galaxies, originally recognized by the American astronomer Carl K. Seyfert from optical spectra. These objects have very bright nuclei with strong emission lines of hydrogen and other common elements, showing velocities of hundreds or thousands of kilometres per second. Most are radio sources.

N: Galaxies with small, very bright nuclei and strong radio emission. These are probably similar to Seyfert galaxies but more distant.

Q: Quasars, or QSOs, small, extremely luminous objects, many of which are strong radio sources. Quasars apparently are related to Seyfert and N galaxies but have such bright nuclei that the underlying galaxy can be detected only with great difficulty.

There are also different schemes used for extremely distant galaxies, which we see in their youth. When a very distant galaxy is examined with a very large telescope, we see its structure as it was when the light was emitted billions of years ago. In such cases, the distinctive Hubble types are not so obvious. Apparently, galaxies are much less well organized in their early years, and these very distant objects tend to be highly irregular and asymmetrical. Although special classification schemes are sometimes used for special purposes, the general scheme of Hubble in its updated form is the one most commonly used.

THE EXTERNAL GALAXIES

Beyond the Milky Way stretches the vast universe filled with billions of galaxies. Astronomers have measured their distances and determined their properties to a degree that would have seemed unbelievable only a few decades ago.

THE EXTRAGALACTIC DISTANCE SCALE

Before astronomers could establish the existence of galaxies, they had to develop a way to measure their distances. In an earlier section, it was explained how astronomers first accomplished this exceedingly difficult task for the nearby galaxies during the 1920s. Until the late decades of the 20th century, progress was discouragingly slow. Even though increased attention was being paid to the problem around the world, a consensus was not reached. In fact, the results of most workers fell into two separate camps, in which the distances found by one were about twice the size of the other's. For this reason, shortly after its launch into Earth orbit in 1990, the Hubble Space Telescope (HST) was assigned the special task of reliably determining the extragalactic distance scale. Led by the Canadian-born astronomer Wendy Freedman and the American astronomer Robert Kennicutt, the team used a considerable amount of the HST's time to measure the properties of the Cepheid variable stars in a carefully selected set of galaxies. Their results were intermediate between the two earlier distance scales. With subsequent refinements, the scale of distances between the galaxies is now on fairly secure footing.

The HST distance scale project established the scale of distances for the nearby universe. Establishing the distances to galaxies over the entire range of present observations (several billion light-years) is an even more difficult task. The process involved is one of many successive steps that are all closely tied to one another. Before even the nearby galaxy distances measured by the HST can be established, distances must first be determined for a number of galaxies even closer to the Milky Way Galaxy, specifically those in the Local Group. For this step, criteria are used that have been calibrated within the Milky Way Galaxy, where checks can be made between different methods and where the ultimate criterion is a geometric one, basically involving trigonometric parallaxes, especially those determined by the Hipparcos satellite. These distance criteria, acting as "standard candles," are then compared with the HST observations of galaxies beyond the Local Group, where other methods are calibrated that allow even larger distances to be gauged. This general stepwise process continues to the edge of the observable universe.

The Local Group of galaxies is a concentration of approximately 50 galaxies dominated by two large spirals, the Milky Way Galaxy and the Andromeda Galaxy. For many of these galaxies, distances can be measured by using the Cepheid P-L law, which has been refined and made more precise since it was first used by American astronomer Edwin Hubble. For instance, the nearest external galaxy, the Large Magellanic Cloud, contains thousands of Cepheid variables, which can be compared with Cepheids of known distance in the Milky Way Galaxy to yield a distance determination of 160,000 light-years. This method has been employed for almost all galaxies of the Local Group that contain massive-enough stars to include Cepheids. Most of the rest of the members are elliptical galaxies, which do not have Cepheid variables; their

distances are measured by using Population II stars, such as RR Lyrae variables or luminous red giants.

Beyond the Local Group are two nearby groups for which the P-L relation has been used: the Sculptor Group and the M81 Group. Both of these are small clusters of galaxies that are similar in size to the Local Group. They lie at a distance of 10 to 15 million light-years.

One example of an alternate method to the Cepheid P-L relationship makes use of planetary nebulae, the ringlike shells that surround some stars in their late stages of evolution. Planetary nebulae have a variety of luminosities, depending on their age and other physical circumstances; however, it has been determined that the brightest planetary nebulae have an upper limit to their intrinsic brightnesses. This means that astronomers can measure the brightnesses of such nebulae in any given galaxy, find the upper limit to the apparent brightnesses, and then immediately calculate the distance of the galaxy. This technique is effective for measuring distances to galaxies in the Local Group, in nearby groups, and even as far away as the Virgo cluster, which lies at a distance of about 50 million light-years.

Once distances have been established for these nearby galaxies and groups, new criteria are calibrated for extension to fainter galaxies. Examples of the many different criteria that have been tried are the luminosities of the brightest stars in the galaxy, the diameters of the largest H II regions, supernova luminosities, the spread in the rotational velocities of stars and interstellar gas (the Tully-Fisher relation), and the luminosities of globular clusters. All of these criteria have difficulties in their application because of dependencies on galaxy type, composition, luminosity, and other characteristics, so the results of several methods must be compared and cross-checked. Such distance criteria allow astronomers to measure the distances to galaxies out to a few hundred million light-years.

Beyond 100 million light-years another method becomes possible. The expansion of the universe, at least for the immediate neighbourhood of the Local Group (within one billion light-years or so), is almost linear, so the radial velocity of a galaxy is a reliable distance indicator. The velocity is directly proportional to the distance in this interval, so once a galaxy's radial velocity has been measured, all that must be known is the constant of proportionality, which is called Hubble's constant. Although there still remains some uncertainty in the correct value of Hubble's constant, the value obtained by the HST is generally considered the best current value, which is very near 25 km/sec (15 m/sec) per one million light-years. This value does not apply in or near the Local Group, because radial velocities measured for nearby galaxies and groups are affected by the Local Group's motion with respect to the general background of galaxies, which is toward a concentration of galaxies and groups of galaxies centred on the Virgo cluster (the Local Supercluster). Radial velocities cannot give reliable distances beyond a few billion light-years, because, in the case of such galaxies, the observed velocities depend on what the expansion rate of the universe was then rather than what it is now. The light that is observed today was emitted several billion years ago when the universe was much younger and smaller than it is at present, when it might have been expanding either more rapidly or more slowly than now.

To find the distances of very distant galaxies, astronomers have to avail themselves of methods that make use of extremely bright objects. In the past, astronomers were forced to assume that the brightest galaxies in clusters all have the same true luminosity and that measuring the apparent brightness of the brightest galaxy in a distant cluster will therefore give its distance. This method is no longer used, however, as there is too much scatter in the brightness of the brightest galaxies and because there are reasons to believe that both galaxies and galaxy clusters in the early universe were quite different from those of the present.

The only effective way found so far for measuring distances to the most-distant detectable galaxies is to use the brightness of a certain type of supernova, called Type Ia. In the nearby universe these supernovae—massive stars that have collapsed and ejected much of their material explosively out into interstellar space—show uniformity in their maximum brightnesses; thus, it can be assumed that any supernovae of that type observed in a very distant galaxy should also have the same luminosity. Recent results have strongly suggested that the universe's expansion rate is greater here and now than it was in the distant past. This change of the expansion rate has important implications for cosmology.

Physical Properties of External Galaxies

Like stars, galaxies display staggering differences. Studies of their physical properties can reveal their origins in the early universe.

Size and Mass

The range in intrinsic size for the external galaxies extends from the smallest systems, such as the extreme dwarf galaxies found near the Milky Way that are only 100 light years across, to giant radio galaxies, the extent of which (including their radio-bright lobes) is more than 3,000,000 light-years. Normal large spiral galaxies, such as the Andromeda Galaxy, have diameters of 100,000 to 500,000 light-years.

The total masses of galaxies are not well known, largely because of the uncertain nature of the hypothesized invisible dark halos that surround many, or possibly all, galaxies. The total mass of material within the radius out to which the stars or gas of a galaxy can be detected is known for many hundreds of systems. The range is from about 100,000 to roughly 1,000,000,000,000 times the Sun's mass.

The mass of a typical large spiral is about 500,000,000,000 Suns.

In the late 20th century it became clear that most of the mass in galaxies is not in the form of stars or other visible matter. By measuring the speed with which stars in spiral and elliptical galaxies orbit the centre of the galaxy, one can measure the mass inside that orbit. Most galaxies have more mass than can be accounted for by their stars. Therefore, there is some unidentified "dark matter" that dominates the dynamics of most galaxies. The dark matter seems to be distributed more broadly than the stars in galaxies. Extensive efforts to identify this dark matter have not yet been satisfactory, though the detection of large numbers of very faint stars, including brown dwarfs, was in some sense a by-product of these searches, as was the discovery of the mass of neutrinos. It is somewhat frustrating for astronomers to know that the majority of the mass in galaxies (and in the universe) is of an unknown nature.

Luminosity

The external galaxies show an extremely large range in their total luminosities. The intrinsically faintest are the extreme dwarf elliptical galaxies, such as the Ursa Minor dwarf, which has a luminosity of approximately 100,000 Suns. The most luminous galaxies are those that contain quasars at their centres. These remarkably bright superactive nuclei can be as luminous as 2,000,000,000,000 Suns. The underlying galaxies are often as much as 100 times fainter than their nuclei. Normal large spiral galaxies have a luminosity of a few hundred billion Suns.

AGE

Even though different galaxies have had quite different histories, measurements tend to suggest that most, if not all, galaxies have very nearly the same age. The age of the Milky Way Galaxy, which is measured by determining the ages of the oldest stars found within it, is approximately 13 billion years. Nearby galaxies, even those such as the Large and Small Magellanic Clouds that contain a multitude of very young stars, also have at least a few very old stars of approximately that same age. When more distant galaxies are examined, their spectra and colours closely resemble those of the nearby galaxies, and it is inferred that they too must contain a population of similarly very old stars. Extremely distant galaxies, on the other hand, look younger, but that is because the "look-back" time for them is a significant fraction of their age; the light received from such galaxies was emitted when they were appreciably younger.

It seems likely that all the galaxies began to form about the same time, when the universe had cooled down enough for matter to condense, and they all thus started forming stars during nearly the same epoch. Their large differences are a matter not of age but rather of how they proceeded to regulate the processing of their materials (gas and dust) into stars.

Some ellipticals formed almost all their stars during the first few billion years, while others may have had a more complicated history, including various periods of active star formation related to the merging together of smaller galaxies. In a merging event the gas can be compressed, which enhances the conditions necessary for new bursts of star formation. The spirals and the irregulars, on the other hand, have been using up their materials more gradually.

COMPOSITION

The abundances of the chemical elements in stars and galaxies are remarkably uniform. The ratios of the amounts of the different elements that astronomers observe for the Sun are a reasonably good approximation for those of other stars in the Milky Way Galaxy and also for stars in other galaxies. The main difference found is in the relative amount of the primordial gases, hydrogen and helium. The heavier elements are formed by stellar evolutionary processes, and they are relatively more abundant in areas where extensive star formation has been taking place. Thus, in such small elliptical galaxies as the Draco system, where almost all the stars were formed at the beginning of its lifetime, the component stars are nearly pure hydrogen and helium, while in such large galaxies as the Andromeda Galaxy there are areas where star formation has been active for a long time (right up to the present, in fact), and there investigators find that the heavier elements are more abundant. In some external galaxies as well as in some parts of the Milky Way Galaxy system, heavy elements are even more abundant than in the Sun but rarely by more than a factor of two or so. Even in such cases, hydrogen and helium make up most of the constituent materials, accounting for at least 90 percent of the mass.

STRUCTURE

The spiral arms of some galaxies are the most notable part of their structure. However, there are other no less important pieces of a galaxy from a halo of old stars to its interstellar gas.

THE SPHEROIDAL COMPONENT

Most and perhaps all galaxies have a spheroidal component of old stars. In the ellipticals this component constitutes all or most of any given system. In the spirals it represents about half the constituent stars (this fraction varies greatly according to galaxy type). In the irregulars the spheroidal component is very inconspicuous or, possibly in some cases, entirely absent. The structure of the spheroidal component of all galaxies is similar, as if the spirals and irregulars possess a skeleton of old stars arranged in a structure that resembles an elliptical. The radial distribution of stars follows a law of the form

$$I = I_e 10^{(-3.33\{[r/re]^{1/4} - 1\})},$$

where I is the surface brightness (or the stellar density) at position r, r is the radial distance from the centre, and I_e and r_e are constants. This expression, introduced by the French-born American astronomer Gerard de Vaucouleurs, is an empirical formula that works remarkably well in describing the spheroidal components of almost all galaxies. An alternative formula, put forth by Edwin Hubble, is of the form

$$I = I_0 (r/a + 1)^{-2},$$

where I is the surface brightness, I_0 is the central brightness, r is the distance from the centre, and a is a scaling constant. Either of these formulas describes the structure well, but neither explains it.

A somewhat more complicated set of equations can be derived on the basis of the mutual gravitational attraction of stars for one another and the long-term effects of close encounters between stars. These models of the spheroidal component (appropriately modified in the presence of other galactic components) fit the observed structures well. Rotation is not an important factor, since most elliptical galaxies and the spheroidal component of spiral systems (e.g., the Milky Way Galaxy) rotate slowly. One of the open questions about the structure of these objects is why they have as much flattening as some of them do. In most cases, the measured rotation rate is inadequate to explain the flattening on the basis of a model of an oblate spheroid that rotates around its short axis. Some elliptical galaxies are instead prolate spheroids that rotate around their long axis.

THE DISK COMPONENT

Except for such early-type galaxies as S0, SB0, Sa, and SBa systems, spirals and irregulars have a flat component of stars that emits most of their brightness. The disk component has a thickness that is approximately one-fifth its diameter (this varies, depending on the type of stars being considered). The stars show a radial distribution that obeys an exponential decrease outward; i.e., the brightness obeys a formula of the form

$$\log I = -kr,$$

where I is the surface brightness, r is the distance from the centre, and k is a scaling constant. This constant is dependent both on the type of the galaxy and on its intrinsic luminosity. The steepness of the outward slope is greatest for the early Hubble types (Sa and SBa) and for the least-luminous galaxies.

SPIRAL ARMS

The structure of the arms of spiral galaxies depends on the galaxy type, and there is also a great deal of variability within each type. Generally, the early Hubble types have smooth, indistinct spiral arms with small pitch angles. The later types have more-open arms (larger pitch angles). Within a given type there can be found galaxies that have extensive arms (extending around the centre for two or more complete rotations) and those that have a chaotic arm structure made up of many short fragments that extend only 20° or 30° around the centre. All spiral arms fit reasonably well to a logarithmic spiral of the form described in chapter 1, The Milky Way Galaxy.

GAS DISTRIBUTION

If one were to look at galaxies at wavelengths that show only neutral hydrogen gas, they would look rather different from their optical appearance. Normally the gas, as detected at radio wavelengths for neutral hydrogen atoms, is more widely spread out, with the size of the gas component often extending to twice the size of the optically visible image. Also, in some galaxies a hole exists in the centre of the system where almost no neutral hydrogen occurs. There is, however, enough molecular hydrogen to make up for the lack of atomic hydrogen. Molecular hydrogen is difficult to detect, but it is accompanied by other molecules, such as carbon monoxide, which can be observed at radio wavelengths.

GALAXY CLUSTERS

Galaxies tend to cluster together, sometimes in small groups and sometimes in enormous complexes. Most galaxies have companions, either a few nearby objects or a large-scale cluster; isolated galaxies, in other words, are quite rare.

Types of Clusters

There are several different classification schemes for galaxy clusters, but the simplest is the most useful. This scheme divides clusters into three classes: groups, irregulars, and sphericals.

Groups

The groups class is composed of small compact groups of 10 to 50 galaxies of mixed types, spanning roughly five million light-years. An example of such an entity is the Local Group, which includes the Milky Way Galaxy, the Magellanic Clouds, the Andromeda Galaxy, and about 50 other systems, mostly of the dwarf variety.

Irregular Clusters

Irregular clusters are large loosely structured assemblages of mixed galaxy types (mostly spirals and ellipticals), totaling perhaps 1,000 or more systems and extending out 10,000,000 to 50,000,000 light-years. The Virgo and Hercules clusters are representative of this class.

Spherical Clusters

Spherical clusters are dense and consist almost exclusively of elliptical and S0 galaxies. They are enormous, having a linear diameter of up to 50,000,000 light-years. Spherical clusters may contain as many as 10,000 galaxies, which are concentrated toward the cluster centre.

Distribution

Clusters of galaxies are found all over the sky. They are difficult to detect along the Milky Way, where high concentrations of the Galaxy's dust and gas obscure virtually everything at optical wavelengths. However, even there clusters can be found in a few galactic "windows," random holes in the dust that permit optical observations.

The clusters are not evenly spaced in the sky; instead, they are arranged in a way that suggests a certain amount of organization. Clusters are frequently associated with other clusters, forming giant superclusters. These superclusters typically consist of 3 to 10 clusters and span as many as 200 million light-years. There also are immense areas between clusters that are fairly empty, forming voids. Large-scale surveys made in the 1980s of the radial velocities of galaxies revealed an even-larger kind of structure. It was discovered that galaxies and galaxy clusters tend to fall in position along large planes and curves, almost like giant walls, with relatively empty spaces between them. A related large-scale structure was found to exist where there occur departures from the velocity-distance relation in certain directions, indicating that the otherwise uniform expansion is being perturbed by large concentrations of mass. One of these, discovered in 1988, has been dubbed "the Great Attractor."

INTERACTIONS BETWEEN CLUSTER MEMBERS

Galaxies in clusters exist in a part of the universe that is much denser than average, and the result is that they have several unusual features. In the inner parts of dense clusters there are very few, if any, normal spiral galaxies. This condition is probably the result of fairly frequent collisions between the closely packed galaxies, as such violent interactions tend to sweep out the interstellar gas, leaving behind only the spherical component and a gasless disk. What remains is in effect an S0 galaxy.

A second and related effect of galaxy interactions is the presence of gas-poor spiral systems at the centres of large irregular clusters. A significant number of the members of such clusters have anomalously small amounts of neutral hydrogen, and their gas components are smaller on average than those for more isolated galaxies. This is thought to be the result of frequent distant encounters between such galaxies involving the disruption of their outer parts.

A third effect of the dense cluster environment is the presence in some clusters—usually rather small dense clusters—of an unusual type of galaxy called a cD galaxy. These objects are somewhat similar in structure to S0 galaxies, but they are considerably larger, having envelopes that extend out to radii as large as one million light-years. Many of them have multiple nuclei, and most are strong sources of radio waves. The most likely explanation for cD galaxies is that they are massive central galactic systems that have captured smaller cluster members because of their dominating gravitational fields and have absorbed the other galaxies into their own structures. Astronomers sometimes refer to this process as galactic cannibalism. In this sense, the outer extended disks of cD systems, as well as their multiple nuclei, represent the remains of past partly digested "meals."

One more effect that can be traced to the cluster environment is the presence of strong radio and X-ray sources, which tend to occur in or near the centres of clusters of galaxies. These will be discussed in detail in the next section.

GALAXIES AS A RADIO SOURCE

Some of the strongest radio sources in the sky are galaxies. Most of them have a peculiar morphology that is related to the cause of their radio radiation. Some are relatively isolated galaxies, but most galaxies that emit unusually large amounts of radio energy are found in large clusters.

RADIO GALAXIES

The basic characteristics of radio galaxies and the variations that exist among them can be made clear with two examples. The first is Centaurus A, a giant radio structure surrounding a bright, peculiar galaxy of remarkable morphology designated NGC 5128. It exemplifies a type of radio galaxy that consists of an optical galaxy located at the centre of an immensely larger two-lobed radio source. In the particular case of Centaurus A, the extent of the radio structure is so great that it is almost 100 times the size of the central galaxy, which is itself a giant galaxy. This radio structure includes, besides the pair of far-flung radio lobes, two other sets of radio sources: one that is approximately the size of the optical galaxy and that resembles the outer structure in shape, and a second that is an intense small source at the galaxy's nucleus. Optically, NGC 5128 appears as a giant elliptical galaxy with two notable characteristics: an unusual disk of dust and gas surrounding it and thin jets of interstellar gas and young stars radiating outward. The most plausible explanation for this whole array is that a series of energetic events in the nucleus of the galaxy expelled hot ionized gas from the centre at relativistic velocities (i.e., those at nearly the speed of light) in two opposite directions. These clouds of relativistic particles generate synchrotron radiation, which is detected at radio (and X-ray) wavelengths. In this model the very large structure is associated with an old event, while the inner lobes are the result of more-recent ejections. The centre is still active, as evidenced by the presence of the nuclear radio source.

The other notable example of a radio galaxy is Virgo A, a powerful radio source that corresponds to a bright elliptical galaxy in the Virgo cluster, designated as M87. In this type of radio galaxy, most of the radio radiation is emitted from an appreciably smaller area than in the case of Centaurus A. This area coincides in size with the optically visible object. Virgo A is not particularly unusual except for one peculiarity: it has a bright jet of gaseous material that appears to emanate from the nucleus of the galaxy, extending out approximately halfway to its faint outer parts. This gaseous jet can be detected at optical, radio, and other (e.g., X-ray) wavelengths; its spectrum suggests strongly that it shines by means of the synchrotron mechanism.

About the only condition that can account for the immense amounts of energy emitted by radio galaxies is the capture of material (interstellar gas and stars) by a supermassive object at their centre. Such an object would resemble the one thought to be in the nucleus of the Milky Way Galaxy but would be far more massive. In short, the most probable type of supermassive object for explaining the details of strong radio sources would be a black hole. Large amounts of energy can be released when material is captured by a black hole. An extremely hot high-density accretion disk is first formed around the supermassive object from the material, and then some of the material seems to be ejected explosively from the area, giving rise to the various radio jets and lobes observed.

Another kind of event that can result in an explosive eruption around a nuclear black hole involves cases of merging galaxies in which the nuclei of the galaxies "collide." Because many, if not most, galaxy nuclei contain a black hole, such a collision can generate an immense amount of energy as the black holes merge.

X-ray Galaxies

Synchrotron radiation is characteristically emitted at virtually all wavelengths at almost the same intensity. A synchrotron source therefore ought to be detectable at optical and radio wavelengths, as well as at others (e.g., infrared, ultraviolet, X-ray, and gamma-ray wavelengths). For radio galaxies this does seem to be the case, at least in circumstances where the radiation is not screened by absorbing material in the source or in intervening space.

X-rays are absorbed by Earth's atmosphere. Consequently, X-ray galaxies could not be detected until it became possible to place telescopes above the atmosphere, first with balloons and sounding rockets and later with orbiting observatories specially designed for X-ray studies. For example, the Einstein Observatory, which was in operation during the early 1980s, made a fairly complete search for X-ray sources across the sky and studied several of them in detail. Beginning in 1999, the Chandra X-ray Observatory and other orbiting X-ray observatories detected huge numbers of emitters. Many of the sources turned out to be distant galaxies and quasars, while others were relatively nearby objects, including neutron stars (extremely dense stars composed almost exclusively of neutrons) in the Milky Way Galaxy.

A substantial number of the X-ray galaxies so far detected are also well-known radio galaxies. Some X-ray sources, such as certain radio sources, are much too large to be individual galaxies but rather consist of a whole cluster of galaxies.

Clusters of Galaxies as Radio and X-ray Sources

Some clusters of galaxies contain a widespread intergalactic cloud of hot gas that can be detected as a diffuse radio source or as a large-scale source of X-rays. The gaseous cloud has a low density but a very high temperature, having been heated by the motion of the cluster's galaxies through it and by the emission of high-energy particles from active galaxies within it.

The form of certain radio galaxies in clusters points rather strongly to the presence of intergalactic gas. These are the "head-tail" galaxies, systems that have a bright source accompanied by a tail or tails that appear swept back by their interaction with the cooler more stationary intergalactic gas. These tails are radio lobes of ejected gas whose shape has been distorted by collisions with the cluster medium.

Quasars

An apparently new kind of radio source was discovered in the early 1960s when radio astronomers identified a very small but powerful radio object designated 3C 48 with a stellar optical image. When they obtained the spectrum of the optical object, they found unexpected and at first unexplainable emission lines superimposed on a flat continuum. This object remained a mystery until another similar but optically brighter object, 3C 273, was examined in 1963. Investigators noticed that 3C 273 had a normal spectrum with the same emission lines as observed in radio galaxies, though greatly redshifted (i.e., the spectral lines are displaced to longer wavelengths), as by the Doppler effect. If the redshift were to be ascribed to velocity, however, it would imply an immense velocity of recession. In the case of 3C 48, the redshift had been so large as to shift familiar lines so far that they were not recognized. Many more such objects were found, and they came to be known as quasi-stellar radio sources, abbreviated as quasars.

Although the first 20 years of quasar studies were noted more for controversy and mystery than for progress in understanding, subsequent years finally saw a solution to the questions raised by these strange objects. It is now clear that quasars are extreme examples of energetic galaxy nuclei. The amount of radiation emitted by such a nucleus overwhelms the light from the rest of the galaxy, so only very special observational techniques can reveal the galaxy's existence.

A quasar has many remarkable properties. Although it is extremely small (only the size of the solar system), it emits up to 100 times as much radiation as an entire galaxy. It is a complex mixture of very hot gas, cooler gas and dust, and particles that emit synchrotron radiation. Its brightness often varies over short periods—days or even hours. The galaxy underlying the brilliant image of a quasar may be fairly normal in some of its properties except for the superficial large-scale effects of the quasar at its centre. Quasars apparently are powered by the same mechanism attributed to radio galaxies. They demonstrate in an extreme way what a supermassive object at the centre of a galaxy can do.

With the gradual recognition of the causes of the quasar phenomenon has come an equally gradual realization that they are simply extreme examples of a process that can be observed in more familiar objects. The black holes that are thought to inhabit the cores of the quasar galaxies are similar to, though more explosive than, those that appear to occur in certain unusual nearer galaxies known as Seyfert galaxies. The radio galaxies fall in between. The reason for the differences in the level of activity is apparently related to the source of the gas and stars that are falling into the centres of such objects, providing the black holes with fuel. In the case of quasars, evidence suggests that an encounter with another galaxy, which causes the latter to be tidally destroyed and its matter to fall into the centre of the more massive quasar galaxy, may be the cause of its activity. As the material approaches the black hole, it is greatly accelerated, and some of it is expelled by the prevailing high temperatures and drastically rapid motions. This process probably also explains the impressive but lower-level activity in the nuclei of radio and Seyfert galaxies. The captured mass may be of lesser amount—i.e., either a smaller galaxy or a portion of the host galaxy itself. Quasars are more common in that part of the universe observed to have redshifts of about 2, meaning that they were more common about 10 or so billion years ago than they are now, which is at least partly a result of the higher density of galaxies at that time.

GAMMA-RAY BURSTERS

In the 1970s a new type of object was identified as using orbiting gamma-ray detectors. These "gamma-ray bursters" are identified by extremely energetic bursts of gamma radiation that last only seconds. In some cases the bursters are clearly identified with very distant galaxies, implying immense energies in the bursts. Possibly these are the explosions of "hypernovae," posited to be far more energetic than supernovae and which require some extreme kind of event, such as the merging of two neutron stars.

NOTABLE GALAXIES AND GALAXY CLUSTERS

These galaxies and galaxy clusters are some of the most astronomically important. They range from the Small Magellanic Cloud to the vast Great Attractor.

ANDROMEDA GALAXY

The great spiral Andromeda Galaxy (M31) is the nearest external galaxy (except for the Magellanic Clouds, which are companions of the Milky Way Galaxy, in which Earth is located). The Andromeda Galaxy is one of the few visible to the unaided eye, appearing as a milky blur. It is located about 2,480,000 light-years from Earth; its diameter is approximately 200,000 light-years; and it shares various characteristics with the Milky Way system. It was mentioned as early as 965 CE, in the *Book of the Fixed Stars*, by the Islamic astronomer aṣ-Ṣūfī, and rediscovered in 1612, shortly after the invention of the telescope, by the German astronomer Simon Marius, who said it resembled the light of a candle seen through a horn. For centuries astronomers regarded the Andromeda Galaxy as a component of the Milky Way Galaxy—i.e., as a so-called spiral nebula much like other glowing masses of gas within the local galactic system (hence the misnomer Andromeda Nebula). Only in the 1920s did the American astronomer Edwin Powell Hubble determine conclusively that the Andromeda was in fact a separate galaxy beyond the Milky Way.

The Andromeda Galaxy has a past involving collisions with and accretion of other galaxies. Its peculiar close companion, M32, shows a structure that indicates that it was formerly a normal, more massive galaxy that lost much of its outer parts and possibly all of its globular clusters to M31 in a past encounter. Deep surveys of the outer parts of the Andromeda Galaxy have revealed huge coherent structures of star streams and clouds, with properties indicating that these include the outer remnants of smaller galaxies "eaten" by the giant central galaxy, as well as clouds of M31 stars ejected by the strong tidal forces of the collision.

COMA CLUSTER

The Coma cluster is the nearest rich cluster of galaxies; it contains thousands of systems. The Coma cluster lies about 33 million light-years away, about seven times farther than the Virgo cluster, in the direction of the constellation Coma

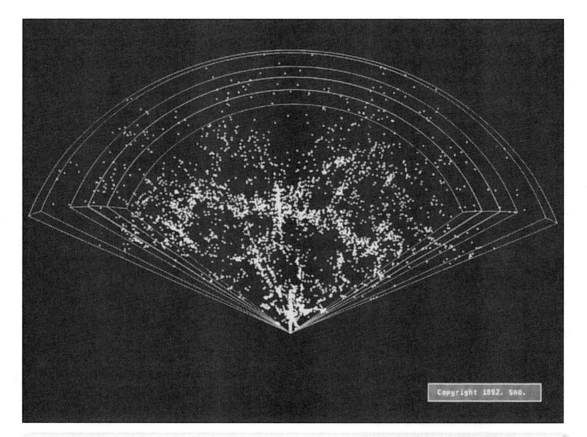

A representation of galaxies distributed on the surfaces of what are thought to be enormous bubblelike voids. The pie-shaped segment of the sky contains about 1,000 galaxies, all located within 300 million light-years from the Earth. The Coma cluster of galaxies, lying near the middle of the segment, seems to occur where several voids intersect. M.J. Geller and J.P. Huchra, Smithsonian Astrophysical Observatory

Berenices. The main body of the Coma cluster has a diameter of about 2.5×10^7 light-years, but enhancements above the background can be traced out to a super-cluster of a diameter of about 2×10^8 light-years. Ellipticals or S0s constitute 85 percent of the bright galaxies in the Coma cluster; the two brightest ellipticals in Coma are located near the centre of the system and are individually more than 10 times as luminous as the Andromeda Galaxy. These galaxies have a swarm of smaller companions orbiting them and may have grown to their bloated sizes by a process of "galactic cannibalism" like that hypothesized to explain the super-giant elliptical cD systems.

The spatial distribution of galaxies in rich clusters such as the Coma cluster closely resembles what one would expect theoretically for a bound set of bodies moving in the collective gravitational field of the system. Yet, if one measures the dispersion of random velocities of the Coma galaxies about the mean, one finds that it amounts to almost 900 km per second (500 miles per second). For a galaxy possessing this random velocity along a typical line of sight to be gravitationally bound within the known dimensions of the cluster requires Coma to have a total mass of about 5×10^{15} solar masses. The total luminosity of the Coma cluster is measured to be about 3×10^{13} solar luminosities; therefore, the mass-to-light ratio in solar units required to explain Coma as a bound system exceeds by an order of magnitude what can be reasonably ascribed to the known stellar populations. A similar situation exists for every rich cluster that has been examined in detail. When Swiss astronomer Fritz Zwicky discovered this discrepancy in 1933, he inferred that much of the Coma cluster was made of nonluminous matter. The existence of nonluminous matter, or "dark matter," was later confirmed in the 1970s by American astronomers Vera Rubin and W. Kent Ford.

CYGNUS A

Cygnus A is the most powerful cosmic source of radio waves known, lying in the northern constellation Cygnus about 500,000,000 light-years (4.8×10^{21} km [3×10^{21} miles]) from Earth. It has the appearance of a double galaxy. For a time it was thought to be two galaxies in collision, but the energy output is too large to be accounted for in that way. Radio energy is emitted from Cygnus A at an estimated 10^{45} ergs per second, more than 10^{11} times the rate at which energy of all kinds is emitted by the Sun. The source of the energy of Cygnus A remains undetermined.

GREAT ATTRACTOR

The Great Attractor is a proposed concentration of mass that influences the movement of many galaxies, including the Milky Way. In 1986 a group of astronomers observing the motions of the Milky Way and neighbouring galaxies noted that the galaxies were moving toward the

Hydra-Centaurus superclusters in the southern sky with velocities significantly different from those predicted by the expansion of the universe in accordance with the Hubble law. One possible explanation for this perturbation in the Hubble flow is the existence of the so-called Great Attractor—a region or structure of huge mass (equivalent to tens of thousands of galaxies) exerting a gravitational pull on the surrounding galaxies. It is estimated that the Great Attractor would have a diameter of about 300 million light-years and that its centre would lie about 147 million light-years away from Earth.

MAGELLANIC CLOUDS

The Magellanic Clouds are two satellite galaxies of the Milky Way Galaxy, the vast star system of which Earth is a minor component. These companion galaxies were named for the Portuguese navigator Ferdinand Magellan, whose crew discovered them during the first voyage around the world (1519–22).

The Magellanic Clouds are irregular galaxies that share a gaseous envelope and lie about 22° apart in the sky near the south celestial pole. One of them, the Large Magellanic Cloud (LMC), is a luminous patch about 5° in diameter, and the other, the Small Magellanic Cloud (SMC), measures less than 2° across. The Magellanic Clouds are visible to the unaided eye in the Southern Hemisphere, but they cannot be observed from the northern latitudes. The LMC is about 160,000 light-years from Earth, and the SMC lies 190,000 light-years away. The LMC and SMC are 14,000 and 7,000 light-years in diameter, respectively, and are smaller than the Milky Way Galaxy, which is about 140,000 light-years across.

The Magellanic Clouds were formed at about the same time as the Milky Way Galaxy, approximately 13 billion years ago. They are presently captured in orbits around the Milky Way Galaxy and have experienced several tidal encounters with each other and with the Galaxy. They contain numerous young stars and star clusters, as well as some much older stars. The Magellanic Clouds serve as excellent laboratories for the study of very active stellar formation and evolution. With the Hubble Space Telescope it is possible for astronomers to study the kinds of stars, star clusters, and nebulae that previously could be observed in great detail only in the Milky Way Galaxy.

M81 GROUP

The M81 group of more than 40 galaxies is found at a distance of 12 million light-years from Earth, one of the nearest galaxy groups to the Local Group (the group of galaxies that includes the Milky Way Galaxy). The dominant galaxy in the M81 group is the spiral galaxy M81. Much like the Andromeda and Milky Way galaxies, M81 is of Hubble type Sb and luminosity class II.

There are two subgroups in the M81 group: one group is associated with

M81 and another is associated with the spiral galaxy NGC 2403. These two subgroups are moving toward each other. The total mass of the M81 group has been determined from the motion of galaxies within it to be $1\ 10^{12}$ solar masses. M81 has a mass of $6.7\ 10^{11}$ solar masses.

The M81 group also has a few galaxies with classifications similar to those of galaxies in the Local Group, and it was noticed by some astronomers that the linear sizes of the largest H II regions (which are illuminated by many OB stars) in these galaxies had about the same intrinsic sizes as their counterparts in the Local Group. This led American astronomer Allan Sandage and the German chemist and physicist Gustav Tammann to the (controversial) technique of using the sizes of H II regions as a distance indicator, because a measurement of their angular sizes, coupled with knowledge of their linear sizes, allows an inference of distance.

MAFFEI I AND II

The two galaxies Maffei I and II are relatively close to the Milky Way Galaxy but were unobserved until the late 1960s, when the Italian astronomer Paolo Maffei detected them by their infrared radiation. Studies in the United States established that the objects are galaxies. Lying near the border between the constellations Perseus and Cassiopeia, they are close to the plane of the Milky Way, where obscuring dust clouds in interstellar space prevent nearly all visible light emitted by external galaxies from reaching Earth.

Maffei I is a large elliptical galaxy. At about 3,000,000 light-years' distance, it is close enough to belong to what is called the Local Group of galaxies, of which the Milky Way Galaxy is a member. Maffei II has a spiral structure and is about three times farther away than Maffei I.

VIRGO A

Virgo A (catalog numbers M87, and NGC4486,) is a giant elliptical galaxy in the constellation Virgo whose nucleus provides the strongest observational evidence for the existence of a black hole. Virgo A is the most powerful known source of radio energy among the thousands of galactic systems comprising the so-called Virgo cluster. It is also a powerful X-ray source, which suggests the presence of very hot gas in the galaxy. A luminous gaseous jet projects outward from the galactic nucleus. Both the jet and the nucleus emit synchrotron radiation, a form of nonthermal radiation released by charged particles that are accelerated in magnetic fields and travel at speeds near that of light. Virgo A lies about 50 million light-years from the Earth.

In 1994 the Hubble Space Telescope obtained images of Virgo A that showed a disk of hot, ionized gas about 500 light-years in diameter at a distance of about 60 light-years from the galaxy's centre. The disk's gases are revolving about the nucleus at a speed of about 550 km per second, or about 1.9 million km (1.2 million miles) per hour, a velocity so great that only the gravitational pull of an object with a mass six billion times that of the Sun would be capable of holding the disk together. This supermassive object could occupy a region as small as the galactic nucleus only if it were a black hole. Gravitational energy released by gas spiraling down into the black hole produces a beam of electrons accelerated almost to the speed of light; the bright gaseous jet that emanates from Virgo A is thought to be radiation from this beam of electrons.

VIRGO CLUSTER

The Virgo cluster is the closest large cluster of galaxies; it is located at a distance of about 5×10^7 light-years in the direction of the constellation Virgo. More than 2,000 galaxies reside in the Virgo cluster, scattered in various subclusters whose largest concentration (near the famous system M87 [Virgo A]) is about 5×10^6 light-years in diameter. Of the galaxies in the Virgo cluster, 58 percent are spirals, 27 percent are ellipticals, and the rest are irregulars. Although spirals are more numerous, the four brightest galaxies are giant ellipticals, among them Virgo A. Calibration of the absolute brightnesses of these giant ellipticals allows a leap to the measurement of distant regular clusters.

Appendix: Other Stars and Star Clusters

Scattered throughout the sky are a myriad of stars and clusters of stars. Some, such as Antares and Spica, are prominent in the night sky or have unusual properties, such as Mira Ceti or Geminga. Others, including HD 209458 or 61 Cygni, have been prominent in the history of astronomy.

61 CYGNI

In 1838, German astronomer Friedrich Wilhelm Bessel obtained a distance of 10.3 light-years for 61 Cygni, the first star whose distance from Earth was measured. The European Space Agency satellite Hipparcos made much more accurate distance measurements than ground-based telescopes had accomplished and obtained a distance to 61 Cygni of 11.4 light-years. The star is a visual binary, the components of which revolve around each other in a period of 659 years, and is located in the northern constellation Cygnus. They are of fifth and sixth magnitudes.

ALCOR

Alcor (Arabic: "Faint One") is a star with apparent magnitude of 4.01. Alcor makes a visual double with the brighter star Mizar in the middle of the handle of the Big Dipper (Ursa Major); however, the two are three light-years apart and thus are not gravitationally bound to each other. The ability to separate the dim star Alcor from Mizar 0.2° away with the unaided eye may have been regarded by the Arabs (and others) as a test of good vision. The pair have also been called the Horse and Rider.

ALDEBARAN

Aldebaran (Arabic: "The Follower") is a reddish giant star in the constellation Taurus. Aldebaran (also called Alpha Tauri) is one of the 15 brightest stars, with an apparent visual magnitude of 0.85. Its diameter is 44 times that of the Sun. It is accompanied by a very faint (13th magnitude) red companion star. Aldebaran lies 65 light-years from Earth. The star was once thought to be a member of the Hyades cluster, but in fact Aldebaran is 85 light-years closer to Earth. Aldebaran was probably named "The Follower" because it rises after the Pleiades cluster of stars.

ALGOL

Algol, or Beta Persei, is the prototype of a class of variable stars called eclipsing binaries, the second brightest star in the northern constellation Perseus. Its apparent visual magnitude changes over the range of 2.1 to 3.4 with a period of 2.87 days. Even at its dimmest it remains readily visible to the unaided eye. The name probably derives from an Arabic phrase meaning "demon," or "mischief-maker," and the Arabs may have been aware of the star's variability even before the invention of the telescope.

The first European astronomer to note the light variation was the Italian Geminiano Montanari in 1670; the English astronomer John Goodricke measured the cycle (69 hours) in 1782 and suggested partial eclipses of the star by another body as a cause, a hypothesis proved correct in 1889. The comparatively long duration of the eclipse shows that the dimensions of the two stars are not negligible in comparison with the distance between them. A third star, which does not take part in the eclipses, revolves about the other two with a period of 1.862 years.

ANTARES

Antares is a red, semiregular variable star, with apparent visual magnitude about 1.1, the brightest star in the zodiacal constellation Scorpius and one of the largest known stars, having several hundred times the diameter of the Sun and 10,000 times the Sun's luminosity. It has a fifth-magnitude blue companion. Antares (also called Alpha Scorpii) lies about 600 light-years from the Earth. The name seems to come from a Greek phrase meaning "rival of Ares" (i.e., rival of the planet Mars) and was probably given because of the star's colour and brightness.

BARNARD'S STAR

Barnard's star is the third nearest star to the Sun (after Proxima Centauri and Alpha Centauri's A and B components considered together), at a distance of about 6 light-years. It is named for Edward Emerson Barnard, the American astronomer who discovered it in 1916. Barnard's star has the largest proper motion of any known star—10.25 seconds of arc annually. It is a red dwarf star with a visual magnitude of 9.5; its intrinsic luminosity is only 1/2,600 that of the Sun.

Because of its high velocity of approach, 108 km (67 miles) per second, Barnard's star is gradually coming nearer the solar system and by the year 11,800 will reach its closest point in distance—namely, 3.85 light-years. The star is of special interest to astronomers because its proper motion, observed photographically between the years 1938–81, was thought to show periodic deviations of 0.02 seconds of arc. This "perturbation" was interpreted as being caused by the gravitational pull of two planetary companions having orbital periods of 13.5 and 19 years, respectively, and masses of about two-thirds that of Jupiter. However, this finding has not been supported by results from other methods of detection.

BETA LYRAE

Beta Lyrae is an eclipsing binary star, the two component stars of which are so close together that they are greatly distorted by their mutual attraction; they exchange material and share a common atmosphere. Beta Lyrae is a member of a class of binary systems known as W Serpentis stars. It is of about third magnitude and lies in the northern constellation Lyra.

The variable character of Beta Lyrae was discovered in 1784 by the English amateur astronomer John Goodricke. Its period of about 13 days is increasing by about 19 seconds per year, probably because the stars are steadily losing mass to a continually expanding gaseous ring surrounding them.

BETA PICTORIS

The fourth-magnitude star Beta Pictoris is located 60 light-years from Earth in the southern constellation Pictor and is notable for an encircling disk of debris that might contain planets. The star is of a common type somewhat hotter and more luminous than the Sun. In 1983 it was discovered to be an unexpectedly strong source of infrared radiation of the character that would be produced by a disk of material surrounding the star. The disk was later imaged and found to have a width roughly 2,000 times the Earth-Sun distance (2,000 astronomical units [AU]). Observations

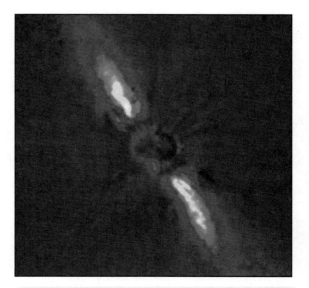

Debris disk surrounding the star Beta Pictoris, in an image gathered by the European Southern Observatory's 3.6-metre (140-inch) telescope at La Silla, Chile. The warping seen in the disk's bright inner region may be indirect evidence for one or more orbiting planets. European Southern Observatory

with the Hubble Space Telescope revealed the disk to be warped and its inner regions to be relatively clear. A likely, but not exclusive, explanation for these characteristics is that one or more extrasolar planets exist there. The outer part of the disk shows rings, possibly caused by a passing star. In 2008, infrared images showed a possible planet orbiting Beta Pictoris. This planet is estimated to have a mass eight times that of Jupiter and to be at a distance from Beta Pictoris of 8 AU.

CANOPUS

Canopus, or Alpha Carinae, is the second brightest star (after Sirius) in the night sky, with a visual magnitude of -0.73. Lying in the southern constellation Carina, 310 light-years from Earth, Canopus is sometimes used as a guide in the attitude control of spacecraft because of its angular distance from the Sun and the contrast of its brightness among nearby celestial objects. The Syrian Stoic philosopher Poseidonius (c. 135–50 BCE) used sightings of Canopus near the horizon in his estimation of the size of Earth.

CAPELLA

Capella (also called Alpha Aurigae) is the sixth brightest star in the night sky and the brightest in the constellation Auriga, with an apparent visual magnitude of 0.08. Capella (Latin: "She-Goat") is a spectroscopic binary comprising two G-type giant stars that orbit each other every 104 days. It lies 42.2 light-years from Earth.

CASTOR

Castor, which is also called Alpha Geminorum, is a multiple star having six component stars, in the zodiacal constellation Gemini. The stars Castor and Pollux are named for the twins of Greek mythology. Castor's combined apparent visual magnitude is 1.58. It appears as a bright visual binary, of which both members are spectroscopic binaries. An additional two component stars form an eclipsing binary system of red dwarfs revolving around each other in less than a day and orbiting the four main stars in a period of 14,000 years. The system is 51.5 light-years from Earth.

COR CAROLI

Cor Caroli, which is also called Alpha Canum Venaticorum, is a binary star located 110 light-years from Earth in the constellation Canes Venatici and consisting of a brighter component (A) of visual magnitude 2.9 and a companion (B) of magnitude 5.5. It is the prototype for a group of unusual spectrum-variable stars that show strong and fluctuating absorption lines of silicon, chromium, strontium, or certain rare earths. Europium apparently is concentrated around one magnetic pole, chromium around the other. Cor Caroli ("Heart of Charles") was named by Sir Edmond Halley for King Charles II of England.

CYGNUS X-1

The binary star system Cygnus X-1 is a strong source of X-rays and provided the first major evidence for the existence of black holes. Cygnus X-1 is located about 7,000 light-years from Earth in the constellation Cygnus. The primary star, HDE 226868, is a hot supergiant revolving about an unseen companion with a period of 5.6 days. Analysis of the binary orbit led to the finding that the companion has a mass greater than seven solar masses.

(The mass has been determined from subsequent observations to be nearly nine solar masses.) A star of that mass should have a detectable spectrum, but the companion does not; from this and other evidence astronomers have argued that it must be a black hole. The X-ray emission is understood as being due to matter torn from the primary star that is being heated as it is drawn to the black hole.

DELTA CEPHEI

Delta Cephei is the prototype star of the class of Cepheid variables and is in the constellation Cepheus. Its apparent visual magnitude at minimum is 4.34 and at maximum 3.51, changing in a regular cycle of about five days and nine hours. Its variations in brightness were discovered in 1784 by the English amateur astronomer John Goodricke, and periodic changes in radial velocity (now attributed to pulsation) were established in 1894.

EPSILON AURIGAE

The binary star system Epsilon Aurigae is of about third magnitude and has one of the longest orbital periods (27 years) among eclipsing binaries. It is located an estimated 2,000 light-years from Earth in the constellation Auriga. The primary star is a yellow-white star about 200 times the size of the Sun. The secondary star, once thought to be thousands of times the size of the Sun, is now believed to be a hot main-sequence star surrounded by an immense ring or shell of gas that eclipses the primary for two years.

ETA CARINAE

Eta Carinae, which is also called Homunculus Nebula, is a peculiar red star and nebula about 7,500 light-years from Earth in the southern constellation Carina and is now known to be a binary star system. It is one of a small class of stars called luminous blue variables. The English astronomer Sir Edmond Halley noted it in 1677 as a star of about fourth magnitude. In 1838 Sir John Herschel observed it as a first-magnitude star. By 1843 it had reached its greatest recorded brightness, approximately –1 magnitude, or as bright as the brightest stars. Unlike the common types of exploding stars called novae and supernovae, it remained bright for several years. From about 1857 it faded steadily, disappearing to the unaided eye only about 1870. Since then it has varied irregularly about the seventh magnitude. The nebula around the star was formed during its 19th-century brightening and is an expanding shell of gas and dust, shaped like an hourglass with a disk at its centre.

In 2005 astronomers studying far-ultraviolet spectral observations of Eta Carinae made by spacecraft found that it is a binary star system with an orbital period of 5.52 years. Its A component has a temperature of about 15,000 K; its B component, about 35,000 K. The main star in Eta Carinae is about 100 times more massive than the Sun. Its luminosity has been estimated as five million times that of the Sun. Flaring events producing not only visible effects but also X-ray, ultraviolet, and radio-wave effects have been observed. It is expected to become a supernova in the next several thousand years.

GEMINGA

The isolated pulsar Geminga is about 800 light-years from Earth in the constellation Gemini and is unique in that about 99 percent of its radiation is in the gamma-ray region of the spectrum. Geminga is also a weak X-ray emitter, but it was not identified in visible light (as a 25th-magnitude object) until nearly two decades after its discovery in 1972. It was the first pulsar not detected at radio wavelengths. It pulsates with a period of 0.237 second, has a radius of about 10 km (6 miles), and probably originated in a supernova explosion about 300,000 years ago.

HD 209458

The seventh-magnitude star HD 209458, 150 light-years away in the constellation Pegasus, was the first star that had a planet detected by its transit across the star's face. The star, which has physical characteristics similar to those of the Sun, was shown in late 1999 to have a planet by detection of the planet's gravitational effects on the star's motion. Shortly afterward, astronomers independently confirmed the planet's presence by observing that HD 209458 changed in brightness with the same 3.5-day period predicted from the discovery data for the planet's orbit. Although the planet could not be seen directly, its passages between its star and Earth provided important information about its physical properties and atmosphere not otherwise available. The extrasolar planet is about 1.3 times the size of Jupiter but has only two-thirds of Jupiter's mass. It orbits surprisingly close to the star—about 10 stellar radii.

HR 8799

The star HR 8799 has the first extrasolar planetary system to be seen directly in an astronomical image. HR 8799 is a young (about 60 million years old) main-sequence star of spectral type A5 V located 128 light-years from Earth in the constellation Pegasus. Observations of this star taken by the Infrared Astronomical Satellite and the Infrared Space Observatory showed a disk of dust such as that expected in the last stages of planetary formation. In 2008 an international team of astronomers released images taken with the telescopes at the Keck and Gemini North observatories of three planets orbiting HR 8799. Observations taken over the period 2004–08 showed that the planets moved with the star and therefore were not background objects. The planets range in mass from 7 to 10 times that of Jupiter and orbit between

3.6 and 10.2 billion km (2.2 and 6.3 billion miles) from HR 8799. These planets are gas giants with temperatures of about 900 to 1,100 kelvins (600 to 800 °C, or 1,200 to 1,500 °F).

HYADES

The Hyades is a cluster of several hundred stars in the zodiacal constellation Taurus. As seen from Earth, the bright star Aldebaran appears to be a member of the cluster, but in fact Aldebaran is much closer to the Earth than the Hyades' distance of about 150 light-years. Five genuine members of the group are visible to the unaided eye. Their name (Greek: "the rainy ones") is derived from the ancient association of spring rain with the season of their heliacal (near dawn) rising.

KEPLER'S NOVA

Kepler's Nova was one of the few supernovae (violent stellar explosions) known to have occurred in the Milky Way Galaxy. Jan Brunowski, Johannes Kepler's assistant, first observed the phenomenon in October 1604; Kepler studied it until early 1606, when the supernova was no longer visible to the unaided eye. At its greatest apparent magnitude (about -2.5), the exploding star was brighter than Jupiter. No stellar remnant is known to exist, though traces of nebulosity are observable at the position of the supernova. Like Tycho's Nova, Kepler's served

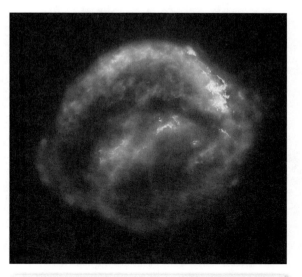

Composite image of Kepler's Nova, or Kepler's Supernova, taken by the Chandra X-ray Observatory. NASA, ESA, R. Sankrit and W. Blair, Johns Hopkins University

at the time as evidence of the mutability of the stars.

MIRA CETI

Mira Ceti, which is also called Omicron Ceti, was the first variable star (apart from novae) to be discovered, lying in the southern constellation Cetus, and the prototype of a class known as long-period variables, or Mira stars. There is some evidence that ancient Babylonian astronomers noticed its variable character. In a systematic study in 1638, a Dutch astronomer, Phocylides Holwarda, found that the star disappeared and reappeared in a varying cycle of about 330 days. It thus acquired the name Mira

(Latin: "Miraculous"). Its brightness varies from cycle to cycle, but generally it is about magnitude 3 at maximum light and magnitude 9 at minimum. Mira is a binary; the red giant primary has a faint bluish white companion. In 2006 the ultraviolet satellite observatory Galaxy Evolution Explorer discovered that Mira had shed material into a cometary tail 13 light-years in length. Mira is about 350 light-years from Earth.

MIZAR

Mizar, also called Zeta Ursae Majoris, was the first star found (by the Italian astronomer Giovanni Battista Riccioli in 1650) to be a visual binary—i.e., to consist of two optically distinguishable components revolving around each other. Later, each of the visual components was determined to be a spectroscopic binary; Mizar is actually a quadruple star. Apparent visual magnitudes of the two visual components are 2.27 and 3.95. Set in the middle of the Big Dipper's handle, Mizar (Arabic: "Veil," or "Cloak") makes a visual double with the fainter Alcor (Arabic: "Faint One"); however, the two are three light-years apart and thus are not gravitationally bound to each other. The ability to separate the dim star Alcor from Mizar 0.2° away with the unaided eye may have been regarded by the Arabs (and others) as a test of good vision.

NOVA HERCULIS

Nova Herculis, or DQ Herculis, was one of the brightest novae of the 20th century, discovered Dec. 13, 1934, by the British amateur astronomer J.P.M. Prentice, in the northern constellation Hercules. It reached an apparent visual magnitude of 1.4 and remained visible to the unaided eye for months. At its centre was found an eclipsing binary pair of small stars, revolving around each other with a period of 4 hours and 39 minutes. One component is a rapidly spinning white dwarf star accreting material from its companion.

NOVA PERSEI

Nova Persei, or GK Persei, was a bright nova that attained an absolute magnitude of –9.2. Spectroscopic observations of the nova, which appeared in 1901, provided important information about interstellar gas. The shell thrown off by the exploding star was unusually asymmetrical, and a bright nebulosity near the star appeared to be expanding incredibly fast, at practically the speed of light. This apparent speed is thought to have been an effect of reflection within a preexisting dark nebula around the star. From this phenomenon, sometimes called a light echo, it is possible to calculate the distance of the nova from Earth, about 1,500 light-years.

OMEGA CENTAURI

Omega Centauri (NGC 5139) is the brightest globular star cluster. It is located in the southern constellation Centaurus. It has a magnitude of 3.7 and is visible to the unaided eye as a faint luminous patch. Omega Centauri is about 16,000 light-years from Earth and is thus one of the nearer globular clusters. It is estimated to contain several million stars; several hundred variables have been observed in it. There is some evidence for a black hole at the centre of Omega Centauri that is 40,000 times as massive as the Sun. The English astronomer John Herschel in the 1830s was the first to recognize it as a star cluster and not a nebula.

PLEIONE

Pleione is a star in the Pleiades, thought to be typical of the shell stars, so called because in their rapid rotation they throw off shells of gas. In 1938 sudden changes in the spectrum of Pleione were attributed to the ejection of a gaseous shell, which by 1952 had apparently dissipated. Pleione is a blue-white star of about the fifth magnitude. Some astronomers conjecture that it may have been brighter in the past; it would then have made a seventh bright star in the Pleiades cluster, which is named for seven mythological sisters.

POLLUX

Pollux is the brightest star in the zodiacal constellation Gemini. A reddish giant star, it has an apparent visual magnitude of 1.15. The stars Castor and Pollux are named for the mythological twins. Pollux is also called Beta Geminorum and is 33.7 light-years from Earth. In 2006, a planet, Pollux b, was discovered. Pollux b has nearly three times the mass of Jupiter, orbits Pollux every 590 days, and is at an average distance of 253 million km (157 million miles). Pollux is the brightest star with a known extrasolar planet.

PRAESEPE

Praesepe, which is also known as the Beehive, is an open cluster of about 1,000 stars in the zodiacal constellation Cancer and is located about 550 light-years from Earth. Visible to the unaided eye as a small patch of bright haze, it was first distinguished as a group of stars by Galileo. It was included by Hipparchus in the earliest known star catalog, c. 129 BCE.

The name Praesepe (Latin: "Cradle," or "Manger") was used even before Hipparchus' time. The name Beehive is of uncertain but more recent origin.

PROCYON

Procyon is the brightest star in the northern constellation Canis Minor (Latin: "Lesser Dog") and one of the brightest in the entire sky, with an apparent visual magnitude of 0.41. Procyon lies 11.4 light-years from Earth and is a visual binary, a bright yellow-white subgiant with a faint, white dwarf companion of about the 10th magnitude. The name apparently derives from Greek words for "before the dog," in reference to the constellation.

RAS ALGETHI

Ras Algethi, which is also called Alpha Herculis, is a red supergiant star, whose diameter is nearly twice that of Earth's orbit. It lies in the constellation Hercules and is of about third magnitude, its brightness varying by about a magnitude every 128 days. It is 380 light-years from Earth. The name comes from an Arabic phrase meaning "the kneeler's head," referring to the Arabic name of the constellation.

REGULUS

Regulus, or Alpha Leonis, is the brightest star in the zodiacal constellation Leo and one of the brightest in the entire sky, having an apparent visual magnitude of about 1.35. It is 77 light-years from Earth. The name Regulus, derived from a Latin word for king, reflects an ancient belief in the astrological importance of the star.

RIGEL

Rigel (Beta Orionis) is one of the brightest stars in the sky, intrinsically as well as in appearance. A blue-white supergiant in the constellation Orion, Rigel is about 870 light-years from the Sun and is about 47,000 times as luminous. A companion double star, also bluish white, is of the sixth magnitude. The name Rigel derives from an Arabic term meaning "the left leg of the giant," referring to the figure of Orion.

SCORPIUS X-1

Scorpius X-1 is the brightest X-ray source in the sky and the first such object discovered in the direction of the constellation Scorpius. Detected in 1962, its X-radiation is not only strong but, like other X-ray sources, quite variable as well. Its variability exhibits two states, one at higher output with great variability on a time scale of minutes and another at lower output with the variability correspondingly lessened.

Scorpius X-1 was observed in visible light for the first time in 1966. Optically it is much less impressive, bluish in colour and appearing only faintly. Scorpius X-1 is a close double star, one component of which is optically invisible—a neutron star. The X-rays are generated when matter from the optically visible, bluish hot star falls onto the neutron star. This matter is tremendously accelerated and crushed by the enormous gravity of the neutron star. Unlike the majority of binary X-ray sources, the visible member does not appear to be very massive; it is only 42 percent the mass of the Sun. The neutron star is 1.4 solar masses. Scorpius X-1 is about 9,000 light-years from Earth.

S DORADUS

S Doradus is a variable supergiant star in the Large Magellanic Cloud. S Doradus (and the Large Magellanic Cloud) is visible to viewers in the Southern Hemisphere in the constellation Dorado. It is one of the most luminous stars known, radiating more than 1,000,000 times as much energy as the Sun.

SPICA

Spica (Latin: "Head of Grain") is the brightest star in the zodiacal constellation Virgo and one of the 15 brightest in the entire sky, having an apparent visual magnitude of 0.98. It is a bluish star; spectroscopic examination reveals Spica to be a binary with a four-day period, its two components being of the first and third magnitudes, respectively. Spica lies about 250 light-years from Earth.

SUPERNOVA 1987A

Supernova 1987A was the first supernova observed in 1987 (hence its designation) and the nearest to Earth in more than three centuries. It occurred in the Large Magellanic Cloud, a satellite galaxy of the Milky Way Galaxy that lies about 160,000 light-years distant. The supernova originated in the collapse and subsequent explosion of a supergiant star, and it is unique in that its progenitor star had been observed and cataloged prior to the event. The fact that the supergiant was hotter than expected for an immediate progenitor led to important improvements in supernova theory. A burst of neutrinos that accompanied the star's collapse was detected on Earth, providing verification of theoretical predictions of nuclear processes that occur during supernovae. Study of the evolving remnant continued into the 21st century.

TYCHO'S NOVA

Tycho's Nova (SN 1572) was one of the few recorded supernovae in the Milky Way Galaxy. The Danish astronomer Tycho Brahe first observed the "new star" on Nov. 11, 1572. Other European observers claimed to have noticed it as early as the preceding August, but Tycho's precise measurements showed that it was not some relatively nearby phenomenon, such as a comet, but at the distance of the stars, and that therefore real changes could occur among them.

The supernova remained visible to the unaided eye until March 1574. It attained the apparent magnitude of Venus (about –4) and could be seen by day. There is no known stellar remnant but only traces of glowing nebulosity. It is, however, a radio and X-ray source. In 2008 a team of international astronomers used light from the original explosive event reflected off nearby interstellar dust to determine that Tycho's Nova was a Type Ia supernova, which occurs when a white dwarf star accretes material from a companion star and that material explodes in a thermonuclear reaction that destroys the white dwarf.

GLOSSARY

binary star A pair of stars in orbit around a common centre of gravity.

black hole An area in space with an intense gravitational field whose escape velocity exceeds the speed of light.

cloud cores The densest regions of molecular clouds, where stars typically form.

dwarf stars Low-luminosity stars.

eclipsing binary Two close stars moving in an orbit so placed in space in relation to Earth that the light of one can at times be hidden behind the other.

extrasolar Revolving around stars other than the Sun.

interferometer An instrument that combines light waves from two or more different optical paths and can be used to measure the angle subtended by the diameter of a star at the observer's position.

kinematics The study of motion.

light-year The distance that light waves travel in one Earth year.

nebulae A mass of interstellar gas and dust.

nova A star that brightens temporarily while ejecting a shell explosively.

photons Packets of radiation.

protostars A contracting mass of gas that represents an early stage in the formation of a star, before nucleo-synthesis has begun.

pulsars Neutron stars that emit pulses of radiation once per rotation.

quasars The abbreviation for quasi-stellar radio sources, which emit up to 100 times as much radiation as an entire galaxy.

recombination The process by which the higher stage of ionization cap-tures an electron, usually at low energies, into a high level of the ion.

thermal ionization The process at higher temperatures where collisions between atoms and electrons and the absorption of radiation tend to detach electrons and produce singly ionized atoms.

z distances Distances above the plane of the Galaxy.

FOR FURTHER READING

Block, David L., and Kenneth C. Freeman. *Shrouds of the Night: Masks of the Milky Way and Our Awesome New View of Galaxies.* Berlin, Germany: Springer, 2008.

Buta, Ronald J., et. al. *The de Vaucouleurs Atlas of Galaxies.* Cambridge, England: Cambridge University Press, 2007.

Clark, Stuart. *Galaxy: Exploring the Milky Way.* New York, NY: Fall River Press, 2008.

Coe, Steven R. *Nebulae and How to Observe Them* (Astronomers' Observing Guides). New York, NY: Springer, 2006.

Eckart, Andreas. *The Black Hole at the Center of the Milky Way.* London, England: Imperial College Press, 2005.

Freedman, Roger A., and William J. Kaufmann, III. *Universe: Stars and Galaxies.* New York, NY: W. H. Freeman & Co., 2008.

Gray, Richard O., and Christopher J. Corbally. *Stellar Spectral Classification.* Princeton, NJ: Princeton University Press, 2009.

Green, Simon F., and Mark H. Jones, eds. *An Introduction to the Sun and Stars.* Cambridge, England: Cambridge University Press, 2004.

Gribbin, John. *Galaxies: A Very Short Introduction.* New York, NY: Oxford University Press, 2008.

Kitchin, Chris. *Galaxies in Turmoil: The Active and Starburst Galaxies and the Black Holes That Drive Them.* London, England: Springer, 2007.

Kwok, Sun. *The Origin and Evolution of Planetary Nebulae.* Cambridge, England: Cambridge University Press, 2007.

Percy, John R. *Understanding Variable Stars.* Cambridge, England: Cambridge University Press, 2007.

Rees, Martin, ed. *Universe.* New York, NY: Dorling Kindersley, 2005.

Salaris, Maurizo, and Santi Cassisi. *Evolution of Stars and Stellar Populations.* West Sussex, England: John Wiley & Sons, 2006.

Sarazin, Craig L. *X-Ray Emission from Clusters of Galaxies.* Cambridge, England: Cambridge University Press, 2009.

Schaaf, Fred. *The Brightest Stars: Discovering the Universe through the Sky's Most Brilliant Stars.* Hoboken, NJ: John Wiley & Sons, 2008.

Sparke, Linda S., and John S. Gallagher. *Galaxies in the Universe: An Introduction.* Cambridge, England: Cambridge University Press, 2007.

Stahler, Steven W., and Francesco Palla. *The Formation of Stars.* Weinheim, Germany: Wiley VCH, 2005.

Wheeler, J. Craig. *Cosmic Catastrophes: Exploding Stars, Black Holes, and Mapping the Universe.* New York, NY: Cambridge University Press, 2007.

INDEX